Copper Country Journal

*The Diary of Schoolmaster
Henry Hobart, 1863-1864*

*A complete listing of the books in this series
can be found online at wsupress.wayne.edu*

Copper Country Journal

The Diary of Schoolmaster Henry Hobart, 1863-1864

Edited with an Introductory Essay
by Philip P. Mason

Bureau of History, Department of State, Lansing, Michigan

 Wayne State University Press, Detroit, Michigan

Library of Congress Cataloging-in-Publication Data

Hobart, Henry, 1841-1920
   Copper country journal: the diary of schoolmaster Henry Hobart,
1863-1864 / edited with an introductory essay by Philip P. Mason.
      p.   cm. — (Great Lakes books)
   Includes bibliographical references and index.
   ISBN 0-8143-2341-3 (alk. paper). — ISBN 0-8143-2342-1 (pbk. :
alk. paper)
   1. Frontier and pioneer life—Michigan—Keweenaw Peninsula.
2. Keweenaw Peninsula (Mich.)—History. 3. Copper industry and
trade—Michigan—Keweenaw Peninsula—History—19th century.
4. Hobart, Henry, 1841-1920—Diaries. 5. Teachers—Michigan—
Keweenaw Peninsula—Diaries. 6. Copper mines and mining—
Michigan—Keweenaw Peninsula—History—19th century.
I. Mason, Philip P. (Philip Parker), 1927- . II. Title. III. Series.
F572.K43H6 1991
977.4'9903—dc20   91-11188

_Cover: This painting "Snap the Whip" (1871) by Winslow Homer
is from the collections of the Butler Museum of Art, Youngstown,
Ohio, and is used with permission. Cover photo inset is of Henry
Hobart circa 1864 and is used with the permission of Mrs. Violet
Hobart, Underhill, Vermont._

ISBN-13: 978-0-8143-2342-7   ISBN-10: 0-8143-2342-1

To George F. Wiskemann
(1904-1988)

"If only he had kept a Journal…"

Contents

EAGLE HARBOR COPPER HARBOR
EAGLE RIVER FORT WILKINS
CLIFF MINE KEWEENAW
LAKE SUPERIOR
CALUMET
HANCOCK LAKE LINDEN
HOUGHTON
COPPER BEARING RANGE
KEWEENAW BAY
ONTONAGON
PORCUPINE BARAGA HURON MOUNTAINS
MTS. L'ANSE
WHITE PINE
ONTONAGON RIVER
HOUGHTON
BESSEMER MARQUETTE
WAKEFIELD ISHPEMING NEGAUNEE
IRONWOOD BARAGA MARQUETTE RANGE
GOGEBIC RANGE ONTON- IRON ESCANABA RIVER
AGON GOGEBIC
MARQUETTE ALGER
DICKINSON DELTA
IRON RIVER
MENOMINEE RANGE
WISCONSIN STAMBAUGH
ESCANABA
IRON MOUNTAIN LITTLE BAY DE NOC BIG BAY DE NOC
NORWAY
MENOMINEE
MENOMINEE RIVER
GREEN BAY

IRON
COPPER

The journal of Henry Hobart was copied verbatim for this edition except for a few minor changes and additions. The editor spelled out abbreviated words and used the correct spellings of names and places. Some punctuation was added to clarify the meaning; however, no attempt was made to correct Hobart's grammar nor to alter his incomplete sentences. His use of quotations, his idiosyncratic capitalization, his unusual spelling of words that are not proper nouns and his French phrases were left in the journal. Hobart scarcely ever used paragraphs; the editor did add them in order to let the reader navigate the journal with pleasure.

There is some repetition in the journal entries but it was decided to include such entries intact. Only one story, repeated word for word a few days previous in the journal, was deleted. Accounts regarding excessive drinking and alcoholism tended to be repeated but the editor left them verbatim in the edited journal. The elaborate stories and statistics Hobart cited on alcoholism most likely came from church sermons and reflect the temperance movement of the era.

The editor made attempts to identify all individuals and families, place names, mining terms, journals and other publications, steamships and sailing vessels, and events. However, the editor chose not to identify the numerous references to the Civil War. The United States census figures for 1860 and 1870 were invaluable for locating pertinent data aboout miners and their families, Hobart's friends and family members, mine company officals and other individuals mentioned in the journal. In many instances, however, the names did not appear in either the 1860 or 1870 census material nor in other sources. The constant movement of workers from one mine to another—often in other sections of the United States and abroad—as well as the varied spellings of the names of immigrants (and Hobart's often imperfect spelling) complicated the search.

The photographs and other illustrations used in this volume were chosen from a large collection amassed from archives and private collections. Credits are listed separately.

Acknowledgements

The editing of the journal of Henry Hobart, the preparation of an appropriate introductory essay as well as documentation for the hundreds of individuals, places and mining terms cited, required a major research effort. I am anxious to acknowledge the help of many people who gave freely of their time, advice, source materials and specialized knowledge of the Copper Country.

The research was further complicated by the fact that Henry A. Hobart, the author of the journal, was not a prominent person who deposited his papers and records in an archives or library. Aside from legal documents filed with public offices in Vermont, Wisconsin and Michigan, the journal is the only major document of Hobart's that has survived. Furthermore, the people mentioned in the journal, the miners and their families, the storekeepers and the stage drivers, were for the most part immigrants who had recently arrived in the United States. They moved constantly—to other copper mines in the Upper Peninsula, to the western states, and even a few to Australia.

I am indebted to archivists and librarians, the keepers of public records who assisted in locating biographical information about Henry Hobart. Connell B. Gallagher and Kevin Graffagnino of the Special Collections Department of the Bailey-Howe Library of the University of Vermont assisted me in locating pertinent records of the Hobart family. Barney Bloom and Mary Pat Brigham of the Vermont Historical Society were also helpful in locating Hobart's Vermont roots. Sandra Kellott, keeper of the Vermont Probate Records, provided copies of the relevant Hobart family wills and death certificates. Mrs. David Yendell of the Williston Historical Society provided valuable information on the Williston Academy where Hobart and his siblings were educated.

At Harvard University, Harley P. Holden, archivist of the University, and Robert Lovett, former director of the Baker Business Library, both close friends and colleagues of long standing, provided leads to sources on Boston investors in the copper mines of the Keweenaw. Barbara Trippel Simmons of the American Antiquarian Society in Worchester, Massachusetts, helped in locating many of the annual reports of the Pittsburgh and Boston and other copper mining companies. Varied parts of the annual reports of the Pittsburgh and Boston Company are referred to in the notes; these can be found in the Harvard University Archives, the American Antiquarian Society and the State Library of Michigan.

For information on Hobart's life in Wisconsin, I received assistance from several sources. James Hansen and Jack Holzheuter of the State Historical Society of Wisconsin helped in locating Hobart's Wisconsin connections. Several Oshkosh residents gave special assistance, including Polly Zimmerman of the *Oshkosh Daily Northwestern*; Helen E. Simpson and Mara B. Munroe of the Oshkosh Public Library; Kitty A. Hobson, archivist of the Oshkosh Public Museum; and George Gunther, superintendent of the Riverside Cemetery. Geraldine N. Driscoll of the Winneconne Historical Society provided me with information about Hobart's teaching career in that community and Arlow Andersen of the Wisconsin Conference of the United Methodist Church and Walter Radley, church historian, First United Methodist Church of Oshkosh, gave data about Hobart's church activities. Patricia H. Ehr, librarian of the Northwestern Mutual Life Insurance Company, made a thorough, although unsuccessful, search of the company's archives for references to Hobart's employment in that company.

I am especially indebted to colleagues and friends in the Upper Peninsula. Theresa Sanderson Spence, and her assistant, Kay Masters, both of the University Archives at Michigan Technological University at Houghton, Michigan, helped in the location of sources on the Cliff and others mines of the area, as well as many of the excellent photographs used in the book. My colleagues, David Halkola, retired professor of history at Michigan Technological University, and Robert Patterson and David Thomas of the Michigan Technological University Library shared their extensive knowledge of the Copper Country. Clarence Monette of Lake Linden, the author of numerous books on Copper Country communities and mines, made many helpful suggestions on sources. I am also indebted to William Foreman, of Calumet, a retired mine inspector for Keweenaw County who spent an afternoon showing me the Cliff mine site, its shafts and building foundations and sharing with me the lore of the Copper Country. James Kliber, an attorney from Hancock Michigan, also gave me a tour of the Cliff site including the remains of the old cemeteries.

Another colleague, William Mulligan, formerly director of the Clarke Historical Collection at Central Michigan University, was also most helpful in sharing information on the mining operations of the Keweenaw Peninsula.

Francis Blouin, director, and Nancy Bartlett, manuscript curator, both of the Bentley Historical Library at the University of Michigan, gave me access to their rich resources on Michigan including the C. C. Douglass and Daniel Brockway collections and the Hotel Register of the Douglass House, where Hobart spent his Christmas vacation in 1863. Joyce Bonk, associate curator of rare books at the William L. Clements Library, University of Michigan, helped in identifying several rare titles mentioned in the journal.

Caroline Scholfield, reference librarian of the Library of Michigan, was most helpful in helping me locate information on the early families of Clifton and the copper mining towns of the Upper Peninsula. David Johnson and his staff at the State Archives were also most cooperative, especially LeRoy Barnett, whose knowledge of Michigan history and its bibliography is without bounds, and John Curry, photo archivist, who helped locate photographs to illustrate the book. Martha Carolyn Bigelow, the recently retired director of the Bureau of History, Department of State, also gave encouragement and approval to the co-publication of the book by the Wayne State University Press and the Bureau of History, Department of State.

The staff of the Burton Historical Collection also assisted me in the research of the Journal, and granted me permission to edit and publish the journal that is in their possession. I would like to give special thanks to Bernice Sprenger and Alice Dalligan, two former chiefs of the Burton Historical Collection.

The descendants of Henry A. Hobart were gracious, helpful and supportive of the project and shared with me all of the information they had about the Hobart family. Edmund F. and William Hobart of Troy, Ohio, offered their assistance and advice on the family and Yvonne Reynolds Whittaker of Monterey Park, California, the granddaughter of Florence Hobart Reynolds, the sister of Henry Hobart, reviewed the family records for references to Henry.

I want to express my profound gratitude to the late Irving Hobart, descended from Henry's uncle, Eli Hobart, and his widow, Violet Hobart of Underhill, Vermont, Mrs. Hobart lives on the Hobart farm located across the road from Amos Hobart's farm, which is no longer standing. She was gracious and helpful in my visits to her home, showing me all of the records, the family Bibles with their genealogical sections, and the family ambrotypes, daguerreotypes, tintypes and photographs. Like her husband she was enthusiastic about the editing project and eager to see the published version.

S. Josiah Penberthy of Farmington, Michigan, the grandson of Edward Penberthy, has been of great assistance in the project. He gave me copies of family letters including a family autobiographical account of Joseph Rawlings and photographs of the Penberthy family.

To Richard Bennett, director of the Special Collections Department of the University of Manitoba, I owe a great deal for his help in tracking Henry Hobart to Wisconsin after his trail had been lost in Vermont. Charles J. Meyers of Southfield, head of the Michigan Indian Commission, shared his extensive library of Michigan books and monographs. So too did George (now deceased) and Geneva Wiskemann, my two dear friends from Lansing who patiently listened for hours while I described the contents and value of the Hobart journal. They also loaned me books from their magnificent Michigan collection. Geneva located many valuable sources in the State Library and State Archives.

I wish to thank also Susan Holleran, associate editor of the American Federation of State, County and Municipal Employees, who read the journal and introductory essay and made many helpful suggestions. To the late professor, Leslie L. Hanawalt of Wayne State University, I also owe a debt of gratitude for he was one of the first to encourage the publication of the journal.

My family also had a part in the preparation of the journal for publication. My son Stephen, then on the faculty at Goddard College, did much basic research in the records in Montpelier, Vermont and the area where the Hobarts lived. Catherine Phillips spent days at the Burton Historical Collection and the State Library examining the rich historical and genealogical sources of those institutions including the United States Census. She also assisted in tracking down and contacting members of the Hobart family throughout the United States. Henrietta Mason read and collated the manuscript and made many helpful suggestions. I am especially indebted to Susan Elaine Mason who assisted in every step of research, editing and preparation of the introductory essay.

I am grateful to Estella Gleason, Alberta Asmar, Colleen Van Auken and Miriam Jones who typed the manuscript, cheerfully working under the kind of pressure an author often applies. Mary Jo Remensnyder of the Bureau of History also gave considerable typing help.

I wish to acknowledge assistance from the Wayne State University Research Stimulation Fund.

Copper Country Journal marks the first in a series of books to be co-published by the Bureau of History, Michigan Department of State, and the Great Lakes Series of the Wayne State University Press. In each and every step, Basil Hedrick, director of the Division of Museums, Archaeology and Publications, Bureau of History, was vital in making this joint publication a reality. Arthur Evans, director of the Wayne State University Press, and his staff gave outstanding counsel and encouragement.

I owe a special debt of gratitude to Saralee Howard-Filler, managing editor of the Book Program, Bureau of History, Michigan Department of State. With her experience as an editor and her extensive knowledge of Michigan history, she made contributions at every stage of the editing project. But more than her specific help in editing matters, her enthusiasm for the journal and her commitment to its publication helped me more than I can say.

To all those mentioned, as well as others whose help and encouragement is less easy to pinpoint, my heartfelt appreciation.

Philip P. Mason
Detroit, Michigan
1991

A Vermonter by birth, Henry Hobart traveled to Michigan's Upper Peninsula in the autumn of 1862 to teach school in the rugged mining community of Clifton (on following page). He began his diary on January 1, 1863.

A young Vermont schoolteacher arrived at the town of Clifton, or "Cliff," as it was known, in the remote wilderness of the Keweenaw Peninsula in Michigan's Upper Peninsula in September of 1862. His name was Henry Hobart, and he had come to teach grades one through twelve at the local school.

Clifton was located twenty-three miles north of the town of Houghton and twenty-two miles due west of the town of Copper Harbor, near the tip of the peninsula, surrounded by the frigid waters of Lake Superior. Its nearest neighbor, Eagle River, was three miles to the north.

The business of the Village of Clifton was copper mining. By 1862, when Hobart arrived to begin his work, the Cliff Mine was one of the most famous and productive of the copper mines in North America and was well known in Europe, especially in England. It had drawn foreign workers, predominantly Cornish, Irish and German, from their homelands, to be joined by closer neighbors, French Canadians and native-born Americans, in this rugged frontier community.

This type of cultural diversity and the challenges it presented greeted Hobart and other contract teachers like him upon arrival in the mining towns of the Peninsula. Some of these teachers had been recruited from New England; others had left homes in the New York, Pennsylvania, Ohio, Michigan and Ontario to work under two- and three-year contracts. They shared the common problems of teaching all grades in a one-room schoolhouse, educating—indeed, communicating—with the children of immigrants, adapting to customs far different from their own, enduring crude frontier living conditions and an often hostile climate and a cost of living nearly out of reach of their ostensibly high salaries.

At the same time, the mining towns of northern Michigan and their inhabitants were not spared the economic, social and political stresses generated elsewhere in the still fledgling American nation. The Civil War was raging, pitting family against family and agriculture against industry. It competed for the time, energies and lives of the miners as well as the copper produced by the mines. The temperance movement had reached the Keweenaw, locking horns with the customary binging and brawling inspired by seventy-hour, six-day work weeks in the mines.

What separated Henry Hobart from other contract teachers and the other inhabitants of the mining towns of the Keweenaw Peninsula was an indefatigible sense of history. Starting in 1863, Hobart recorded a detailed account of life in Clifton. For twenty months of his two years as a resident and educational leader of the community, he chronicled daily what he saw and his reactions to it in a large, eight by fourteen inch journal. In these pages, Hobart described the routine of daily life in the mining town, the social and cultural issues facing the struggling inhabitants, the achievements of his students as well as his own professional and personal successes and disappointments during his years in Clifton.

Descriptions of life in Clifton, working conditions in the mine, the influence of alcohol, leading families of the town, the schools, the effects of the Civil War, and copper—the valuable metal that brought them all together—flowed from his pen.

Hobart's observations provide a unique window on the world, fully accompanied by the biases, prejudices and sensitivities of a young man sufficiently disciplined to make a daily record of what he saw. They bring us back in time in a way no less contemporary an account could do and bring alive a culture and community long since passed from the American landscape.

Henry Hobart

The author of the journal, Henry Hobart, was born in
Chittenden County, Vermont on March 4, 1841. He was the eldest
child of Amos and Clarissa Fullington Hobart, both of whom were
born and raised in the Burlington, Vermont area, near Lake Champlain. Henry was one of six children. Another son was Homer,
who was born in 1842 and died in 1861 at the age of nineteen while
a student at the University of Vermont. The eldest daughter was
Jane who died in 1849 at the age of five. The Hobart family twins
were born in 1847; one, Florence, died at age thirty, and the other,
DeForest, died at age two. Gertrude, born in 1855, lived until age
sixty-nine. Like so many families of that time, Amos and Clarissa
suffered the loss of young children.[1]

By 1860, Amos Hobart was a successful farmer in Westford, Vermont. In the 1870s, he moved to nearby Essex Junction. According
to the 1860 Census of Chittenden County, the Hobart farm was
worth $6,000 and Hobart's personal property was valued at
$2,000.[2]

The Hobart livestock included 3 horses, 31 milk cows, 4 working
oxen, 15 cattle, 12 sheep and 2 swine. The farm produced, in 1860,
100 bushels of Indian corn, 300 bushels of oats, 5 bushels of barley,
15 bushels of buckwheat, 50 pounds of wool, 200 bushels of Irish
potatoes, 120 tons of hay, 2000 pounds of butter, 3000 pounds of
cheese and 14,000 pounds of maple sugar.

A decade later, in 1870, the farm had increased in value to
$16,000 and Hobart's personal property was valued at $5,700. By
standards of the day, Amos Hobart was considered a well-to-do
farmer.

Amos Hobart took part in community and civic affairs in
Westford. He served on the Board of Selectmen and ran for the
state legislature in 1864. The Hobart family regularly attended the
local Methodist Episcopal Church.

It was fifteen miles from his first home in Westford that the
young Henry Hobart spent his formative high school years at the
Williston Academy, founded in 1828 by Peter Chase. By the 1850s,
when Henry was a student at Williston, the Academy was widely
recognized for its academic program and attracted students from
other New England, Middle Atlantic and Midwest states. The
school had strict rules governing the behavior of students, not only

The Hobart farmhouse in Westford, Vermont, is shown circa 1920. On March 8, 1863, twenty-two-year old Hobart wrote, "It is Sunday today & sitting in my snug little room my mind wanders to home and home scenes...."

in the classroom but after classes as well. For example, the catalog of the Academy proclaimed:

That the hours of evening be properly spent by the pupil is deemed to be of special importance. Hence all are required to spend the evening at their homes or boarding houses, and a proper amount of it in preparation of lessons for the ensuing day. In no case are students allowed to attend parties or gathering for amusement, during term time; nor are they excused from their rooms at all during the evening, except it be by parental authority for the transaction of necessary business, or by special permission of the Principal.[3]

The Academy also forbade "profane swearing, vulgarity and every other practice calculated to debase the mind and corrupt the heart."[4]

Williston's annual catalogs describe the general areas covered by the curriculum and list the textbooks studied by the students. These documents shed light on his educational background. Among the academic staples and texts required at Williston Academy were:

Common English Branches—Wilson's *Series of Readers*; Cornell's *Geography*; Greenleaf's *Common School Arithmetic*;

High English—Willard's *Universal History*; Cutler's *Anatomy and Physiology*; Parker's *Natural Philosophy*; Porter's *Chemistry*; Burritt's *Geography of the Heavens*; Wayland's *Moral Science*; Greenleaf's *Algebra and Geometry*; Loomis's *Trigonometry*;

Latin—Andrew's *Grammar and Lexicon*;

Greek—Crosby's *Grammar*; Crosby's Xenophon's *Anabasis*; Jacob's *Greek Reader*; Liddell and Scott's *Lexicon*;

French—Fasquelle's *Grammar*; Noel and Chapsal's *Grammar*; *Telemaque*, with notes by Fasquelle; Racine; Mme DeStael; Lamartine; Moliere; Spiers and Surenne's *Dictionary*.[5]

In 1859, Henry Hobart graduated from Williston Academy with a specialization in French. In the fall, he accepted a teaching position on Grand Isle, a large island village in Lake Champlain, north of Burlington. No records have been found to tell the nature of his first teaching experience. There are only passing references to it in his journal.

Archival sources, including the Hobart journal, are silent on how Hobart learned about the teaching opportunity at the Cliff Mine, or who might have recommended him for the position. The

catalog of Williston Academy for 1859 gives a clue.[6] A fellow student of Henry's at Williston was Ascher Robinson of Underhill,
Vermont, a town adjacent to Hobart's home in Westford. In 1860,
Ascher Robinson is listed on the *U.S. Census* as a resident of Clifton, Michigan. His occupation: "teacher"; his birthplace: "Vermont." Robinson may have encouraged Hobart to take his place as
teacher in Clifton when Robinson left in 1862. The Vermont "net-
work" may have again been in action in 1864 when another gradu-
ate of Grand Isle, Maria Hyde, wrote to Henry Hobart seeking
information about a teaching position at Clifton.

Another of the perplexing questions about Henry Hobart was
his status in the Civil War. His daily journal leaves no doubt of his
views on the war. He staunchly defended the Union cause and
President Abraham Lincoln. Anxiously he awaited letters from
home and newspapers to give him news about the war's progress.
He lamented the death of young friends from the Burlington area
who were killed in the war. But why did Hobart not enlist in a Vermont or Michigan regiment? It is true that he had signed a contract
to teach for two years at the Clifton. Yet this responsibility ended
in August 1864 when he returned to his home in Vermont.

Hobart was eligible for the draft under the Militia Act of 1862
that gave the President authority to draft 300,000 militiamen for
nine months as well as the Draft Act of 1863 that provided the first
federal compulsory recruitment of manpower. Under this act, men
between twenty and thirty and unmarried men between thirty-five
and forty-five were drafted first. In 1863, Hobart, a bachelor of
twenty-two, would have been high on the list of eligible draftees.

To evade the draft, Hobart could have hired a subsitute to serve
for him or paid the government three hundred dollars for a communtation by which a drafted man could gain release. There appears to be no record that Hobart enlisted or served in the Union
Army nor is there any record of a communtation or mention of hir-
ing a subsitute. His journal suggests that he would abhor such a
course of action. One explanation is that he lived in areas that met
their quotas and thus avoided service.

We do know that in 1862 this young man accepted an offer to
teach at Clifton. Late in the summer of 1862, he arrived there to
take up his duties in the frontier mining town. Hobart travelled
from Burlington to Detroit by train and then embarked upon a
four- or five-day trip (depending on the weather and connections

at Sault Ste. Marie) from Detroit to the Keweenaw Peninsula. If the harbor at Eagle River was clear, the steamer would have stopped there; otherwise, Hobart would have disembarked at Copper Harbor and taken a stagecoach to Clifton.

Hobart had several choices of living accommodations in Clifton. There were boarding houses that catered to single miners. A log house was available if he could afford the rent and had the time and inclination to cook for himself. Another option was boarding with one of the established families. He chose the last alternative and boarded with Joseph Rawlings, a prominent mine engineer and mechanic, his wife, the former Johanna Penberthy, seven children, and servants, in a large frame house.

Living at the Rawlings home in 1862 were five Penberthy boys, born of Johanna Penberthy's previous marriage: Edward, age twenty; James, age sixteen; William, age fourteen; Josiah, age thirteen; and Stephen, age eleven. The last three boys were enrolled in Hobart's class. The two children of Joseph Rawlings and Johanna Penberthy were Eliza, age five, and Samuel, age three.

At the Rawlings-Penberthy home, Hobart shared a room with Josiah, the youngest Penberthy child; a hoard of ravenous bedbugs who visited during the summer months; and mosquitoes on hot and humid days. In his entry of May 29, 1863, as the warm weather arrived in Clifton, Hobart complained: "The mosquitoes are giving me fits as I am writing in my room this evening and when I retire the bed bugs will be more ravenous." He reported he had "killed nearly a pint of these sweet creatures . . . Oh horrors, covered with the little biters, how can one sleep."

Hobart shared meals with the Rawlings family although he balked at Cornish food and its manner of preparation.

> Very invigorating weather it is true but there is a great scarcity in the eating line—no meat, stale butter, old molasses & white bread which I like if there was some corn bread once in a while. But I get tired of it without milk, no pies or anything inviting. One of my little girls brings me an apple once in a while which is a fine treat. I have had one or two eggs just enough to inform me that they go fine but I cannot have them. The warehouse pork would do for one to eat who had lost the sense of smell. In any other circumstances it is no go.

Hobart especially disliked breakfast, writing on one occasion about the "dry wheat bread and water." He described the butter as

23

"so filthy, I can hardly get along with it on the table much less try to eat it." He longed for New England cooking during his stay at Clifton, and wrote invidiously of the meals at the Rawlings home. "My mouth fairly waters for a home meal." Whenever Hobart went to Eagle River or Houghton, he revelled in the taste of the culinary specialities of the hotels there that included oysters, fresh meat and apple pie.

Hobart's relationships with members of the Rawlings-Penberthy family were complex as evidenced by the frequent attention given to the subject in his journal. On the one hand, Hobart had the highest respect for and a close and warm friendship with forty- year-old Joseph Rawlings. Hobart had daily contact with Joseph, and the two had long conversations about the operation of the Cliff Mine, Rawlings' early years in Cornwall and his interest in cartography. Hobart clearly enjoyed Rawlings's sharp wit and humorous anecdotes.

His views on Mrs. Rawlings, however, were different. He found her garrulous, argumentative and a poor cook and housekeeper. He was revolted by the lack of cleanliness in the kitchen: "Wipe the knives and forks on the towel, wash the plates in the wash dish and perhaps in the same water that some nasty little urchin has used." She was "well versed in tyrannizing over all who came under [her] authority," Hobart wrote. "She has had four girls this summer who have left rather than listed to her jawings."

At the same time, Hobart developed close personal and friendly relationships with the Penberthy boys. Although there was intense competition between Hobart and Edward Penberthy—they were the same age—they spent much time together, travelling to Eagle River, Houghton and Eagle Harbor and on expeditions to hunt and fish. William, Josiah and Stephen Penberthy were among Hobart's "scholars" and he saw them constantly.

Existing archival sources give us no clue as to the origin of Hobart's strong feelings on subjects such as temperance but there was a series of public temperance meetings in Burlington, Williston and other Vermont communites during the 1840s and 1850s. The Methodist Episcopal Church where the Hobart family worshipped strongly supported the temperance cause.[7] Temperance societies were formed in many communities, sponsoring weekly meetings and rallies and campaigning for legislation that curbed the use of alcohol.

Whatever the source of his conviction, he brought his strong opposition to the use of alcohol with him to Clifton. There it received reinforcement from his observations of the constant abuse of beer and liquor as well as from the Methodist Church that shared Hobart's temperance stance. The sermons of local and visiting ministers stressing the value of abstinence often made their way into Hobart's journal and he cited examples, arguments and statistics of the speakers. Hobart held out no hope for those addicted to strong drink until they took the pledge of total abstinence. Repeatedly, he described and bemoaned the drunken brawls that characterized the weekends and holiday celebrations in town. In one of his frequent journal entries on the subject, Hobart observed:

> I witnessed several who used the "eye water", and were *hors de combat*, or in other words tight as Nooies [Cornish], raving mad under the influence of Gin. What disgraceful scenes for grown men to enact. I have seen them abuse their wives and kick them & beat them, pursue them from one place to another until they would hide in some house until the man was no longer drunk....

On another occasion, Hobart looked at Mrs. Carter, a fellow teacher and wife of a mine carpenter, who had violated the oath of abstinence: "I say hunt her out of the place. Shun her always."

More than a mere observer and scribe, Hobart took an active part in the temperance movement. He was a leader in founding a branch of the Independent Order of Good Templars, a temperance organization, in Clifton, and took regular part in its meetings and work. He founded and directed the Band of Hope, a "juvenile" temperance group, similar to those he had known in Vermont, for his students and other young citizens of Clifton. The way Hobart brought and shared his views of temperance is an example of how ideas and social movements established in communities of the East were carried and spread to frontier areas.

Hobart's two years as schoolmaster—in the years when he finished his teen years and entered his twenties—had a profound effect upon him. The experience created a lasting bond with the Midwest, deepened his awareness of the perilous existence of copper miners, and renewed his dedication to his early Christian beliefs.

Hobart the Teacher

When Henry Hobart arrived in Clifton in the late summer of 1862, he found a schoolhouse built in 1859 when the Clifton School District was first organized. It was already too small for the student body, having been designed for one hundred students. By 1862, the student population had risen; the facilities were totally inadequate.

During his first year of teaching in Clifton, Hobart had 224 pupils, or "scholars," as they were called, ranging in age from five to twenty. For an average of twenty-six days a month, Monday through Saturday, ten months of the year, teacher Hobart averaged eighty students a day. When the daily attendance exceeded 125, the school was so overcrowded it put the education of the diverse student body nearly out of reach.

The schoolhouse and land on which it was built were worth $2,000 in 1863.[8] During the summer of that year, the school house was enlarged to a building seventy-five feet long and divided into two large rooms to separate the primary from the upper grades. A wood stove provided heat for each room.

There were 320 volumes in the school's library, including books of literature, arithmetic, spelling, algebra, geography, grammar and natural philosophy. In addition, the Public Library of Clifton was housed in the schoolhouse in a large wooden bookcase. There is no record of the contents of the Public Library in 1862-64, but by 1870 it contained 504 books including a "judicious selection from various fields of English literature."[9] During his two years at Clifton, Hobart was responsible for the operation of the Public Library and his journal reveals that the citizens of Clifton made frequent use of it.

Public records show the Clifton school budget for the year ending September 7, 1863, was $1,716.29, raised as follows: [10]

Money on hand	$57.20
Two Mill Tax	$756.29
Primary School Fund	$118.40
Other District Taxes	$650.00
Library Money	$134.40
Total	**$1,716.29**

This schoolhouse was enlarged in the summer of 1863. The building contractor left without finishing the job; Hobart arranged for the building construction to be completed and painted the structure himself.

The expenditures for the school for the same period were:

Paid Male Teacher	$405.00
Paid Female Teacher	$180.00
Building Repairs	$650.00
Library Books	$95.43
Other Purchases	$175.00
Total	**$1,505.43**

For his first year at Clifton, Henry Hobart received $405.00 for teaching twenty-six days a month for ten months. During the summer of 1863, he earned an additional $52.00 for painting the schoolhouse and $20.00 for taking care of the Public Library collection. During the 1863-64 academic year, he received $50.00 a month, or an annual wage of $500.00.

Hobart's salary at the Clifton school does not compare to modern standards, but, for the time, it was better than the salaries paid in many eastern states. In Vermont, for example, the average salary for a male teacher in 1860 was $17.40 a month, exclusive of room and board; for a female teacher it was $7.80 a month. In Clifton, nearly $20.00 a month was paid for a female teacher.[11]

Perhaps the most interesting and surprising attribute that Hobart brought to his task was his philosophy of teaching. Despite his own rigid and disciplined experience, he was not a stern disciplinarian. He developed and preferred a gentler approach. In his journal entry on November 23, 1863, Hobart wrote:

> I have become a disbeliever in punishment in the school room. I believe in mild means for I have found it the best. I have not been governed by anyone's theory—it is a result of my own experience and I can show as fine a school as anyone. I have no rulers or whips. I have scholars who love me and who are willing to act as I desire. How pleasant.

Even with the most positive of attitudes, Hobart faced difficult conditions for his objectives. The constant turnover of students, frequent absences due to illness, and the problem of attempting to teach 80 to 125 students each day in a single room made Hobart's task more than an ordinary challenge. His journal made frequent reference to the frustration he felt in trying to teach so many:

This evening I can say that it has been a very warm day and one that has placed me in a position that I was never in before viz. to have the charge of one hundred and thirty students in a school room large enough to accomodate seventy-five. It has been a severe day's labor for me. . . . .

On an autumn day, four month later, during his second year at Clifton, he lamented:

I had a few new scholars yesterday which makes a large school for me to manage. I have hard work and from this constant confinement I feel lazy or as if my life were worn out. I long for some smart exercise, for a change. Confinement with such care as I have is very severe. It can hardly be endured.

The problems facing Henry Hobart as Clifton's schoolteacher were not different from those encountered by other school teachers in mining towns of the Keweenaw Peninsula. Lack of interest by parents was evidenced by the meager turnout at school board meetings and other school functions. Hobart and other teachers often commented that only members of the school board attended. In addition, the constant mobility of miners during the 1860s resulted in continual turnover of the student body. Miners left Clifton to work at other mines on the peninsula paying higher wages, with shallower mine shafts than those at the Cliff Mine. Of course, many young students between the ages of fourteen and twenty left school to work in the mines.

The health hazards of the day including head lice also took their toll on Hobart's wards. Hobart wrote: "Black hair white with the eggs of the sweet animal. There are lice enough in the head of most any child to make a Cornish pasty."

Beyond such sufferable although unpleasant infestations, the epidemics of scarlet fever and influenza as well as kidney disease in 1862, 1863 and 1864, caused frequent absences from school. As one would expect, the funerals of young scholars who failed to survive sudden and unexpected illnesses disrupted many school sessions and added a truly melancholy dimension to Hobart's responsibilities as teacher. Among the most poignant entries in Hobart's journal are his accounts of the losses of his young wards to accident and illness.

On January 23, 1864, Hobart attended the funeral of one of his favorite "scholars," Isabella, the nine-year-old daughter of Harlow and Jane Everett. She had died of typhoid after an illness of four weeks. Although a quiet sufferer in her last moments, Hobart wrote, "she died happy kissing her little sister and saying she was going to Jesus. She was a member of the Sunday School and loved by all."

Other young children died that winter, some suddenly, prompting Hobart to lament: "How sad to see the young die when giving promise of future excellence. . . . No one can tell who may be called next." Hobart also mourned the tragic loss of four of the five children of James Souden, mining engineer at the Cliff, including two who died within a week, of scarlet fever. "It seems impossible for some to raise a child. . . . I am feeling very lonesome."

Meanwhile, the mine took its toll. The death of Henry Benney, a boy of thirteen who had left school to work with his father underground, is reported on the journal on February 18, 1864. Young Henry fell to his death from a slippery ladder. "His poor father feels very bad and his mother and sister have met with a severe loss. How they grieve the sad death of their boy who was full of promise and hopes."

Despite the emotional strains of watching his students fall prey to the rigors of the rugged times and lifestyle in the mining village, Hobart was still able to take great pleasure in their academic successes. One of Hobart's special interest was training students for spelling bees. This required hours of extra practice sessions often held in the evenings and on weekends, as well as trips to Eagle River, Eagle Harbor and nearby mining villages to compete with other contestants. In February 1863, in preparation for a challenge to a spelling bee from students in Eagle River, Hobart noted: "There is great excitement in consequence of this affair. My scholars are working day and night. I have met them every night this week."

Hobart made sure the students were recognized for their efforts. On one occasion when returning from a victorious expedition to Eagle River, he led his students through the village of Clifton singing, "Three cheers for the Clifton School. . . . " He then treated them to candy and "went home feeling well." Judging from the number of victories by the scholars of Clifton, Hobart's efforts in inspiring the students to participate in this discretionary intellectural pursuit were successful.

Hobart also made a vital contribution to the educational program of Michigan when he opened an evening school for mine workers. Starting in January 1863, he held classes each evening from five to nine. The ages of the evening students ranged from fifteen to fifty; many were the parents of the young charges he taught during the day. Most of the evening students were German workers unable to read English; others could speak a limited amount of English. All were interested in bettering themselves.[12]

Unfortunately, many of the students could not keep up with the pace of evening classes. Because of the shortage of laborers at the Cliff Mine in 1863, miners were ordered to work additional shifts and were unable or too exhausted to attend night school. Nevertheless, it was a credit to Hobart that he responded to the needs of the immigrant workers and attempted to provide them with educational opportunities.

Meanwhile, the school faced other challenges peculiar to the Keweenaw Peninsula. The blustery, frigid winters, with weeks of snowy sub-freezing weather, made it difficult to keep the school rooms evenly heated. As teacher, Hobart had to gather wood for the stove and attend to it regularly. Even then, the wind blew through the cracks in the walls of the school house. Snowdrifts, sometimes six to ten feet high, required constant shoveling to clear the way for students to enter and leave the building, as well as to locate wood needed to fuel the stoves.

The frustrations and challenges of teaching in a frontier mining community did not prevent Hobart from gaining the respect of his students. He developed close rapport with many, visited their homes and shared meals with their families. Of his students, he said: "They all like me and speak well of their teacher. This is pleasant and right. I hold that there should be good feeling and perfect love between pupil and teacher."

In the winter of 1864, Hobart hired two teams of horses, at his own expense, and borrowed a third, to take a group of students on a special outing.

At 9:00 the teams were ready and with three flags flying we left the Cliff singing "Rally round the flag boys." We went through the villages of Eagle River, Garden City, Humboldt, Copper Falls etc. Arrived at the harbor at half past twelve.

Had the large hall warmed and there we all took a fine lunch that we brought with us. We returned our sincere thanks to the proprietor and his wife, sung them a song, gave them three cheers for the Cliff and went home. The day was beautiful and my scholars had a fine treat. This is a great encouragement to them. They will always remember the ride Mr. Hobart gave them.

Before he left Clifton, he hired a photographer to take "likenesses" of several of his favorite scholars. The admiration held for Hobart by his students and their families led the town's leaders to try to encourage him to renew his contract and remain in Clifton as their schoolmaster. On March 3, 1864, Hobart recorded: "Mrs. Souden was in last night and said she did not know what would be done if I did not come back next summer." He noted with satisfaction: "The children all love their teacher." Indeed, parents from other mining communities in the area, familiar with Hobart's teaching skills, tried to secure him as their children's teacher when his contract in Clifton ran out.

On July 16, 1864, the last day of school, Hobart wrote in his journal: "Every pupil is anxious to have me return again and the final class caused them sadness."

Life in Clifton

What greeted Henry Hobart when he arrived in the village of Clifton in the fall of 1862 may not have been the Old West, but it was a rugged frontier community nonetheless. Far different from the farms of Vermont, Clifton was more the rural industrial environment, with the attendant characteristics and problems of a centrally employed, laboring populace. Interdependence and isolation, epidemics and death, drinking and brawling, and crimes and violence challenged the residents of Clifton and characterized their lives.

In the 1850s and 1860s, Clifton was an isolated frontier community with few good roads to travel to nearby towns. There was a military road that ran through Clifton, connecting Copper Harbor on the northern tip of the Keweenaw Peninsula and Ontonagon, but it was impassable for many months of the year. During winter

Above is the village of Clifton with the Methodist Episcopal Church at the far left; inset is a view from atop the bluff looking down upon the village and the Cliff Mine.

months when snow covered the ground, more reliable transpora-
tion from the Cliff Mine to Hancock, Houghton, Ontonagon and
other mining towns was by sleigh, operated by the Anderson Stage
Company. During the late spring and summer, it was often much
easier to travel by steamer or other vessel between Eagle River and
Ontonagon.

The macadam road between Clifton and Eagle River was kept in
good condition by the Cliff Mine Company, for it was in constant
use for mining business. In 1860, one writer described travel on
this busy thoroughfare: "Masses of copper from four to eight tons
weight are loaded on great groaning trucks and hauled by four to
six yoke of oxen go slowly down the smooth road . . . to Eagle
River."[13]

In addition to wagon roads on the Keweenaw, there were paths
and trails running from Clifton to the bluff above the town and to
the nearby Delaware, North Cliff, North Western and Central
mines. On Sundays and holidays, Cliff miners and their families
visited friends and relatives at these mines and in other nearby
communities.

The coming of snows and blizzards in November and December
marked the end of the shipping season and the beginning of six
stark months of isolation for the village of Clifton. It was not only
impossible to reach Clifton from Detroit and the lower Lakes during the winter; it was also virtually impossible to leave Clifton and
reach other cities in the Midwest. A few hardy travelers made the
trip overland by sleigh, wagon and on foot to central Wisconsin
where there were railroad connections to Chicago, Detroit and
eastern cities.[14] One writer described the isolation as "being so far
outside of the track of civilization, that reckoned by present standards any point in Alaska's interior would seem in close touch."[15]

The only other contacts Clifton residents had with "down state"
Michigan—and other areas of the country called "below" by local
residents—during the harsh and snowbound months of winter
were the unreliable overland mail deliveries via Green Bay and
Appleton, Wisconsin. An account left by a local miner in 1858 described the precarious state of the mails:

> The mail bags were securely strapped onto a small sleigh
> which is drawn by five dogs, the whole being in charge of an
> Indian who runs by their side . . . it being a novel sight to
> many of us as well as a matter of much importance seeing our

correspondence with distant friends depend upon its safety. Large numbers of miners assembled in front of the Company's big store to see it off.[16]

The mail service seldom brought prompt contact with friends and relatives. In fact, mail delivery was the center of bitter controversy pitting Upper Peninsula residents, businessmen and merchants against the United States Postal Service and their contractors. According to complaints in 1863, it took thirty-five days to send a letter, and to get an answer, from New York City to Ontonagon via Green Bay, Wisconsin. Mail arrived at the post office in Clifton on the average of every twelve days in 1863, although a record was set in March 1864 when mail delivery from Green Bay to Rockland near Ontonagon, took only four days.[17]

Hobart remarked in his Journal about the problem, attributing it to poor mangement:

Last night there was a mail in but no news of importance. The contractor, Mr. Harvey, who is the person to furnish this upper country with the mail is a penurious scapegoat like most Government contractors and has hired a set of lazy fellows because he could get them cheap to bring it from below and the consequence is we receive it very irregular

The condition of the mail and parcels delivered to residents of Clifton was also a target of sharp and frequent criticism. On one occasion in 1863, an indignant businessman from Hancock, a mining town about twenty miles south of Clifton, described the mail as "resembling more the contents of bleaching vat than a U. S. Mail." On another occasion, mail bags were found "hanging from a tree" on one of the mail routes from Green Bay. They were left there to lighten the carrier's load, to be picked up on the next run.[18]

The frequency of mail deliveries at Clifton was carefully recorded in Henry Hobart's journal, as he awaited news from home and reports on national events. Mail arrived at the post office and was picked up there. On January 8, 1864, Hobart ended his journal entry with word of mail from home:

I heard that there was a mail and went over to the Office and found a letter from Mother, Gertie and Florence. How glad I was to hear from home for it has been a long time since I received any news. It is very cheering to read Mother's kind letter full of good advice which I shall ever remember and try to heed. Florence wrote a good one. She is at school which I am glad to hear. Gertie's little letter caused me to laugh very much. How I would like to see them all. There is nothing like home which I long to see. *Je Fini Pour Cet Temps.*

After navigation on Lake Superior was opened, around May 1 of each year, mail delivery was more reliable and regular. Most steamers bound for Keweenaw Peninsula ports stopped at Copper Harbor and Eagle River to deliver and pick up mail. On one tragic occasion, the postmaster at Eagle River was blown out into Lake Superior and lost after he had rowed out to pick up mail from steamer anchored outside the harbor.[19]

Like the mail, newspapers were anxiously awaited by Cliff residents. Among those regularly received in the mining town were *Harper's Weekly, Frank Leslie's Illustrated Weekly, Harper's New Monthly Magazine, Scientific American, Godey's Lady's Book,* the *London News,* the *New York Tribune* and the *Detroit Free Press,* along with newspapers from Cleveland, Milwaukee, Chicago and other cities. German newspapers published in Detroit, Milwaukee and other Midwest cities were also popular.

By 1860, there were three local newspapers available to Clifton residents. The *Lake Superior Miner* was published in Ontonagon; the *Lake Superior News* and *Mining Journal* in Marquette; and the *Portage Lake Mining Gazette* in Houghton. All of these were published weekly and delivered promptly to the mining communities. The *Lake Superior Journal,* originally published in Copper Harbor as the *Lake Superior News and Mining Journal* from 1846 to 1850, had many subscribers and readers in Clifton, especially in the summer months when delivery was regularly scheduled.

News accounts gave Clifton residents information on the latest developments in national and international affairs. Fires, natural disasters, riots, wars and weather conditions were covered. *Godey's Lady's Book* and *Harper's New Monthly Magazine* provided accounts of social life in America, with special attention to women's fashions.

The Upper Peninsula newspapers reported the local news. Mining was given extensive coverage. The annual reports of the Pittsburgh and Boston Mining Company, for example, were published in full each spring in the *Portage Lake Mining Gazette.*[20] The arrival of the mail and, during open navigation, the schedules of the steamers were announced. Local elections and social functions, including meetings of the Masons, Odd Fellows, Knights of Pythias,

Good Templars, and church services were noted. Interestingly, mining accidents and deaths were mentioned but seldom given lengthy coverage. Such occurrences were either taken for granted or understated by newspaper editors.[21]

The isolated location of Clifton, far from adequate medical facilities, seriously compromised the health of its residents. The practice of medicine at the Cliff Mine and in other mining communities was crude and suffered from lack of proper supplies and equipment. There were no hospitals in the Upper Peninsula at this time; the nearest was in Detroit, over five hundred miles away. Because of the dangers posed by underground mining activities and machinery operations on the surface, most of the larger mining companies did employ physicians, domiciled at the mine sites. To pay the doctor's salary, mine workers contributed wages.[22] This was simply a version of the "bal surgeon" system long used at Cornish mines. For the period from 1862-1864, Dr. Senter and Dr. A.I. Lawbaugh served as doctors in Clifton.[23]

There were, however, no trained nurses or other medical personnel to assist the physicians. On one recorded occasion, when surgery was necessary, Dr. Abram S. Heaton had to train a mine employee to assist him in giving the anesthesia.[26]

For dental work, Clifton residents had to trek to Eagle River. Hobart's journal entries bear personal testimony that dental work of the day was painful indeed:

> Last Saturday I went to the Doctor's office and had Dr. Greelee commence the job of filling my teeth. Three or four of the front ones with Gold and other with tin foil. It is a severe task to remain quiet and let a dentist fill decayed teeth after going through the painful operation of having them dug out.

Hobart may have considered himself lucky. Far worse fates than toothaches befell many other Clifton residents. Epidemics of influenza and scarlet fever took their toll. During the winter of 1863-64, according to Hobart, "most everyone is or has been sick with influenza." Dropsy and scarlet fever spread throughout the Peninsula, taking the lives of many young children, often with only a few hours warning. In January and February of 1863 alone, nearly one dozen died. The headstones of the period found in the cemeteries in Clifton and nearby Eagle River bear silent testimony to the losses borne by so many families.

As the rugged frontier life at the Cliff Mine was a constant threat to the health and survival of miners and their families, it curtailed leisure pursuits. The underground miners, surface laborers, teamsters and mining company staff worked six days per week and averaged ten hours a day. By 1862, when the copper country was suffering an acute labor shortage, workers were often assigned an additional half shift. If a worker refused to work, he was fired and forced to leave Clifton. As a result, the mine workers had little time available for socializing, recreation, athletics, reading or other leisure activities.

To many, Sunday, the day off, was the only opportunity for relaxation and release from the long hours underground, or in the stamp, washing and engine shops. For those families with deep religious convictions, it was a day of mandatory rest, with church services in the morning and evening. Each of the churches in the vicinity of Clifton held Sunday School classes for the children.

In 1862, when Hobart arrived in Clifton, there were three churches with active congregations: the Grace Episcopal, the Methodist Episcopal and the Catholic. The Methodist Episcopal, which had the largest congregation, was the oldest church in Clifton. It had been organized by eight miners with the assistance of the Reverend John Pitezel.[25] Pitezel preached the first service in the coopers shop at the mine in 1846. During the next year, a church building was constructed in Clifton.

The Cornish formed the nucleus of the Methodist Episcopal congregation in the 1860s. They followed a practice of encouraging lay participation in church services, and on numerous occasions young Cornish miners gave the church sermons.[26]

It was the Methodist Episcopal Church that formed the center of temperance movement in the town. Perhaps in part because of its view on alcohol, the Methodist Episcopal was Hobart's place of worship and he taught Sunday School there. Hobart praised the example set by the church pastor, the Reverend John A. Baughman:

> We are blessed here with the very best preaching. Rev. Mr. Baughman, the Methodist preacher, is a man of superior talents and takes a great interest in my school. [He] has held the highest position as a divine Presiding Elder Agent of the American Bible Society and etc. He is now 61 years of age, weighs 251 lbs. and has never taken intoxicating drink in any form or tobacco. Would that every man might say the same.

The following year, Hobart repeatedly lamented the Reverend Baughman's departure from Clifton and the weaknesses of his replacement, the Reverend Wright, who, when younger, had been a sailor and "a drinking man."

The Grace Episcopal was the second church established in Clifton. It was organized in 1855 through the efforts of Hervey C. Parke, the chief clerk at the Cliff Mine. The church building opened in August 1856 and was consecrated by Bishop Samuel A. McCoskey. It offered active church and Sunday School programs.[27]

Meanwhile, the congregation of the Church of the Assumption was made up mostly of Irish and German residents. The only Catholic church in Clifton, it was built in 1859 at a cost of $1,860. Bishop Frederic Baraga preached the first sermon in the new church.[28]

The rigorous schedule of worship on the one day off each week left little time for play. Rawlings, mine engineer and Hobart's host in Clifton, observed: "there was no ball playing, or sports of any kind allow'd on Sundays, in public; so everybody had to be 'as good as they knew how' or woe to the transgressor, for the 'good people' were very 'goody goody.'"[29] Rawlings also described the special Sunday dress in Clifton: "all the young men on Sundays wore 'pepper and salt' pants, high boots or moccasins and a red/blue flannel shirt with a silk sash or scarf twisted around the body a few times instead of suspenders; vests or coats were seldom worn in summer or winter, and an overcoat was a rarity."[30]

The churches played a central role in the lives of many of the Cliff miners and their families. Despite some friction among the three denominations and even some competition for parishioners, the regular Sunday services and Sunday Schools at all three churches in Clifton were well-attended.

For the less religious, Sundays and holidays were occasions for revelry. As in many, more urban, mining communities, drinking and gambling were two of the few outlets for the miners and other workers. In Clifton, the many single men, unmarried or separated from their families, led the pack and intensified the toll such activities took on the village. Brawls and holiday drinking binges punctuated the weekend, leading to many arrests and stiff fines.

Celebrations regularly began Saturday night at the end of the last shift, or at the beginning of a holiday recess. Some miners left Clifton on Sunday to travel to saloons in Eagle River and Eagle Harbor. In

Eagle Harbor, there were a reported twenty-seven saloons in the 1860s, as well as a brewery. In describing miners' propensity for drink, one writer observed: "Much drinking, much blasphemy, much fighting. . . roughs, maddened with whiskey, ruled the roost."[31] A sober citizen, another wrote, "could only hide himself in his house til the storm blew over."[32]

Mine officials at the Cliff Mine, who had almost complete control of life at Clifton, could have prohibited the importation and sale of beer and whiskey in the village. However, they owned most of the dwellings and boarding houses where beer and liquor were served and sold. Clifton was not unique in this regard.

Beyond the profits realized by mine officials through the sale of alcoholic beverages, mine officials believed drinking had a useful and restorative purpose in providing miners, especially those who lived alone, a release or escape from the drudgery and exhaustion of long days of dangerous and arduous work. And they preferred to provide alcohol in Clifton rather than to have miners travel to Eagle River or Eagle Harbor for their supply.

Contributing to the violence that often accompanied binging in Clifton and other mining communities was the long-standing hostility between the Cornish and Irish. Separated by religious affiliation, custom and culture, the two groups were polarized by feuding and fighting. Violence erupted at the Quincy Mine in January 1863 when a Cornish miner was stabbed by a group of Irish workers. Thirteen Irishmen were arrested in connection with the assault. [33]

Elsewhere, in mining communities with a large German population, the Germans helped to maintain law and order and balance between the Irish and the Cornish, curbing open violence. Cliff engineer Rawlings noted in his reminiscences that after the larger contingent of Irish workers left the Minesota Mine for the smaller mines in the area, "peace returned" because the Cornish and Irish populations were more equally balanced. [34]

The Cliff Mine suffered its share of alcohol-driven violence. In 1864, Hobart described in his journal an incident following a night of drinking by Irish workers. One of them, Mr. More, was beaten and buried under a cord of wood and snow. He was discovered and saved by a teamster who saw his boot sticking out of the snow. Hobart blamed drinking: "Strange to say he was alive though out of his mind. He will probably recover. Drink is the cause of this outrage. It will not be noticed." Two arrests followed.

Far sadder was the toll taken on families. Hobart described, on December 7, 1863, the tragic death of a mother and child, thrown out of the house after a drunken argument:

I hear that a drunken husband drove his wife out doors at midnight with a little boy at the Phoenix mine. The mother and child were without clothing and were found the next morning frozen in the cold snow a few rods from the house without any clothing. It is stated that they were both drunk and he has turned her out before. It was not so cold but what she might have found shelter in houses near by if she had been sober. If she was drunk she would not think of the thing. It is a sad affair. How that little boy must have felt taken from a warm bed out into the cold to be frozen to death on the body of his mother. This is one of the results of drinking. It should be put down. A man going to church the next morning saw them by the road side. He went to the house and called the husband asking who it was. He replied he did not know but imagine his feelings on seeing them dead. He is free by a jury.

Although not much of a match for the incentives to drink, the temperance movement in Clifton did what it could. A Lodge of the Independent Order of Good Templars was founded in Clifton in January 1863. A secret society, all of its members were "sworn to use no kind of intoxicating drink." It met frequently and campaigned regularly against the use of alcohol.

There were also crimes of passion in the mining town. In December 1862, Clifton was a scene of a crime involving the town blacksmith, Mr. Richards, and Mr. Harris, a miner. Harris's wife ran one of the local boarding houses. Harris suspected Richards had an interest in his wife and warned Richards to stay away from her. On the evening of December 9, Harris purposely missed his shift underground and returned to the boarding house, where he found Richards and his wife together. He fatally wounded Richards but, before he could reload his shotgun to turn it on his wife, other miners restrained him and turned him over to the sheriff in Eagle River. Accounts of the shooting and subsequent trial were covered in detail in the local newspapers.

While the village of Clifton attempted to cope on a local scale with the drinking and the accompanying violence of its citizenry, it was not spared the profound effects of violence raging on a national scale in the American Civil War. The Union effort created a dramatic increase in demand for copper. The sheathing on wooden warships, naval equipment, bronze cannons, pots and pans, brass buttons and coins were all produced from copper and caused a constant demand for Lake Superior ore.

Ironically, at the same time that the war stimulated a sharp increase in the production of copper, the campaign to recruit volunteers to join Union regiments decimated the labor force, particularly at the Cliff Mine. The Cliff Mine was assigned a quota of thirty-two recruits in response to a call for 11,298 volunteers to fill the ranks of Michigan regiments, which were floundering in October 1863 after two years of conflict.[35]

The offerings of bounties by federal, state and local governments of up to one thousand dollars per recruit swelled enlistments from the Cliff area and further depleted the work force. In order to counteract the enlistment of mine workers, mining companies paid for substitutes to meet enrollment quotas for the Keweenaw Peninsula.[36]

Each major battle of the war was described in local papers in detail; speeches of President Abraham Lincoln and other leaders were repeated verbatim. Hobart reported on one such speech by General Butler:

> I notice in the [*Independent*] an extract of a speech of Gen. Butler's delivered in New York April 2. It is a very good thing and shows that he is deeply imbued with pure love for the Union and Government. He is one of our best Generals and should have a high position.

Local war recruiting campaigns, parades and patriotic meetings were reported as well. Letters from local soldiers describing the battle campaigns appeared frequently and there was a continuous string of reports and obituaries on local soldiers.

On May 7, 1863, Hobart wrote of a battle report received by mail from "below," and in it reveals his keen interest in the War and its progress.

> We have just received a heavy mail from below with dates as late as the first of May. Frank Leslie's has several pictures of the bombardment of Fort Sumter by our ironclads which was a failure, or we could not reach the city of Charleston owning to obstructions in the river. The month of April has been one

of the most eventful in our nation's history. The rebellion culminated into open war two years ago and Fort Sumter was
take by the rebels after fighting with only seventy men to defend her against thousands. . . .

It was a frustration and sense of disappointment Hobart expressed often. His comments demonstrate a good contemporary
appreciation for the impact of the War for one so far away. On the
Fourth of July in 1863, Hobart wrote:

A terrible civil war, unparalleled in history is raging and desolating the fairest portions of our Land. It is a result of slavery
of the same aristocratic feeling that was planning our submission and carrying it out at the time of the revolution. It originated from the dregs of aristocracy, the seed from England
that were sown in the parts of our land. Slavery extended its
influence under the protection of Government until it received a check by the election of an administrator whose
views were for liberty, then it came out in open war with the
Government.

Meanwhile, the Civil War caused bitter feelings among Clifton
residents. Many of the Cornish, Irish and German immigrants had
little interest in the war and refused to participate in patriotic rallies at the mine; some even expressed sympathy for the Confeder-
ate cause, resulting in nasty exchanges with Union supporters.
Hobart criticized the Cornish residents' lack of patriotism at the
news of the Union victory:

The boys were out playing the fife and drum and all were jubilant. Cornishmen care nothing about it only hoping it will
prevent a draft. They would do almost anything rather than
go fight for the country. Those who enlisted from here after
getting their advance pay deserted in Detroit fleeing to Canada. Very little sympathy is manifested here for the Government, that is, among a certain class of Cornishmen.

Despite the pressures of work, illness and the effects of national
affairs on the little village of Clifton, the residents found time for
play and celebration. Aside from Sundays, holidays provided time
off from the mine and an excuse for recreation and relaxation.

During the last day of each month, for example, mine operations
shut down except for the work of "measuring the number of feet each
miner has cut or drifted." After the tabulation was made and recorded,

a miner could go to the mine office and receive his pay, "not to exceed his wages after deducting his expenses." Like Sundays, this was a "jolly day for the miners" and many, according to one observer, "went to the beer shop and enjoyed a 'drop of beer.'"[37]

The Christmas season was an occasion for great celebration. As Hobart recorded in his journal, the mine was closed for eight to ten days around Christmas and New Year's, providing a much welcomed respite during the frigid days of winter in Lake Superior. Church services were held Christmas Eve, and groups of children, families and single workers went from house to house singing Christmas carols. A common practice among the Cornish was to "sing for beer." Many families at Clifton trimmed a tree in their homes and exchanged presents on Christmas Day. During the Christmas recess, some Clifton residents visited friends and relatives in nearby towns. Hobart described his activities on his first Christmas in Clifton :

> Christmas night I spent at a social party at Mr. Brockway's Hotel in Eagle River. Custom makes it binding on the respectable class to attend this party. Thus I passed one Christmas very pleasantly in the northern part of Michigan.

The following year, on December 26, 1863, Hobart and his friends, Joe Retallick and Edward, John and William Penberthy, took the Anderson Company sleigh to Portage Lake and stayed at the Douglass House, a well-known hotel in the Keweenaw Peninsula. They spent several days visiting friends and touring the mining operations of the area.

St. Patrick's Day was celebrated by the Irish residents at Cliff, although it was not considered a formal holiday. There were usually parades, music, speeches and religious services.[38] The Fourth of July was well-celebrated at Clifton, especially during the Civil War years when patriotic feelings ran high.[39] Hobart described the 1863 festivities:

> The Methodist Sunday School started the thing and it was on their behalf. First there was marching after martial music, the committee acting as marshals for the scholars who made a long procession with banners flying. They then stopped by the side of the church where there were seats and a platform built. After Prayer and singing I read the Declaration of Independence and the Rev. Mr. Baughman followed with a fine

speech. The committee were then very busy passing lemonade, candy, nuts, provisions to the satisfaction of all.

Meanwhile, there were celebrations of a different character in
other parts of Clifton for, that evening, a brawl led to the arrest of
several miners "for drunkenness and fighting."

Throughout the year, fraternal organization sponsored activities.
In 1862, the Independent Order of Odd Fellows, Lodge #79, established in Eagle Harbor in 1859, moved to Clifton. This secret fraternal order held meetings every Saturday and assisted members and
the community in a variety of ways. Members of the Good Templars Lodge, the local temperance contingent, took turns watching
over fellow members who were sick or dying and handled funeral
arrangements and services for deceased members.[40]

Hobart, an active member and secretary of the good Templars
Lodge for most of his stay in Clifton, also formed the Band of
Hope, a juvenile temperance organization and served as its president.[41] At one time in May 1864, the Band had seventy members.
During the Fourth of July celebration that year, the group raised
money to sponsor a "temperance party" featuring nonalcoholic re-
freshments as an alternative to those offered at other festivities.

During the winter months, sleigh riding was a popular pastime
in Clifton, especially for women and children. Although horses
were sometimes used, more often dogs were harnessed to power
the sleigh. Hobart observed in March 1863, "an old lady out the
other evening who has a family of six or eight children enjoying
the sport [of sleigh-riding] with the others."

In the summer months, there were other attractions. The game
of marbles was popular. The Cornish were fond of wrestling
matches and pole climbing Hobart describes one such event in his
journal entry for May 7, 1864:

> I witnessed a few tumbles. . . for a prize of $30. There was a
> crowd of men and women, ladies etc. Present also several bar-
> rels of ale on the ground. The wrestlers took off their shirts
> and put on a very loose jacket made of bagging tied with cord
> up and down in front. It was then a rough and tumble game,
> twisting each other in all shapes. Most of them were full of
> "Beer," swearing, fighting etc. I never witnessed such a tight,
> rough set of men in my life. I cannot tell all the Cornish talk
> and will not try. Some are very good on a hitch.

Streams, rivers and lakes near Clifton attracted fishermen, and the woods were full of small game for hunters. For the naturalist, Lake Superior provided a site for the search for agates along the rocky shores. Hobart writes of one such outing in his journal entry for May 25, 1863:

> We ... looked around to see what kind of place we had landed in, and found that it was a good place between two rocky points—the beach was composed of round stones quite small and mostly of a red color piled up about ten feet high by the waves and extending back about thirty feet to the woods. The rock is visible on the shores of Lake Superior either on the beach or out in the water a short distance. Every few miles that we passed rocky points extend into the water composed of a round red stones cemented together with a substance like or partaking of the nature of sandstone. . . . .

Travelling shows also provided entertainment. In July 1863, "Warren Bardwell and Lady with a Panorama of the War," opened at Clifton Hall.[42] This exhibition consisted of Civil War photographs and featured a "lady singer" who sang "many touching songs." In June of 1864, a "program" with "magic and sleight of hand" also opened at the Hall.

Daguerreotypists, photographers and artists also visited Clifton in the 1860s to take "likenesses" of the citizens, especially the children. Hobart had several made of his favorite "scholars" so that he could take them back to Vermont when his contract expired in July 1864.

Copper in the Upper Peninsula

Any reader of the journal of Henry Hobart must measure Hobart's observations against the historical perspective of the time and events preceding the copper mining boom. The 1840s witnessed the first two major mining booms in the United States following the discovery of iron near Marquette, Michigan in 1844, and public reports of the rich copper deposits in the nearby Keweenaw Peninsula. Thousands of men from all parts of the United States rushed to northern Michigan to seek their fortunes in copper and iron. Women were recruited to run the boarding houses, serve as cooks and provide other services in the mining towns.

Above is an 1880s engraving of copper miners with candles set into their hard hats. This is a somewhat idealized image of what was an exhausting and hazardous occupation.

Unlike iron, which was first discovered in the Upper Peninsula of Michigan by William A. Burt in 1844, the existence of copper in the Upper Peninsula had been known for centuries. Thousands of years earlier, Native Americans had mined the pure copper on the Keweenaw Peninsula and on Isle Royale, located about sixty miles from the tip of the Peninsula in Lake Superior. They hammered and fashioned copper into ornaments, tools and weapons. Even today, the sites of their crude mines can be seen in the forests near Ontonagon and other parts of the Keweenaw Peninsula and Isle Royale.[43]

The Indian copper pieces attracted the attention of the French who controlled the Lake Superior region until 1760. French explorers and others assigned to posts on Lake Superior searched for copper along the southern shore of Lake Superior and, in the 1690s, a French mining company was formed to locate and mine copper. Internal political bickering in Montreal ended this operation. It was not until the 1730s that another French mining venture was started at Lake Superior. This enterprise continued long enough to procure and send samples of copper to Paris for testing and evaluation, but the mining operation failed when a Sioux-Chippewa conflict erupted along the shore of western Lake Superior. The French tabled their interest in copper.

Copper also attracted the interest of British explorers and fur traders whose homeland won tentative control from the French in 1760. In 1766, the English fur trader, Alexander Henry, who in 1763 had survived the massacre at Fort Michilimackinac, located a huge mass of copper on the bank of the Ontonagon River thirty miles from where it flows into Lake Superior. He organized a company to mine the area but abandoned the venture in 1772 after a year with no success.[44]

Not until the southern Lake Superior region came under American control was interest in mining copper renewed. In 1820, Lewis Cass, governor of the Michigan Territory, set out to explore northern Michigan and to examine personally the region's natural resources. When the expedition reached the mouth of the Ontonagon River, Indian guides led Governor Cass and Henry Rowe Schoolcraft, the geologist of the exploring party, thirty miles up the river to where they came upon a huge nugget of pure copper encased in rock, partly lying in water. Schoolcraft's account of the expedition and find, published in 1822, called attention to the need for government action to ensure the mining of copper.[45]

In a published account of the 1830 and 1832 expeditions to locate the course of the Mississippi River, Schoolcraft again described the rich copper deposits along the shoreline of the Keweenaw Peninsula and the potential for profitable mining ventures there.[46] Of special significance on the 1832 expedition was the presence of Dr. Douglass Houghton who served as its geologist and botanist. Houghton also visited the famous Ontonagon Boulder and chipped off pieces as specimens. He examined the copper outcroppings along the western shore of the Keweenaw Peninsula and kept detailed records of his findings in his journal of the expedition. After returning from the trip, Houghton announced his discoveries in "A Report of the Existence of Copper in the Geological Basin of Lake Superior." He sent the report to Cass, who by then was President Andrew Jackson's Secretary of War. The report was later published as a congressional document and also in Schoolcraft's account of the 1830 and 1832 expeditions, both of which were widely circulated and read. The publicity that the Cass expeditions engendered stimulated further interest in the natural resources of the Upper Peninsula.

Shortly after he became the State Geologist of Michigan, Houghton conducted a careful survey of the Keweenaw Peninsula to determine the location and extent of copper desposits. In his 1841 report to the Michigan State Legislature, he announced he had found extensive deposits on the Keweenaw Peninsula, although he qualified his conclusions with warnings of the many difficulties standing in the way of quick profits for would-be copper mining ventures.[47]

The Houghton report received widespread attention in Lower Michigan and in the East. Soon after it was circulated, adventuring prospectors by the hundreds entered Michigan's northern peninsula seeking to make it rich in copper.

As a result of the influx of prospectors, the United States Congress appropriated funds to purchase the Chippewa lands in the western Upper Peninsula. In the treaty of La Pointe, signed in October 1842, 25,000 square miles of land west of Marquette and east of Duluth came under federal jurisdiction. Houghton immediately undertook the survey of this land and, in 1843, a federal mineral agent was sent to Copper Harbor, at the northernmost tip of the Keweenaw Peninsula, to process land claims.[48] To protect miners from the Indians of the area, the United States War Department built Fort Wilkins at Copper Harbor between Lake Fanny Hooe and Lake Superior and stationed federal troops there.[49]

The mineral agent at Fort Wilkins, under the authority of the War Department, issued the first mining permit in 1845. Following the precedent established for the mining of the western lead lands, early permits were issued. At first, permits for nine square mile parcels, for a three-year period, were available. In 1845, the amount of land covered by a permit was reduced to a section or one square mile. The leases were renewable for two terms in a nine-year period. Each lessee was required to report his returns to the mineral agent and to pay the government six percent of profits in royalties for the first three-year term and ten percent thereafter.

Congress transferred the custody of mineral lands from the War Department to the Treasury Department in 1847 and authorized the outright sale of mineral lands in quarter sections for $2.50 an acre. By September 1847, the price per acre was reduced to $1.25.

By 1843, the stage was set for the first major mining rush in the United States. During of the summer of 1843, more than one hundred mining permits were issued by the mineral agent at Copper Harbor; by 1846, approximately a thousand such permits were outstanding. Hundreds of prospectors swarmed into the Keweenaw Peninsula. Some came overland from the lead mines of Wisconsin. Most, including explorers and speculators, came by schooner or steamer from Detroit and the lower Great Lakes, changing vessels at Sault Ste. Marie and portaging around the falls of St. Mary's River to pick up passage on one of the schooners bound for the Keweenaw.

Despite the initial optimism, would-be miners soon learned that locating copper was not only difficult but treacherous as well. There were no roads and only a few scattered Indian trails; swamps and cedar thickets covered much of the Keweenaw Peninsula. Supplies were scarce and, when available, the cost was often exorbitant. The harsh winters on Lake Superior further discouraged many miners. Even of those prospectors who endured these inhospitable conditions, few were successful. Searching for an outcrop of copper with only a pick and a shovel and a few pounds of gunpowder, one could accomplish little.

An effort of a well-financed, experienced entrepreneur ended in failure due to government intervention. A wealthy Detroit businessman, Julius Eldred, arrived in the Upper Peninsula in 1841 with a plan to acquire the by then famous Ontonagon Boulder and return it to Detroit where he planned to place it on display. First, he paid $150.00 to a Chippewa chief who asserted a claim to it. Then, he paid $1,365 to a Colonel Hammond who had taken a permit to mine the land on which the boulder sat. Finally, Eldred received a permit from General Walter Cunningham, the local government agent. After a long, tedious process with block and tackle, and removable tracks, he transported the copper nugget to the shores of Lake Superior and shipped it to Detroit. Eldred placed the copper on exhibit in a building on Jefferson Avenue and charged a twenty-five cent admission fee to view the nugget. This venture was terminated abruptly when the Secretary of War seized the boulder and sent it to Washington for display at the Smithsonian Institute. [50]

Within a year or two after the first miners arrived and started their search for copper, it was clearly evident that individual miners, or even small groups of prospectors, would have little success in mining copper. Masses of native copper, like the Ontonagon Boulder, located directly on the surface were uncommon. Successful copper mining required extensive financial resources to provide the necessary equipment, supplies, transportation, housing and wages for the work force. Such an undertaking required a well-financed and experienced mining company, owned either by a single individual or a group of investors. In 1843, the first such company, the Lake Superior Mining Company, was formed. It operated on a site near Copper Harbor. This venture lasted until 1849, when the company folded, like the majority of those that followed. In 1845, the famous Cliff Mine, around which the Hobart journal is centered, was founded. For the next two decades it stood as one of the leading producers of copper in the world.

The year 1846 marked the opening of another famous Upper Peninsula mine, the Minesota, located near the present town of Rockland, Michigan. Like the Cliff Mine, the Minesota produced mass or "native" copper. For years it vied with the Cliff Mine as the leading producer of copper.

In the following decade, the Portage Lake District located in the central part of the Keweenaw Peninsula near the cities of Hancock and Houghton, became the center of copper mining with the opening of the Pewabic, Franklin and Quincy mines. Unlike the Cliff and Minesota, copper in the Portage Lake mines was found in amygloid and conglomerate rock formations. Interestingly, in the long run, this type of mine produced more copper than the Cliff and Minesota mines with their pure mass copper lodes.

Cliff Mine

The discovery and mining of the Cliff Lode exemplifies the unique development of the Copper Country. The exploitation of the generous deposit of copper at the Cliff meant good fortune for many.[51]

In the summer of 1843, John Hays, a well-to-do druggist from Cleveland, Ohio, headed for the Upper Peninsula in search of copper. He had read about copper deposits described by Houghton and other geologists and seized the opportunity to seek his fortune. He had perhaps an additional reason for going north; he had a respiratory ailment that promised improvement in the climate of Lake Superior.

Hays arrived at Copper Harbor, at the tip of the Keweenaw, in 1843 after a three-day voyage aboard the steamboat *Chesapeake*. He had traveled from Cleveland to Sault Ste. Marie and from there to the Keweenaw by the schooner *Algonquin*. Before setting out on his journey, Hays discussed his plans with Curtis Hussey of Pittsburgh, a wealthy friend and hunting companion. Hussey too was excited about the prospect of a profitable investment in copper and agreed to pay half of Hays' expenses in return for a share in the fortune he anticipated Hays would make.

Hays travelled to a number of the mining towns in the Keweenaw. He examined the mining sites and talked to geologists, prospectors, speculators and miners who frequented the hotels and taverns of the area. He heard the gossip and exaggerated tales of their copper finds.

While at Copper Harbor, Hays met James Raymond, a mining speculator from Boston, who represented a group of investors who had staked three land claims in the northern end of the Keweenaw Peninsula. Each of the claims was three miles square. One was located at Copper Harbor, one at Eagle River and the third just south of Eagle River. Hays was impressed with Raymond's accounts of the potential of these claims and purchased, on behalf of Curtis Hussey, a one-sixth interest in the three claims. He then returned to Pittsburgh to report his findings. Dr. Hussey was obviously pleased with Hays' progress and thereupon founded the Pittsburgh and Boston Mining Company.

Hoya, Hoya, and geologist Alfred Randolph, along with eight experienced coal miners and some mining equipment, returned

A large iron stamp at the Cliff Mine crushed the rock mined by Cliff miners. The rock was then washed to separate out the copper that was shipped to smelters in several eastern cities.

Hays, Hussey and geologist Alfred Rudolph, along with eight experienced coal miners and some mining equipment, returned in the spring of 1844 to Copper Harbor to work their claim. Attention centered on the "green rock" vein near Fort Wilkins and, later, inland where they discovered a continuation of the vein in the form of a black oxide of copper. Two shafts were excavated and twenty-six tons of black oxide were brought to the surface. Unfortunately, the yield was less than three thousand dollars on an investment of more than twenty-five thousand. The first venture of the Pittsburgh and Boston Mining Company had failed.

At this point, fate intervened in a dramatic way. While sailing south along the shore of the Keweenaw Peninsula, a schooner carrying Hays and several of his colleagues was blown ashore near Eagle Harbor in a squall. This gave Hays the opportunity to visit the third Raymond claim near Eagle River. There, at the top of a huge 200-foot bluff running parallel to the Peninsula, Hays discovered a vein of pure exposed copper.

There are conflicting stories as to whether Hays discovered the copper on his own, or whether Raymond or another prospector told Hays of its location. Regardless of the source, Hays recognized the importance of the discovery and acted promptly. Although winter had arrived in northern Michigan, Hays immediately headed for Pittsburgh, travelling by boat, sleigh, stage coach and finally, by railroad. Enroute, he stopped in Detroit and discussed his proposed mining venture with State Geologist Houghton.

No record seems to exist of Houghton's advice, but it did not deter or discourage Hays. Arriving in Pittsburgh, he reported his discovery to Hussey who, in turn, persuaded his wealthy friends, Dr. Charles Avery, Thomas Howe and Dr. William Petit to invest sufficient funds in the Pittsburgh and Boston Mining Company in order that it purchase a controlling share from Raymond's group of investors.

Hays returned again to the Keweenaw in March of 1845 with additional supplies, mining equipment and miners. They soon discontinued the work on the mine at Copper Harbor and moved the equipment to the Cliff claim near Eagle River. They continued to explore the land at the top of the bluff and found a vein containing copper and silver stretching half way down the cliff.

During the winter of 1845-46, Hays hired a group of German miners to clear the rubble that had accumulated at the base of the cliff. When the lower cliff was exposed, the miners found the continuation of the copper vein. Later, after digging an adit (horizontal opening) into the side of the cliff, they discovered a mass of native copper, even larger than the famous Ontonagon Boulder.

This find was historically important to the future of copper country for it came at a time when many prospectors were discouraged and losing faith in the mining future of the Keweenaw. It also marked the real origin of one of the most famous copper mines in all of North America.

The kick-off of operation of the Cliff Mine took place in 1846. Under the supervision of Captain Edward Jennings, an experienced Cornish mining engineer, a work force was hired, log houses built and work commenced. Shafts were excavated, each about 125 feet deep, reaching tons of valuable copper. In July 1846 alone, more than 500,000 pounds of copper were taken from the Cliff Mine, dwarfing in comparison the output of other companies. During that year, miners discovered a mass of native copper at the Cliff Mine weighing more than 100,000 pounds. The copper was transported by schooner to Sault Ste. Marie, unloaded, drawn by wagon over the portage, and reloaded on steamers bound for the lower Great Lakes and, ultimately, to the Roxbury and Revere Copper Works outside of Boston, Massachusetts.

Despite the spectacular discovery of a large mass of native copper in 1846, the Cliff Mine did not immediately realize a profit. The costs of bringing in expensive equipment, recruiting workers and building mine facilities and living quarters precluded early returns on the venture. It was not until the stockholders of the Pittsburgh and Boston Mining Company invested in additional mining equipment that copper yields, and therefore income, exceeded expenses. In 1849, the Company announced a dividend of $60,000 on six thousand shares or $10.00 per share. [52]

The Cliff Mine continued its remunerative operation during most of the decade of the 1850s. Substantial dividends were declared each year, although Curtis Hussey, the president of the company, wisely insisted that adequate funds be set aside for the purchase of the latest and most efficient mining equipment to assure productivity of the mine.

A forty-five ton engine was installed at the base of the cliff in a new five-story engine house in 1851. It was used for crushing rocks, washing the copper and pumping water from the underground shafts and drifts. [53]

Several years later, Cliff officials recognized the depth of underground workings required different equipment and reorganization of surface and underground operations. In 1858, shafts were straightened and enlarged to facilitate removal of ore from depths exceeding a thousand feet; wire ropes replaced chains; and more powerful and efficient hoisting equipment was installed, including skips which held two and a half tons of rock, replacing one-ton capacity kibbles.[54]

On the surface, new and more powerful stamps were installed, with iron heads substituted for wooden ones. By 1856, as the supply of nearby wood was running out, coal was imported to provide fuel for stream-driven equipment.[55] The Cliff Mine was not the only mine to make these changes and improvements; but it was the leader and set the pace for technological advances in the industry.

Copper prices declined worldwide beginning in 1856. With the increased costs of bringing copper miners and rock to the surface as the mine shafts exceeded a thousand feet, the Cliff Mine faced its most serious challenges since opening in 1845. Production dropped from 3,363,557 pounds of copper in 1857 to 2,199,632 pounds in 1859, and profits declined proportionately. The Cliff Mine did not declare a dividend in 1860 for the first time since 1849.[56]

The Cliff recovered its profitable status in 1861 when production increased to 1,928,011 pounds with mass copper accounting for forty-eight percent; barrel work, twenty-one percent; and stampings, thirty-one percent. Eighty thousand dollars were paid to stockholders in dividends.[57] During the following year, there began a sharp rise in the demand for copper as a result of the war effort, and a concurrent rise in prices. The Cliff Mine responded to this demand. Despite a critical shortage of laborers, the mine increased its production to 2,004,960 pounds in 1862 and 2,100,354 pounds in 1863, before falling to 1,351,334 in 1864. The dividends for these years were $80,000, $180,000 and $32,000, respectively.[58]

The Pittsburgh and Boston Mining Company purchased 2,300 acres from the North American Mining Company in 1860. Located near the Cliff Mine, and renamed South Cliff, the mine on this land had been in operation since 1852 and was placed on "tribute," whereby operators of the mine paid the Cliff stockholders one-eighth of the net proceeds.[59] The company also continued to improve its equipment and facilities, installing in 1862-63 a stone mineral house at the No. 4 shaft, "an addition to the Blacksmith Shop, 54 feet in length; and the Wash Floor by 50 feet." Thirty new log houses for miners were also constructed during 1861-63.[60]

By the autumn of 1862 when Hobart arrived, the Civil War had created a great demand for copper for use in the Union war effort. Despite the shortage of miners and other workers, the citizens of Clifton were optimistic about the future of their community and its life blood—the Cliff Mine.

Working at the Cliff Mine

The miners were mostly Cornish, Irish or German immigrants. A superintendent—reporting directly to the officers of the Pittsburgh and Boston Mining Company—directed all mine operations. In 1862, this position was held by James Watson.[61]

The staff consisted of Percival H. Updegraff, chief clerk; Samuel Updegraff, storekeeper; and mine captains Henry George, Samuel Bennetts and Thomas George. E. M. Green was in charge of the Cliff Mine warehouse, docks and shipping operations at Eagle River.

Details of mine management are not available, except for some routine information found in the mine company's annual reports. It is known that in 1863, James Watson instituted the new procedure of formally calling together his staff for discussions of the operation of the mine.[62] Up to that time, the superintendent operated independently.

Of all the immigrant groups who came to the Upper Peninsula of Michigan to work in the copper mines, none made greater contributions than immigrants from Cornwall, England. The harsh climate of the Keweenaw Peninsula did not discourage the Cornish as it did many immigrants. In fact, the area, with Lake Superior's waves breaking on rocky shores, was similar in many ways to Cornwall, with its craggy shores jutting into the Atlantic Ocean. Like Cornwall, the Keweenaw was isolated and situated at the periphery of the communication system. The huge bluff at the Cliff had been in operation since 1882 and was placed on "tribute," whereby operators of the mine paid the Cliff stockholders one-

The miners at Clifton worked over a thousand feet under the ground. Toiling an arduous ten to twelve hours at work every day except Sunday, miners faced accidents and sickness from unsafe working conditions.

Mine reminded many Cornish settlers of the sea cliffs of Cornwall and eased the adjustment they faced.

Cornish miners were experienced in deep mine operations and familiar with the design, construction and operation of the hoisting and pumping machinery used in mines like the Cliff. Through years of work, they had mastered techniques of removing ore to the surface from hundreds of feet below and crushing rock to release the copper trove it held. They knew drilling techniques— in particular, the use of the three man team—to cut copper into manageably-sized pieces. They were experts in blasting.

Cornish miners also contributed management skills in the daily operation of the Cliff. Most of the mine captains were Cornish; with the families of Vivian, Hall, Bennetts, George and Paull playing prominent roles at the Cliff Mine. The mine engineer, machinists and other skilled personnel involved in the design and installation of mining engines and other equipment were also Cornish.

In Cornwall, it was the very decline of the copper mining industry that led displaced workers to come to North America, seeking similar lifestyles and occupations. As the Cornwall mines went deeper, profit margins dwindled and investment capital dried up. At the same time, the supply of copper was running out.

Although the copper mining industry in Cornwall did not collapse until the mid 1850s, it was evident in the 1840s the end was in sight. The depression in England, competition from copper mines in Chile, Spain and Michigan, and over-population in Cornwall, triggered massive unemployment.[63]

As a result, Cornish miners left Cornwall by the thousands. Many went to work in South American copper mines, but most emigrated to North America to find employment in the coal mines of Pennsylvania, the lead mines of southwestern Wisconsin, the Bruce Mines of northern Ontario, and the iron and copper mines of Lake Superior. In the 1850s, Cornish miners also contributed to the mining rush in Arizona and California.

To pay for passage to the United States, Cornish miners sold their homes in Cornwall or borrowed from friends and relatives. Most of the miners first went alone and later sent for their families. As news spread of the rich copper lodes in the Keweenaw, Cornish emigration swelled.

Despite the favorably disposed audience, the Cliff Mine undertook a variety of recruitment efforts directed at Cornish miners. Mine agents visited Copper Harbor and Eagle River frequently to meet immigrants arriving by steamer from the lower lakes. Networks of families and friends helped as well. Cornish families in Clifton wrote to relatives back home describing excellent job opportunities and high wages. The John Penberthy family, for example, heard about opportunities at the Cliff Mine from Mrs. Penberthy's mother and aunt who ran a boarding house in Clifton. Although John Penberthy died of cholera in Montreal, en route to Michigan, his widow and sons continued on their journey to Clifton and settled there, where she later met and married Joseph Rawlings.

Germans, the second largest ethnic group in the work force at the Cliff Mine, were recruited directly from Germany as well as from German settlements in the United States. Starting in the early 1840s, Michigan had immigration agents, on location, in Germany, encouraging people to migrate to Michigan and settle the rich farm lands. The agents served, at the same time, as recruiters for the copper and iron mines of northern Michigan.[64]

The political upheavals in Germany during the 1840s and 1850s accelerated emigration to the United States and particularly to Michigan and other midwestern farming communities. In Detroit, where there was a large German settlement, the *Michigan Volkshatt* the *Das Tagliche* and the *Michigan Journal*, carried news about Copper Country and job opportunities there. In fact, in June 1864, C. Marxhausen, the editor of the *Michigan Journal*, came to the Keweenaw to solicit subscribers and obtain information on jobs.[65]

Nearly ten percent of the work force at the Cliff Mine in 1860 had been born in Ireland. The 1840s potato famine in Ireland was a driving force behind Irish immigration to the United States. Most of the Irish immigrants settled in urban centers along the East Coast, in Boston, New York and Philadelphia, but others migrated to the Midwest. The copper and iron mining areas of the Upper Peninsula attracted significant numbers of Irish settlers.

For the recruitment of Canadian workers, the mining companies used services like the Mining Emigrant Association. In June 1863, 250 Canadian workers arrived in the Keweenaw under the charge of E. Brule, the agent of the Association.[66]

The officers, agents and stockbrokers of the Pittsburgh and Boston Mining Company actively recruited workers from the coal fields of Pennsylvania and assisted the workers and their families in arranging transportation to the Keweenaw Peninsula. On several occasions, mine officials actually accompanied the miners on their voyages to Lake Superior.

Boston investors in the copper mines of northern Michigan provided close contacts between these mining centers and eastern sources of skilled labor. There was a similar close relationship between the mining communities of the Keweenaw and those of Wisconsin, which assisted in the recruitment of miners.[67]

Labor shortages also led to an ultimately unsuccessful effort to recruit Scandinavian settlers to work in the copper mines of the Keweenaw. Shortly after the beginning of the Civil War, when the shortage became critical, mine companies raised $90,000 to recruit and transport workers from Norway and Sweden to the mining region. Several hundred Scandinavian workers accepted the passage money, but when they arrived in the United States, many refused to work in the mines. Many enlisted in the Union Army and received substantial bounties from the government; others landed other jobs. This type of recruiting project, at mining company expense was not repeated.[68]

These miners working below the surface built the six to eight foot vertical shafts downward to the location of the veins of copper. At different depths, they constructed horizontal openings ("drifts") measuring four by six feet in size to reach the lode. Once a vein or mass of native copper was discovered, the miners excavated the rock above the drift, a process called "stoping." They used black gunpowder to separate the copper from the rock attached or adjacent to it. This was a dangerous operation in the underground drifts and required the judgment of an experienced miner. If a large quantity of powder was needed, the work was scheduled for Saturday evening after the last shift returned to the surface, allowing the air in the mine to clear by the return of the first shift on Monday morning.

After the rock had been blasted loose from the mass of copper, the miners had to determine whether the hanging rock above the copper vein was strong enough to stand alone or if timber supports were needed. If the exposed copper mass weighed less than ten tons, it was usually removed to the surface intact. If larger, it had to be cut on location into smaller pieces and transported to the main shaft to be raised to the surface.

The cutting of copper was done by teams of three miners. One held a chisel which varied in size from one to six feet; the other two wielded sledge hammers averaging eight and a half pounds. Each team worked eight to ten hour shifts and, in that time, were able to cut about nine inches of copper. It took several weeks to cut through a large mass of copper. In fact, one expert noted that an ordinary mass of fifty or sixty tons "required the labor of three men, working at it continuously, for from three to four months, before it is ready to come to the surface."[68]

In addition to the mass copper, miners at the Cliff removed thousands of tons of rock containing small pieces of copper. Once removed to the surface, the rock was taken to the stamp mill where it was crushed and washed, separating out the pieces of copper. The concentrate was then placed in barrels and, along with the mass copper, hauled by wagon to Eagle River to be loaded on steamers for shipment to Detroit, Chicago, Cleveland and other lake ports.

A large work force was also employed on the surface. During the period from July 1, 1862 to November 30, 1863, 427 individuals worked for the Cliff Mine, 232 underground and 195 above. The surface workers included the following:[70]

Agent and office clerks	3
Mining captains and timbermen	7
Storekeepers and assistants	6
Engineers and machinists	4
Carpenters	7
Blacksmiths and helpers	6
Engine drivers and firemen	20
Men in mineral yard	9
Cleaning mass copper	3
Washing floors	40
Wheelers, landers and fillers	65
Road and burrow men	4
Changing house	2
Farm work	3
Sundry surface work	2
Cutting and hauling wood, etc.	14
Total	**195**

In addition to the work available at the Cliff Mine, there were other job opportunities directly related to mine operations. The boarding houses hired housekeepers, servants, cooks and washer women. Carpenters, painters, masons, shoemakers and merchants found employment in the village to support the mining population. There were two schoolteachers (including Hobart) and three clergymen in residence. Contracts were let to workers to haul timber, lumber and supplies.

In 1860, the year for which the U. S. Census provided accurate information on the inhabitants of Clifton, most of the miners, laborers and other workers were between the ages of twenty and forty. Some of the mine captains, mechanics and engineers, like Joseph W. Rawlings and Samuel Bennetts, were in their forties and others, like Thomas Paull, a hotel keeper and merchant, were in their fifties.

There were many younger men working in the mine. One worker was listed as fifteen, three at age sixteen, fifteen were age eighteen and seven, age nineteen. Young girls were also listed on the employment rolls. According to the 1860 Census, fifteen girls, ages fourteen through nineteen, were employed as servants in boarding houses and households in Clifton.[71]

The wages of Cliff Mine workers varied according to the nature of the work performed and demand for labor. Those employed on the surface worked ten hours on each shift and received a flat wage each week. For a four-week period, surface workers were paid on the following schedule:[72]

1860	$29.89
1861	$29.03
1862	$32.16
1863	$39.10
1864	$58.68

The sharp seventy-four percent increase in wages between 1863 and 1864 was attributed by mine officials to the improved efficiency of the newly installed copper washing machines, allowing far greater production for the same hours of effort. It is likely that the labor shortage and the intense competition from other mines in the Keweenaw and the Marquette Iron Range as well as Civil War inflation were also responsible for driving up wages.

The wages for the miners who worked underground were based on a different system of compensation, yielding higher pay, called the contract or "Tutwork" system. This wage system was widely adopted in the copper mines of the Keweenaw. It allowed a miner, on behalf of a few colleagues making up a team, to bid on the excavation of a certain section of a shaft, drift or stope, or the cutting of a designated mass of copper.[73]

On occasion, the mine captains set a stipulated price per fathom and selected the best qualified team of those expressing an interest in the work. The miners, as well as the mine captain, would carefully examine the work involved before making or accepting a bid.

There was always an element of chance or luck in this system. A shrewd and experienced team of miners could make a substantial profit or at least a decent wage if unforseen obstacles or accidents did not result in delays.

Although the contract system pitted one group of miners against another and tended to depress wages overall, it was favored by the Cornish miners. It was the system they had worked under in Cornwall, England. The system favored them in competition with German miners, because the Cornish had more experience in deeper mines. It yielded these monthly wages:[74]

July 1860	$31.96
July 1861	$29.81
July 1862	$39.90
July 1863	$48.75
November 1864	$64.14

At the end of each month, on the Friday before payday, work underground stopped while the mine captain examined the excavation, determined the amount owed to the miners and announced the contracts for the following month. The wages were credited to each miner's account, and after his room and board and other expenses at the company store were deducted, he could draw upon the balance.

Another source of income for those miners and surface workers who worked in the stamp and washing mills was silver. It was commonly found along with copper deposits in Keweenaw mines, especially with the mass copper lodes. According to Joseph Rawlings, the chief mechanical engineer at the Cliff Mine during Hobart's stay in Clifton, the "miners got the largest share [of silver] generally; . . . good many hundred pounds . . . the Stamps was a great place for picking up small pieces, the apron in front was frequently cover'd over with pieces the size of pin-heads, which the boys pick'd and pocketed."[75] Another observer noted that "Cliff silver bought a good many farms in the 'old days.'" Angus Murdock, the author of the popular book, *Boom Copper*, said the Cliff Mine "had more than four million dollars worth of silver bars credited to the company at the U. S. Mint in Philadelphia."[76]

In determining the overall income of the workers at the Cliff Mine, one must also take account of their "fixed" expenses. In 1860, for example, the cost of room and board at one of Clifton's seven boarding houses was $10.00 a month; a single bed with mattress, pillow, but no sheets, $3.50 a month. According to Hobart, it cost from $20 to $25 a month for the "Yankee style" of food. By March 1864, the cost of room and board had risen to $15 a month, with predictions that it would increase to $20 before the year was over.

Workers had other expenses essential to their jobs. They had to provide their own powder and fuses for blasting, as well as special clothing for work underground, including hard hats with candles, drills, and sledge hammers. Each month, a worker had to pay the company doctor fifty cents for medicine and treatment.[77]

The Cliff Mine owned and operated a company store. It was one of the few such facilities available in Clifton for miners and their families to shop. The store stocked mine tools and equipment, food stuffs, cooking and household utensils, hardware, sundries, tobacco, combs and brushes, health tonics and medicines, herbs, spices, coffee and tea. In effect, the company store was similar to the typical general store common in the towns of rural America. There was one major difference, however, the prices were high and controlled by the company, rather than by natural competition with other stores.

The only shopping alternative for Cliff residents was to go to Eagle River, Eagle Harbor, or Houghton, where there could be found a variety of grocery, hardware, jewelry and meat, at competitive prices.[78] Some of the more well-to-do Cliff residents ordered supplies and foodstuffs from Detroit and other lower lake cities and had them sent by steamer to Eagle River.

Working conditions at Clifton in the 1850s and 1860s were marked by the constant threat of accidents in the engine houses and other mine facilities utilizing steam-driven machinery, and especially underground. The ladders in the vertical shafts, used by miners to descend into the depths of the Cliff Mine and to "return to the grass," were wet and slimy in the hot summer months and icy during the winter, making them treacherously slippery. The Cornish expression, "hold on with your hands when your feet go to the Devil," refers to the danger of climbing these ladders.

Visitors to the Cliff Mine, like Henry Hobart, Robert Clarke, Horace Greeley, and others, commented on the high incidence of accidents caused by falls, from slippery, icy or broken ladders. As the main shaft of the Cliff Mine passed the thousand-foot mark, the use of ladders became even more dangerous. Miners, weary from an eight to twelve hour shift underground, had to climb for nearly an hour to reach the surface. The introduction of the "man machine" designed and first introduced in the Copper Country at the Cliff Mine by Joseph Rawlings in 1864 facilitated the transportation of miners up and down the main shaft. Still it did not eliminate serious accidents caused by falls.

More serious and frequent than falls from ladders were accidents caused by falling rock, cascading down shafts and long drifts. Because of the method of mining veins of copper, a hanging wall was often left above the miners as they worked to cut or free the copper masses below. The use of gunpowder and hand drills often caused huge rocks to loosen and fall. This fate befell Henry Jenkins, a young Cornish miner, who, on the morning of September 20, 1858, was working in one of the lower drifts of the Cliff Mine. While cutting a vein of copper, rocks fell from the roof of the drift, crushing him to death.[79]

Two months later, on November 26, an accident occurred at the 480-foot level "to Henry Goniwan and William Willis when a large rock falling on them whilst engaged at the work. Willis had one of his legs broken. Goniwan's ribs and breastbone were crushed and his spine injured."[80]

Yet another source of danger was rock and copper pieces falling from the buckets or skips as they were hoisted to the surface. Falling machinery, buckets, tools, and timbers likewise posed a hazard. On June 16, 1859, a newly arrived Cornish miner, Richard Richards, age sixteen, was knocked into a shaft by a piece of falling timber and fell eighty-four feet to his death.[81]

Many miners were injured, some fatally, by explosives, most resulting from premature blasts. Late blasts that occurred when miners returned to what they thought to be a safe location, also took their toll in miners lives. Asphyxiation from fires and smoke filled tunnels was always a hazard and claimed the lives of many miners.[82]

Workers involved in the use of steam engines, hoisting equipment, stamps, and other mine machinery were the victims of serious accidents and injuries as well. The number of such accidents increased sharply after 1850 when copper mines became more mechanized. The local newspapers, mine company reports and the firsthand accounts in Henry Hobart's journal provide further details. In March 1860, for example, John Pope recorded a German employee at the stamps "being crushed to death and mutilated."[83]

There were accidents involving surface hands, woodsmen, teamsters and the dock hands, who loaded the copper aboard steamers at Eagle River. The young and inexperienced were especially vulnerable as were the older workers. Mine captains, engineers and even bystanders were injured in accidents. The mining of copper in the 1850s and 1860s was a treacherous occupation.

Despite the increasing number of serious accidents, mine operators did little to provide safer working conditions. Nor did workers and their families campaign for safety improvements. Perhaps this was due to the character of the workers who cherished their image of employment in a "rugged, all-male industry. . . where the peril of sudden injury or death" was imminent. One writer described miners as "risk takers" who considered these "perilous hazards" as "part of the job."[84]

Working conditions at the Cliff Mine were similar to those at other mines throughout the country. Long hours and a lack of safety measures were balanced by reasonably good wages and pride in a day's work for the miner. The company's need to make a profit always controlled the operation of the mine and workers were always available.

As an interested observer of the miners' work life, Henry Hobart might well have been grateful that he had chosen the profession of a schoolteacher.

Notes for Introductory Essay

1. Information on Henry Hobart and his family can be found in the *8th* and *9th U. S. Census*, Chittenden County, Vermont. See also Percy Hobart Titus, ed., *The Hobart Family of America* (Boston: 1943) and Vital Statistics Office, State of Vermont, Montpelier, Vermont.

2. *8th U. S. Census*, Chittenden County, Vermont, 1860; *9th U. S. Census*, Chittenden County, Vermont, 1870; *Burlington Free Press*, July 5, 1861.

3. Quoted in F. Kennan Moody and Floyd D. Putnam, *The Williston Story* (Essex Junction, Vermont: Roscoe Printing House, 1961), p. 36.

4. Ibid., p. 36.

5. Ibid., pp. 36-37.

6. *Catalogue of the Trustees, Officers, Teachers and Students of Williston Academy* (Burlington, Vermont: Free Press Print. 1859), p. 8.

7. For a list of the various Burlington area temperance societies in the 1840s and 1850s and the temperance lectures and programs, see the Temperance File at the Vermont Historical Society, Montpelier, and the University of Vermont, Special Collections Department. For a typical temperance sermon, see Dr. Robert Moody, *Temperance* (Burlington,Vermont: Chauncey Goodrich, 1832).

8. Michigan School Inspectors Report for Year Ending September 7, 1863, in State Archives, Lansing, Michigan.

9. Michigan School Inspectors Report, 1870, in State Archives, Lansing, Michigan.

10. Michigan School Inspectors Report for Year Ending September 7, 1863, in State Archives, Lansing, Michigan.

11. Mason S. Stone, *History of Education in State of Vermont* (Montpelier, Vermont: Capital City Press, 1900), p. 114.

12. Marquis Shattuck, "Adult Education Childhood," *Michigan Educational Journal* 35 (January 1958), pp. 188, 198-202.

13. John Forster, "Lake Superior Country," *Michigan Pioneer and Historical Collections* VIII (1885), pp. 138-139.

14. In the winter of 1862-63, Percival Updegraff, the agent at the Cliff Mine, transported the body of his mother from Clifton to Appleton, Wisconsin. For an account of this trip see Clarence Monette, "Opening 1862 Mail Route to Area," *Copper Island Sentinel*, December 27, 1979.

15. *Military Order of the Loyal Legion of the U. S....In Memoriam: Lieut. Col. William B. Wright* (Detroit:1902).

16. *Report of S. S. Robinson, Hancock and Green Bay Mail Stage Co.*, (Houghton, Michigan: Mining Gazette Printing Co., 1866), pp. 3-20.

17. *Portage Lake Mining Gazette*, January 24, 1863; *Lake Superior Miner*, March 26, 1864; *Report of S. S. Robinson, Hancock and Green Bay Mail Stage Co.*, pp. 3-20.

18. *History of Upper Peninsula of Michigan* (Chicago: The Western Historical Company, 1883), p. 135.

19. *Portage Lake Mining Gazette,* November 11, 1864.

20. See for example the *Portage Lake Mining Gazette,* May 23, 1863, for the company's 1862 Annual Report.

21. Larry Lankton, "Died in the Mines," *Michigan History* 67 (November-December, 1983), pp. 39-41.

22. James Fisher, "Michigan's Cornish People," *Michigan History* 29 (Summer, 1945) p. 382; A. C. Todd, *The Cornish Miners in America* (Glendale, California: Arthur H. Clark Co., 1967), p. 120.

23. A. I. Lawbaugh, "A Physician's Life in the Copper Country's Early Days," in Michigan Technological University Archives, Houghton, Michigan; Pittsburgh and Boston Mining Company Annual Reports, 1862-1864. Copies of the Pittsburgh and Boston Company reports may be found at the Harvard University Archives, Cambridge, Massachusetts, the American Antiquarian Society, Worcester, Massachusetts and the State Library of Michigan, Lansing, Michigan.

24. Lambaugh, "A Physician's Life."

25. John Pitezel, "Fresh Breezes from Lake Superior," in Pitezel Collection, Clarke Historical Library, Central Michigan University, Mt. Pleasant, Michigan; *Houghton Daily Mining Gazette,* September 2, 1955.

26. John Rowe, *Hard-Rock Men: Cornish Immigrants and the North American Mining Frontier* (New York: Barnes and Noble, 1974), p. 15; A. L. Rowse, *The Cornish in America* (London: Macmillan, 1969), p.17; Fisher, "Michigan's Cornish People," *Michigan History* 29 (Summer, 1945), p. 383; Angus Murdock, *Boom Copper* (New York: Macmillan, 1943), pp. 202-203.

27. *Houghton Daily Mining Gazette,* September 2, 1955, April 5, 1969; *Hancock Journal,* December 18, 23, 1908; *Pathfinder,* March, 1905.

28. *Houghton Daily Mining Gazette,* August 6, 1966.

29. Joseph Rawlings, "Reminiscences," in the Michigan Technological University Archives, Houghton, Michigan.

30. Ibid.

31. "Keweenaw County Centennial, 1861-1961," in Michigan Technological University Archives, Houghton, Michigan.

32. Forster, "Lake Superior Country," *Michigan Pioneer and Historical Collection* VIII (1885), p. 141.

33. *Portage Lake Mining Gazette,* January 17, 1863.

34. Rawlings, "Recollections of a Long Life"in Roy Drier, ed. *Copper Country Tales* (Roy W. Drier: Calumet, Michigan, 1967), pp. 101-102

35. *Lake Superior Miner,* October 3, 1863, December 5, 1863.

36. *Portage Lake Mining Gazette,* August 23, 1862.

37. Nicholls, "'Saarvey Day,' An Old Mining Custom," in the Keweenaw Historical Society Collection, Michigan Technological University Archives, Houghton, Michigan.

38. In Houghton, Michigan in 1863, 312 miners marched in a St. Patrick's Day Parade, *Portage Lake Mining Gazette*, March 21, 1863.

39. For accounts of the 4th of July celebrations in Ontonagon and Houghton in 1864, see *Portage Lake Mining Gazette*, July 11, 1864. An account of a similar celebration in 1846 in Ontonagon is found in the Diary of William Spaulding, Spaulding Collection, Bentley Historical Library, University of Michigan.

40. The Independent Order of Good Templars was founded in Utica, New York in 1851 and spread throughout the United States and Canada and after 1868 in England and Scotland, Ireland, Wales and other countries in Europe. Based upon the pledge of total abstinence and prohibition for the state, the organization boasted several hundred thousand members. It was recognized as one of the strongest organizations opposed to legalized liquor traffic in the United States. Arthur Preuss, Compiler, *A Dictionary of Secret and Others Societies* (St. Louis: Herder Book Co., 1924), pp. 187-189; William D. P. Bliss, *The New Encyclopedia of Social Reform* (New York and London: Funk and Wagnalls, 1908), pp. 555-556.

41. Bands of Hope, temperance organizations for juveniles, were first established in 1847 and spread throughout English-speaking countries. The pledge taken by its members was: "I hereby solemnly pledge myself to abstain from the use of all intoxicating drinks, including wine, beer and cider as a beverage; from the use of tobacco in every form, and from all profanity." Preuss, *A Dictionary of Societies*, p. 57; Bliss , *Encyclopedia of Social Reform* , p. 89.

42. Douglass House Register, July 18, 1863, in the Bentley Historical Library, University of Michigan.

43. For an account of the Indian and French exploration of copper, see Grace Lee Nute, *Lake Superior* (New York: Bobbs Merrill, 1944), pp. 156-163; and David J. Krause, "The Secret of the Keweenaw: Native Copper and the Making of a Mining District," Ph.D. dissertation, University of Michigan, 1986, pp. 7-28.

44. William B. Gates, Jr., *Michigan Copper and Boston Dollars* (Cambridge: Harvard University Press, 1951), pp. 5-6, and Robert Hybels, "The Lake Superior Copper Fever," *Michigan History* 34 (December, 1950), pp. 97-119, 309-326.

45. Philip P. Mason, *Schoolcraft's Expedition to Lake Itasca* (East Lansing: Michigan State University Press, 1958).

46. Ibid., pp. 290-294.

47. Douglass Houghton, *Annual Report of the State Geologist. Michigan Joint Documents*, Vol. 1, No. 11 (Lansing, Michigan: 1841). Also George N. Fuller, editor, *Geological Reports of Douglass Houghton* (Lansing, Michigan: Michigan Historical Commission, 1928), pp. 483-654.

48. See Murdock, *Boom Copper*, and Hybels, "The Lake Superior Copper Fever," *Michigan History* 34 (December, 1950), pp. 312-317.

49. Hybels, "The Lake Superior Copper Fever," *Michigan History* 34 (September, 1950), p. 226.

50. Gates, *Michigan Copper and Boston Dollars*, pp. 14, 16.

51. For accounts of the John Hays and the founding of the Pittsburgh and Boston Mining Company and the discovery of the Cliff Mine, see Donald Chaput, *The Cliff: America's First Great Copper Mine* (Kalamazoo: Sequoia Press, 1971), Hybels, "Lake Superior Copper," *Michigan History* 34 (September, 1950), pp. 223-234. According to John Forster, one of the early pioneers of the Keweenaw Peninsula, there were numerous pits and excavations left by the "ancient miners." In fact, he reported that "the number of ancient (stone) hammers . . . took from this and other excavations exceeded ten cart loads." Forster, "Lake Superior County," *Michigan Pioneer and Historical Collections* VIII (1885), p. 137; Ralph Williams, *The Honorable Peter White* (Cleveland: Penton Publishing Co., 1907); Murdock, *Boom Copper*, pp. 48-58; "Curtis Hussey," *Magazine of Western History* III (February, 1886), pp. 334-335; T. A. Rickard, *The Copper Mines of Lake Superior* (New York: The Engineering and Mining Journal, 1905). See also Pittsburgh and Boston Mining Company Report, 1849.

52. For dividend payments of the Cliff Mine, see Gates, *Michigan Copper and Boston Dollars*, pp. 215-221 and Pittsburgh and Boston Mining Company Annual Reports, 1847-1879.

53. Pittsburgh & Boston Mining Company, Report, January, 1852.

54. Pittsburgh & Boston Mining Company, Report of the President and Directors, Annual Report, November, 1860, pp. 6-11.

55. Pittsburgh & Boston Mining Company, Annual Report, 1857.

56. Pittsburgh & Boston Mining Company, Annual Report, November 1860, p. 7.

57. Pittsburgh & Boston Mining Company, Annual Report., November, 1861, p. 6.

58. Pittsburgh & Boston Mining Company, Annual Report, March, 1864, p. 33.

59. Pittsburgh & Boston Mining Company, Annual Report, November, 1860, p. 12-13; Pittsburgh & Boston Mining Company, Annual Report, November, 1861, p.1.

60. Pittsburgh & Boston Mining Company, Annual Report., March, 1864, p. 16.

61. Ibid. T. Egleston, "Copper Mining on Lake Superior," *Transactions of the American Institute of Mining Engineers* Vol. VI (1879) p. 287; Egleston gives an excellent account of the mining of mass copper, pp. 275-288.

62. Ibid.

63. Todd, *Cornish Miners in America*, pp. 23-24.

64. Commissioner of Immigration, Governor's Files, Michigan State Archives, Lansing, Michigan.

65. *Lake Superior Miner*, June 11, 1864

66. *Portage Lake Mining Gazette*, June 27, 1864.

67. Forster, "Lake Superior Country," *Michigan Pioneer and Historical Collections* VIII (1885), p. 142.

68. See Pittsburgh and Boston Mining Company, Report of the Superintendent, December 1, 1864, p. 14.

69. Ibid.

70. Pittsburgh and Boston Mining Company, Annual Reports, 1861-1864.

71. *8th U. S. Census*, 1860, Houghton County.

72. Pittsburgh and Boston Mining Company Annual Reports, 1861-1864.

73. For an account of the contract system see Todd, *The Cornish Miners in America*, pp. 23-24 and Alfred Nicholls, "'Saarvey Day,' and Old Mining Custom," in the Keweenaw Historical Society Collection, Michigan Technological University Archives, Houghton, Michigan.

74. Pittsburgh and Boston Mining Company, Annual Reports, 1861-1864.

75. Rawlings, "Reminiscences," Michigan Technological University Archives. See also T. A. Rickard, *Copper Mines of Lake Superior*, p. 235.

76. Murdock, *Boom Copper*, p. 99. Murdock provides no documentation for this claim, which, based upon the financial reports of the Pittsburgh and Boston Mining Company, appears to be greatly exaggerated. According to the Commissioner of Mineral Statistics of the State of Michigan, the Cliff Mine yielded from 25-50 pounds of silver annually at a value of from $1500 to $5300. The Commissioner noted also that "but a small portion of the silver found its way into the coffers of the company; not infrequently the miners regarded such 'finds' as their peculiar prize, and so appropriate it to themselves." *Annual Report for 1880* (Lansing: W. S. George Company., 1881), p. 21.

77. Todd, *The Cornish Miner in America*, p. 120; Fisher, "Michigan's Cornish People," *Michigan History* 29 (1945), p. 382.

78. For a list of the stores in Eagle River in 1863 see *Michigan State Gazetteer and Business Directory* (Detroit: Charles Clark, 1863). p. 292; *History of the Upper Peninsula of Michigan*, pp. 339-340.

79. John Pope, "Diary," September 20, 1858. Unpublished manuscript in the LaTrobe Library, Melbourne, Australia.

80. Ibid., November 16, 1858.

81. Ibid., June 16, 1859.

82. See Larry D. Lankton, "Died in the Mines," *Michigan History* 67 (November-December, 1983), pp. 33-41.

83. Pope, "Diary," March 2, 1860.

84. Todd, *The Cornish Miner in America*, p. 26; Lankton, "Died in the Mines," pp. 40-41.

Copper Country Journal

The Diary of Schoolmaster
Henry Hobart, 1863-1864

Copper Country Journal

CLIFF.MINE.

JOURNAL.

BY.

H.A.HOBART.

1863.

Henry Hobart's journal (cover above) showed the world of Cliff miners (on opposite page) and their children from the vantage point of a young New Englander during the Civil War.

January—February 1863

January 1, 1863

It is proper to form good resolutions at the commencement of a new year, if every possible effort be made to carry them out, to live up to them in the business of life, and use proper efforts or means to improve by them each day. Very many will promise, in their more serious moments, to live more in accordance with the principles of virtue and Christianity, but since, they make no effort to verify such promises, they fail to secure the good to be derived from a course of conduct in accordance with such principle of action. If a resolution is formed to improve in any business a strong effort should be made to carry that out in every particular, for it is contrary to the principles of morality & right to utterly disregard the principles of truth and honor.

In looking over my conduct for the past year, I find that I have committed sins and errors and I feel it a duty to commence this year with good resolutions formed and labor to carry out those resolutions. In my present situation I have an excellent opportunity to do *good* and *improve*. The present welfare of many young minds is under my care and instruction requiring a good example on my part and a great effort to give thorough and proper instruction. I have the charge of 150 scholars and I trust I may be able to give sufficient instruction and of such a nature as will fit them to occupy honorable positions in life....

I am desirous of keeping a journal as far as time will permit, and I shall express myself on the events and everything connected with my stay *here* in plain language without any attempt at show or flourish. The affairs of the [Cliff] mine as far as I may be able to learn I will speak about. The weather and the important events in my own history.

The holidays "Christmas" and "New Year's" are celebrated by all the mining class. No business is transacted and everyone *old & young* is on a spree. Ale & Liquors of all kinds are made free use of; therefore to see persons in a state of beastly intoxication is a common sight. Ale is used very freely to fit each one to enjoy the sprees. At Christmas the miners go round to each house singing Christian songs for which they are well treated with ale etc. It is very amusing to one unaccustomed to such scenes. To see a party of fifty or one hundred men with *enough down* to make them lively, all singing a song is a very amusing sight. To be a *sober* witness of the antics and speeches of a part of men, who have labored under ground for a long time without having a spree, in a state of semi-intoxication, has been my fortune the past Christmas.

I had no school for four days at Christmas time which I spent in preparing and decorating the Episcopal Church preparatory to the "Festival." Christmas night I spent at a social party at Mr. Brockway's Hotel [in] Eagle River.[1] Custom makes it binding on the respectable class to attend this party. Thus I passed one Christmas very pleasantly in the northern part of Michigan.

Today is a day for general pleasure and I have no school for the rest of the week, I have taken a tramp to the [Eagle] River where drunkeness & carousing seems to be the main thing.[2] I make a few calls during the day in the afternoon.

I receive by mail two papers from home and very discouraging news from "Dixie" viz Burnside's army driven back across the Rappahannock with great slaughter. I hope it may not prove true. The day before we raised the "Stars and Stripes" for the news that Fredericksburg was taken and the enemy routed. Quite a change in a short time.

January 2, 1863

All who have lived in this section for any length of time agree in the opinion that this winter is remarkable above all others for its mildness and splendid sleighing. The weather has been very favorable with no severe changes even [though] for the past two or three days it has the appearance of a thaw. With fine splendid weather the scholars have had an excellent opportunity to attend school and the consequence has been that is has averaged more in number than any previous winter. We have had mails from below twice a week but they do not contain the latest war news. Everyone who has an interest in war matters is very much discouraged here from the late news. We expect a mail from below tonight.

January 4, 1863

It is a little cooler today and very cloudy with a slight breeze blowing from the South. Last night the Society of "Odd Fellows" had a public installation of officers which...I attended. This society has a good object in view the assistance of brothers in want and sickness. It is governed by such principles as "Truth, Love and Friendship" and holds regular meetings every Saturday evening for the transaction of its business.[3] After returning from the public library room last evening, I found a letter in the post office from Father & Mother which I was anxiously looking for. It was very cheering to receive good news from home and I spent a pleasant evening in looking over its contents and thinking how things must look! I was glad to hear that Florence was attending school.[4] I have taken charge of a class in the Episcopal Sunday School which was never done by a School teacher in this place before.

January 6, 1863

It is very cold this morning and it is the general expectation that a severe change will soon take place. It snows a very little today. Yesterday I commenced School again and had six or seven new scholars. The day passed away pleasantly & in the evening I commenced Evening School but had no new scholars and most of the old ones have gone to other mines. I shall keep evening school no more this winter as I cannot get Scholars enough to make it pay. Most of my scholars have gone to the Portage and all of the men are on ten-hour shift and cannot get time to attend school although they wish to very much. The time that I can get evenings will give me a good opportunity to improve in reading History etc. which I will gladly improve it and spend my time in storing my mind with useful knowledge. My Expenses are very great and I regret that I cannot have a good large Evening School for a short time to cancel necessary Expenses. But with ten-hour shifts the men have no time.

January 8, 1863

We are now having still freezing weather but not severe. Yesterday it snowed one or two inches in the afternoon. The indications are small for a heavy fall of snow. I am very much disappointed in the weather so far for by report I expected by the first of January it would be very severe but instead of that we have had fine weather & sleighing.

Yesterday I had 110 scholars and it was a severe task to go through with the recitations. William Benney, one of my best scholars, has gone to work in the Wash House. [5]

Last night we had mail from below but there was no particular news. Today has been a day of severe labor for me. There was more than one hundred scholars and they have been there so long that the place seems tiresome and in order to manage everything and...I find it a severe tax. The scholars are making good progress in their studies which is very encouraging to a teacher. I shall make an attempt in the Spring to have the [school]house built over and two apartments made one for the small scholars and one for the large ones. With such an arrangement the school would make much more rapid progress.

January 14, 1863

Since I last wrote the weather has been very fine up to yesterday when it commenced blowing very hard & snowing some. It still continues to blow and is much colder than it was yesterday. We have not yet experienced the severe weather peculiar to this place. The clear waters of Lake Superior are in a state of terrible commotion and we can almost hear the waves as they dash against the icy shore three miles away. The wind is prevented from having a full sweep over our little mining village by the high bluff and tall trees in the forests. If this section were level it would be almost impossible to live here at times. I received a letter a day or two since from Cousin Hobart Shipman.[6] He says he has been acting as agent for *Lloyds Military Magazine* of the United States & intends to come into the States to take an agency of some kind.[7] I should think it would be very slim business for wartime.

I had three new scholars yesterday & my school is now prospering finely. The day before Mr. Trezites brought up the Black Board that he promised to make three months ago and today I intend breaking it in. Last night there was a mail in but no news of importance. The contractor, a Mr. Harvey, who is the person to furnish this upper country with the mail, is a penurious scapegoat like most Government contractors & has hired a set of lazy fellows because he could get them cheap to bring it from below & the consequence is we receive it very irregular. [8]

There is a prospect of a fall of some snow tonight and it is evident that we shall have a very severe change very soon. Edward P[enberthy] is quite unwell after having a tooth pulled & an[other] filled. [9] There is no news in this vicinity.

January 15, 1863

As I leave my virtuous couch this morning the frost on the windows is a sure indication that Jack Frost is hard at work. I find that this is very true. The wind is blowing very hard from the Lake & the air is filled with Frost. Snow fell about one foot last night. The cold increases through the day. My school was quite small today averaging about sixty which gave one an excellent opportunity to use the Black Board. Spent some time in the afternoon with the Grammar classes at the Board. I found it quite difficult to warm the house today & it must be very cold in severe weather.

There has nothing worthy of note taken place for me to write about today. I am now reading *The History of the U. S.* by Bancroft in six or eight large volumes.[10] I shall finish one this week in relation to the colonization of this country. I find it very interesting and instructive. *Il est temps pour manger mon super etsrene ecrieperai pas qulque chose ce nuit. Il est tres froid dans mon chambre.*

January 16, 1863

I learn this morning that the "mercury" is at zero and this is the coldest morning that I have seen on Lake Superior. Still it is nothing to what I expect to see. There is quite a strong wind this morning. I am informed that there was a mail in last night & General Rosecrans has had a severe battle in the west with the enemies of the country. Our loss was very heavy & we gained a victory. I have not seen a paper and do not know the result.

I must now start for school. My school has been quite small, sixty in all, which is owing to the cold weather. There has a man come here, to teach an evening school and his prospects are very small for any scholars. He is from Marquette and can find no employment. Tonight I intend going down into the mine with Captain Josiah Halls.[11] I have often mistaken him for my father whom he resembles very much a short distance away—he has red whiskers like him etc. Captain Josiah, as he is called, is a man of fine principles & a firm friend of my school.

January 18, 1863

Friday evening after partaking of a hearty supper I went over to the captain's office and putting on a miner's suit of clothes I started with Captain Josiah Halls at seven o'clock to visit the mine. It was a very pleasant evening and the thermometer was at zero. With a hard skullcap on my head and a miner's candle on the top of it, I commenced descending the ladders after Captain who gave me the caution to hang fast with my hands so that I should not be dashed in pieces in case my feet should slip. It is a common expression among miners to say "hang fast with the hands if the feet go to the Devil." The ladders were quite slippery with ice etc. They are set almost straight & some of them incline under.

At the distance of thirty feet or so there is a flooring and a hole through it just large enough to admit the body of a man down through these places the ladder run. The water dripping down the shaft freezes on the ladders and makes some of them quite dangerous. The pump extends down this shaft on one side for drawing the water out of the mine. It is over one foot in diameter and goes to the bottom. On the other side of the shaft separated from the

Pump & Main ladder by a partition is the place where the Bucket draws up the copper & rock. This is a large shaft.

Down I go after the Captain into the bowels of the earth. Soon three or four men come behind us & we let them pass. It is very surprising to see the men down so fast. After passing down some distance we start off in one of the levels or drifts running from the shaft. These drifts are about feet wide & four feet high. They are blasted through the solid rock by the side of a vein of copper which may be from one foot to three feet in thickness & very high. The top of this drift is blasted down [in a process] called stoping. Then by drilling in behind the vein of copper it is thrown out by powder & wheeled to the shaft to be raised to the surface.

We find here & there men at work drilling. The appearance of the drifts is the same as the pictures in different papers of Foreign Mines. Down to the one-hundred fathom level there is a mass of copper of upwards of one hundred tons. It is over thirty-six foot long, fifteen high & one or two thick. Here were several men cutting it up & I took a chip from this large mass. We then pass down ten fathoms lower — the lowest drift in the mine & passed through here 1100 feet in length. In one place they are sinking a shaft which is now seventy feet lower than this drift. I looked down and saw the bottom of this shaft as one of the men went down in the bucket by a windlass. We then started for the surface & I sweat very much climbing the ladders. We arrived at the surface at half past twelve tired enough.

I would dislike to work in a mine very much & incur the danger that miners run. Sometimes they will fall through a shaft several hundred feet, sometimes a rock will crush them into atoms. Cliff Mine is one of the richest mines on the Lake. The expenses of working this Mine one month are more than twenty five thousand dollars.

January 20, 1863

Last Saturday I went to the Doctor's office and had Dr. Greelee commence the job of filling my teeth.[12] Three or four of the front ones with gold & others with tin foil. It is a severe task to remain quiet & let a dentist fill decayed teeth after going through the painful operation of having them dug out. I am now taking great comfort with solid teeth.

In the evening my friend, John Penberthy, Clerk in the office, took his cousin, Miss Mary Edwards, living here, down to Squire Vivian's & was married.[13] They make a nice little couple & I wish them long life & much happiness. Sunday we had some oysters & much pleasure over the event. In the afternoon went to meeting & took charge of my class in the Sunday School.

Monday was a very fine day & I had a good time in school. In the evening a number of miners & boys came around the house with guns, old pans & sticks to get a treat. Friend John was ready for them & their clamor was stopped by bringing forth plenty of States Ale bought for the time. This "shivereeing" is a detestable thing in my opinion, and is practiced only by a low class of rowdies.[14] Had some tall singing in the evening after the beer commenced operating. Everything passed off nicely today. Scholars labored hard in study which is pleasing to a teacher.

January 24, 1863

The weather since last Tuesday has been very mild & comfortable & last night it commenced snowing and is much colder. The wind is blowing quite hard this morning & snow fell about one foot. Last night it looked very cold & rough and I expect a small school which is always the case Saturdays. Last night my scholar Josiah Penberthy & myself made a visit to Captain Paull's & passed a very pleasant evening.[15] The Captain is a fine old Fellow. His wife is a noble looking woman & they have a family of five children—one little boy & two girls who attend my school. The oldest is twelve. The other little girl has a very large head and is one of the class of children who live only until about fourteen years of age on account of possessing too large a brain. She is a fine little scholar.

In visiting Captain Paull's I am reminded of the comfort of families in Vermont. The Captain's new house furnished in good style [is] quite a contrast with the miners' houses. The sitting room is decorated with Paintings & Profiles etc. The Captain has made his money out of a small store in selling Goods & Double refined Liquors.

January 26, 1863

We are now enjoying very pleasant weather although there is a strong wind almost every day. There was an appearance of a thaw yesterday but it is cooler now. Saturday evening I had an invitation to attend a social party at Mr. Brockway's. Had a very pleasant time. The lawyers from Portage Lake were there & Solomon Cundy, a brother of my assistant teacher who is a clerk in a store at the Portage.[16] Everything is very quiet here. There is no news of importance.

The science of metaphysics is a study that every professional man should devote much of his time & thought. He should understand thoroughly the operations of the mental powers. The mind is not a material substance for if it were it would be subject to the common properties of matter viz location etc. The mind has intelligence or the power of progression and where there is intelligence there is design and this is not the case with matter. Matter is confined or limited; it has not the power of transmitting itself from one place to another. The stone is moved only as it is acted upon by some force or agency & it has not power to stop itself. It comes in contact with some force or agency and is stopped. Here it must remain until acted upon again.

This is a common property of all kinds of matter but is the mind so limited in its powers, not at all. Before I can speak it I can send my thought to London & back almost instantly or up to the sun & moon or Jupiter & back. And this power of the mind some would term the action of matter of a material substance. This cannot be for if it were this would become a common property of matter— but the stump, the block of wood, has no such property. Therefore we conclude that the mind is an immaterial substance. I strike the desk; it is not my hand that does it. It is my mind or will, through the agency of my hand. Take away my mind or will & my hand cannot perform the act. Take the dead body immediately after death—perfect—as the living body it cannot act; therefore it is that immaterial substance the mind that performs the action through the agency of matter.

But one says we are to deal with a living body very well. The life of that body is this immaterial mind. The cause must always be equal to the effect & no effect can be greater than its cause. There is always an equality between the two. We have already shown that matter possesses no such property as the mind. Therefore, if it is a material substance, it must be the result of the organization of matter. Matter may be put in two different ways, mechanically and chemically. It is done mechanically by putting two pieces together or in contact by a mechanical process.

It has already been shown that matter does not possess the properties [and] that the mind does; therefore if it is made to possess them by organization either chemically or mechanically, then we have an effect greater than the cause or in other words:

> Matter not possessing any of these properties cannot be made to possess them by conbination for we should have an effect greater than the cause which is contary to an established truth, it is reasonable to conclude that the mind is immaterial.

January 27, 1863

It is quite cool today but not uncomfortable. I find no occasion to use an overcoat in walking out. How unlike the weather that I was told I should find on Lake Superior. All here speak of this as a remarkable winter very favorable for children to attend school etc. I have the largest school that was ever known in this vicinity. There...[were] 110 scholars today.

After school I paid a visit to the houses of some of my pupils viz Mike Hanley & Dan Sullivan where the following scholars live—John Hanley & Julia Sullivan.[17] I find my way into Hanley's log cabin. The old man has just come out of the mine & taken supper & the old lady, a short, fat, not over clean, specimen of solid Irish, is taking her case in a chair. The cabin is a log one like all miner's homes with one small room below.

I enter into conversation & praise the sterling qualities of John, his success etc. to the joy of all. "Re gannies John is a fine lad. Sure," says the old lady. Finally I speak of the following. John got into a squabble one day at noon in the fore part of school and got a little too much. He goes home and reports & the next day the old lady comes down which was the first I heard of it. I made it all right & told John to report to me next time. I now inquired if John got any thrashings & found that John was full of glee as he could now fist Mike Hanley, who a short time since was too much for him. So Mike would not touch him. I have often seen two of these fellows go out to play & one would be too much for the other when the one who was whipped would come to me & say some one was beating him. I make a short speech to them and depart & Sure the master is a fine fellow & John must go every day.

I find it an excellent plan to go into these hovels and take up their little urchins and make ones self at home—in spite of the *sickening inconveniences* which I will not mention. My stay at Sullivans was short & pleasant. The old paddy was in ecstacy over his daughter's success. "Master, you are a fine hand at teaching."

I went into a house a short time since & among the many animals to be seen was a brace of dogs—half hound & so poor that their hair was coming off like the wool on an old sheep. What a family of different kinds of animals & what a place to live in when compared with Captain Paull's snug clean little home. The one is unfit for cattle; the other is a fine place for civilized persons to live in. Received a letter from Jesse Bushnell tonight.[18]

January 29, 1863

Very pleasant this morning and so warm that I can go out without a coat on. It is very cloudy & a little fine snow is falling which does not render it uncomfortable. Paid a visit with my assistant after school on the Bluff at Miss Harper's came down & had a good spelling school in the evening.[19] My scholars are learning to spell very fast which is always the case under my instruction. I say it with no intention of bragging.

The trial of Mr. Harris is progressing at the river. It is to see if he shall be confined to await his trial for the murder of his wife's seducer.[19] My name is down as a witness; still I do not expect to be called until the last trial. There was a mail in last night but no news from below. The days are growing longer and we do not expect but little severe weather. The crystal waters of Lake Superior will not be covered with a sheet of ice this winter.

January 30, 1863

There was quite a change in the weather last night. The wind blew cold & hard from the north drifting the snow very much. It is not as cold this morning as it has been before. Edward Penberthy is quite sick with the toothache resulting from filling one after killing the nerve. John's new wife was taken sick this morning "vomiting etc." My school has averaged more than a hundred scholars this week. I must now go to begin my day's work. The mail came in at four o'clock PM and I received a letter from Florence who is going to Mr. Cilley's School.[20] Had one from Jesse also.

February 3, 1863

The weather since last Friday has been increasing in cold until the present time. Last night it was fifteen degrees below zero and the wind blowing strong from the north. Snow has been falling most of the time and drifting very much. The air is filled with a fine snow or frost which I suppose results from freezing the fog from the Lake. This evening it is milder; still it will freeze very severe tonight. The snow is very deep and drifted very much. February will doubtless be a month of very cold weather. The people prepare against severe weather very well; the most of them wear shoe-packs and German socks—very comfortable things. Quite a change in school yesterday as it was very stormy and cold. I had only twenty-five students and I took some comfort.

I am now having the toothache quite hard as the Dentist is trying to separate a couple of the double ones so as to fill a hole between them. This is done by crowding in cotton batten which expands as it is moistened & crowds them apart. The pressure makes them very sore & painful. It is a horrible feeling.

February 4, 1863

Last night was the coldest that we have had yet. The clouds cleared away just at dusk and it was as fine an evening as we have yet seen here. It was thirty-two degrees below zero during the night which would be very severe for anyone to be exposed to any length of time if the wind was blowing. But it was very still and clear—the stars shining very beautiful in the sky. What a healthy invigorating air there is in this region. The wind has been blowing quite strong today and the air is full of blustering snow rendering it quite disagreeable for anyone traveling. The snow is very deep.

Charlie Lewis, the first man who settled in this country and owned a good share of the Mine for some time & through drinking lost it & spent his time as a ditch drunkard ever since, died last night and was buried this afternoon.[21] This old man knowing his fondness for strong drink gave his property to the [Central Mine] Company with the agreement that they should support him as long as he lived. So he spent his time as a miserable drunkard.

There has been some exitement here to invest money in the Central Mine. Last September the shares were selling for four dollars per share & now they are selling for thirty dollars per share and will soon be up to sixty dollars.There is a great show of copper & with more money it will be one of the best mines on the Lake. Many are investing largely. If I had brought up two thousand dollars last fall & invested I should be a rich man now.

February 10, 1863

It is some time since I wrote last still nothing has taken place worthy of note. The weather has been quite rough & snowing much of the time. My school moves quietly and pleasantly. Last night I went to the river with Edward; had a jolly time. It cost me nineteen dollars to save my teeth. They were in a very bad condition.

February 15, 1863

I am aware that I am sadly neglecting my Journal but I cannot help it. There is not any news worth relating. Everything is quiet. The changes in the weather are the most worthy of note. For the past two or three days it has snowed very hard & last night it turned into a drizzling rain of short duration. It is very cold today & windy. The snow is about six feet deep and drifted badly.

No war news of importance. I have longings to join the army & cannot take up a paper without wishing that I had a hand in helping crush this Rebellion.

Oh don't you remember sweet Alice, "Ben Bolt',"
Sweet Alice, with hair so brown.
She wept with delight when you gave her a smile,
And trembled with fear at your frown.
In the old churchyard in the valley "Ben Bolt".
In a corner, obscure and alone,
They have fitted a slab of granite so grey.
And sweet Alice lies under the stone.
Oh don't you remember the wood, "Ben Bolt",
Near the green sunny slope of the hill
Where oft we have sung 'neath the wide spreading shade,
And kept time with the click of the Mill
The Mill has gone to decay, "Ben Bolt"
And silence now reigns all around;
See the old rustic porch with its roses so sweet,
Lies scattered and fallen to the ground.
Oh! don't you remember the school, "Ben Bolt",
And the master so kind and so true,
And the little nook by the clear running brook
Where we gathered the flowers as they grew.
O'er the master's grave grows the grass "Ben Bolt"
And the running little brook is now dry.
And of all the "friends" that were schoolmates then,
There remains "Ben" but you & I.
There remains "Ben" but you & I.[22]

February 18, 1863

For the past two or three days the weather has been very mild and pleasant. Yesterday the snow was soft enough for snowballing and my scholars engaged in the sport with animation. The snow packs down quite hard & is so deep that the fences are covered & those who engage in the sport of hunting go into the woods on snowshoes. Today it looks very much like a thaw.

My school now averages one hundred. They are all progressing very fast and I have become master of them without now inflicting punishment. They all like school. The old Catholic priest declares that the Irish children must not go any longer as a Yankee teacher will corrupt them. They are intending to build a school for the Catholic children & put them under the charge of a Nun.

Misses Cundy & Harper made a trip underground last Saturday night. They went as far as the ninety fathom level on the ladders and up again.

February 20, 1863

We now have a change in the weather. It was colder yesterday than it had been for some time & last night it froze very hard. The frost on the windows is quite thick. It was very cloudy and may snow in a few days. I met my best spellers at Captain Harry George's house last night and had a pleasant time drilling in spelling.[23] They spell very well. After we were through spelling, Captain Harry thought it very strange how I could put out words so very fast and tell when they were missed. I put out over four thousand in one hour and three quarters.

February 24, 1863

The weather is milder this morning with some appearance of snow and rain. I left my couch quite early & cut up some wood for Mrs. Rawlings. I cut some almost every day. There is now a challenge between my school and Eagle River to come off at the River. The schools are to be examined in geography, arithmetic and spelling. When the battle takes place I will give the particulars. Captain Halls has hired Mr. Chapman's team to carry my scholars down.[24] There is great excitement here in relation to my spelling schools which I am glad to see. I met the scholars in arithmetic last night and commenced drilling them—all meet the classes in spelling & geography tonight.

February 26, 1863

It commenced snowing a very little this morning and has been a very stormy day. The wind is strong from the north yet it is not very cold. I think that the weather will be very severe to night. The Examinations to come off Saturday are to be in spelling and Grammar, & I am glad that I have made such an arrangement. There is great excitement in consequence of this affair. My scholars are working night and day. I have met them every night this week. Last night I had a spelling school at the schoolhouse. Quite a large number were in & everything passed off pleasantly.

February 29, 1863

It is very pleasant weather this morning although there is now and then a slight fall of snow. Quite a number of the people here have gone to the River today for a sleigh ride. The only news we have here is the following.

Spelling Schools

Yesterday the trial between this school & the school at the River was to come off in the afternoon in "Spelling & Grammar." I had met my scholars every evening for a week & equally as great preparations had been made on the other side. Captain Halls provided us with a double team & driver & at twelve noon, a load of thirty of us set out for the River. The weather was fine and we had a joyful time on the way. After arriving at the place of trial we made ourselves at home, and were told by all present that we should go back like whipped dogs—but my scholars were well trained & kept up good spirits.

We very soon made the necessary arrangements & Mr. Northmore, the teacher, & myself put out a few words when we commenced spelling down. I put out the words once & they tried once on a word. I soon had the River school down on words of one syllable & one half of mine (twelve in number) were still up. Their teacher then took the book & gave them a chance to try twice on each word. He went all through the book after hard words & his school was soon down and ten of mine were still up.

Next came Grammar. The two classes were called out on the floor in a line, & Mr. Northmore went through with a lengthy examination. My class were well prepared. I did not question them in Grammar but sent mine to the board & had them write down a sentence & analyze it. His class were afraid that I should call on them & took their seats.

Our team was then ready and after getting in I raised the "stars and stripes" which my scholars did not know I had brought along but I was determined that if I whipped I should rejoice some way. We drove through the village quietly & then my scholars sung the "Red, White & Blue" as we drove back through the village for the

Cliff. Crowds in the doors saw us pass. When we arrived at the Cliff, we went through the village singing the following:

Three cheers for the Clifton School etc.
The Clifton School forever etc.
Three cheers for the Red White & Blue.

Also "John Brown." We halted before the store where the crowd gave the school & teacher three hearty cheers. I then had the scholars give Captain Halls three cheers for his kindness in furnishing us with a team. Treated the scholars with candy & went home feeling well. The parents are all rejoicing & the scholars are working very hard. Many of them are making remarkable progress. Much good will result from this affair.

Notes for January-February 1863

1. Daniel D. Brockway (1815-1899) was one of the early pioneers of the Keweenaw Peninsula. Born in Franklin County, Vermont on May 2, 1815, he moved to Washtenaw County, Michigan, in 1831. He was appointed blacksmith and mechanic to the Indian Department of the Upper Lakes in 1843 and was stationed at L'Anse at the foot of Keweenaw Bay, Lake Superior. He moved to Copper Harbor in 1846 and opened a hotel and became involved in various copper mining ventures. In 1861 he moved to Eagle River where he opened the hotel that Hobart visited during Christmas of 1862. Brockway sold the hotel in 1863 and moved to Copper Harbor to run a mercantile business. In 1872 he returned to the Cliff Mine to open a store; from 1882-1895 he served as superintendent of the Cliff property. See *History of the Upper Peninsula of Michigan* (Chicago: Western Historical Company, 1883), p. 344; *Michigan State Gazetteer and Business Directory for 1863-64* (Detroit: Charles Clark, 1863), p. 292; Alvah L. Sawyer, *History of the Northern Peninsula of Michigan* (Chicago: Lewis Publishing Co., 1911), p. 1326. The Brockway Papers are in the Bentley Historical Library, University of Michigan, Ann Arbor, Michigan.

2. Located on Lake Superior, three miles from Clifton, Eagle River had a population of about three hundred in 1863. The village had three churches, one lodge of Odd Fellows, one ashery, two breweries, three general stores, two sawmills, several saloons and a hotel. Its docks stretching into Lake Superior were built and owned by the Pittsburgh and Boston Mining Company and provided access for steamers to load the copper of the Cliff, Phoenix, Central, Copper Falls and other nearby mines. See *Michigan State Gazetteer, 1863-64*, p. 292.

3. The first Lodge of the Odd Fellows (No. 68) was established in Eagle Harbor in October of 1859 and later was moved to Clifton. See *History of the Upper Peninsula of Michigan*, pp. 337-338.

4. Florence Hobart, Henry's younger sister, was born April 9, 1847, and died December 20, 1877.

5. William Benney, age 13, was the son of John, age 39, and Elizabeth Benney, age 35, and one of six children, as of the *8th U. S. Census*, Houghton County, 1860.

6. Hobart Shipman, born in 1841, was the son of John and Rachel Hobart Shipman of East Whitby Township, Ontario. The other cousins were Wilbur, age 16, John Jr., age 6, and Julie, age not known. *United States Bureau of the Census*, Ontario Census, Ontario County, East Whitby Township, 1861; Percy Hobart Titus, ed., *The Hobart Family in America* (Boston: 1943).

7. This may possibly refer to the Henry H. Lloyd who published a number of military maps and campaign charts during the Civil War.

8. C. T. Harvey received the contract for mail delivery between Green Bay and the Keweenaw Peninsula at the rate of $13,500 a year. The *Portage Lake Mining Gazette* published many articles complaining about the poor mail service, lost mail and other related problems. See *Portage Lake Mining Gazette*, January 24, 1863, and *Lake Superior Miner*, January 9, 1864.

9. Edward R. Penberthy was born June 24, 1841, in Cloumel County of Tipperary, Ireland. The Penberthy genealogy was provided by S. Joseph Penberthy of Farmington, Michigan.

10. George Bancroft, *History of the United States from the Discovery of the American Continent* (Boston: Charles Little and James Brown, 1854-1875).

11. Josiah Halls was born in Cornwall, England, in 1826 and came to Cliff Mine in 1851 with his wife, Fannie Grove of England, who was born in 1830. He began employment at the Cliff Mine as a miner and later as a "timber man" and "pit man." In 1860 he was promoted to mining captain at the Cliff Mine and later worked at the Pewabic Mine in Hancock, Michigan. By 1860 they had six children, ages 7, 6, 5, 4, 4, and 2. By 1883 the Halls' had eleven children. Several of the children were "scholars" in Hobart's school. See *8th U. S. Census*, Houghton County, 1860; *History of the Upper Peninsula*, p. 317.

12. Dr. Greelee does not appear in the *U. S. Census* of 1860 or 1870 for Houghton or Keweenaw County.

13. According to the Penberthy family genealogy, John Penberthy was born in Marazion, Cornwall, England in 1836. The *8th U. S. Census*, Houghton County, 1860, lists John, age 22, as an engineer. John Vivian was born in Cornwall on February 11, 1827, the son of Nicholas Vivian, and was married to Sarah Landor who was born in Lancashire, England, in 1827. He worked as a miner at the Cliff Mine until injuries from falling rocks forced him to give up underground work. He taught school for two years and then was elected county clerk for Keweenaw County in 1860

and held that position for four years. He served as Justice of the Peace from 1861-1891. He also served as supply clerk at the Osceola Mine. According to the *9th U. S. Census,* Keweenaw County, Copper Harbor, 1870, John and Sarah Vivian had six children—Nicholas J., age 16, Robert, age 12, John L., age 10, Ellen, age 9, David L., age 8, and Mary A., age 1. See *Memorial Record of the Northern Peninsula of Michigan* (Chicago: Lewis Publishing Company, 1895), pp. 429-430, and Clarence J. Monette, *The History of Eagle River, Michigan* (Lake Linden: 1978), p. 46.

14. "Shivaree" is a corruption of "charivari," a mock serenade of discordant noises often made with kettles and tin horns.

15. Josiah Penberthy was born in Ireland in 1849, according to the *8th U. S. Census,* Houghton County, 1860. Captain Joseph Paulls was born in Cornwall, England, in December 1822. He came to the United States in 1844. After sixteen years in mining he opened a general store at the Cliff Mine in 1860 and remained there until 1869. In 1860 he and his wife, Mary, had six children— Mary, age 9, Sarah, age 7, Joseph, age 5, Isabelle, age 3, and Ralph and Thomas, twins— age 7 months. His real estate was valued at $5,000 and his personal property at $5,000, according to the *8th U. S. Census,* Houghton County, 1860. See *History of the Upper Peninsula,* p. 311.

16. According to the *8th U. S. Census,* Houghton County, 1860, Solomon Cundy was born in Ireland in 1832. He and his wife May had one son, Mathew, born in 1856.

17. Mike Hanley, was listed in the *9th U. S. Census,* Keweenaw County. 1870, as age 16, born in Virginia, the son of Patrick and Mary Hanley. A Dan Sullivan is listed in the *8th U. S. Census,* Houghton County, 1860.

18. Jesse H. Bushnell was a classmate of Hobart's at Williston Academy in 1859, according to the *Catalogue of the Trustees, Officers, Teachers and Students of Williston Academy* (Burlington, Vermont: Free Press Print, 1859). He was the son of Hiram, age 61, and Jerusha, age 39, Bushnell. Jesse was 20 in June 1860 and his brother Edgar was 18 in the *8th U. S. Census,* Chittenden County, Vermont, 1860.

19. For additional information on the Harris murder trial, see Donald Chaput, *The Cliff: America's First Great Copper Mine* (Kalamazoo: Sequoia Press, 1971), p. 86. Under the headline, "Shocking Murder at the Cliff Mine," the *Lake Portage Mining Gazette* of December 13, 1862, ran the following account of the incident: "We are indebted to A.F. Leld, Esq., of Hancock, for the following particulars of the murder of Cliff Mine last week. The murdered man was a blacksmith, named Richards, who had been in the employ of the Company for a considerable time. Harris, the dealer of such summary justice, was a miner and kept a boarding house, and Richards was formerly one of his boarders, until his intimacy with Mrs. Harris became the subject of remarks by all in the house, when he was ordered to leave. He went off, but was seen making occasional visits to the house, when Harris was underground on nightshifts. These visits became so notorious as to cause the mining captains to severely reprimand

him, and make him promise to keep away from the house. Harris became informed of the proceedings, from persons outside and also from his wife, who seemed to delight in annoying him by speaking of Richards' visits. Tuesday, of last week, Richards and Mrs. H. indulged in a sleighride, and Harris duly informed of it in the evening, on his return from work. He, of course, was very indignant, and quietly procured a double-barreled gun, loaded it with shot, and placed it under the stairway. One or two evenings after this, he pretended to his wife that he would be obliged to work that night, took his candles and put on his mining clothes and went out, but instead of going to the mine, he came back by another street, and got under the house, where he remained for more than two hours. In the meantime his wife went out, and after being absent some little time, came in again and put the children to bed. Not long after this Harris heard some one conversing with his wife, and thought that he recognised Richards' voice. Coming out from his place of concealment, he attempted to enter the house, but found the door fastened. He then picked up an axe which was lying ouside, and raising a window stepped into the front room, and, through a half open door, saw Richards and his wife in the adjoining room sitting by the stove drinking a glass of "hot stuff." The moment they saw him, they both rushed at him, and endeavored to take the axe away. Harris, fearing he would be worsted by the two, called for help and some of the boarders, who were in their rooms, came to his assistance. They took the axe away, and one of them held the woman. Harris then told Richards that he would not be harmed if he would sit down, and talk the matter over. This threw the rest off their guard, and allowed Harris an opportunity to step to the stairway and get his gun, one barrel of which he discharged at Richards, the load striking him a little below the heart and inflicting a mortal wound. He then turned and pointed the gun at his wife, who was begging of him not to shoot

20. J. S. Cilley was principal of Williston Academy in Willison, Vermont, while Henry was a student there. The strict rules of behavior for the Academy were introduced by Cilley. F. Kennan Moody and Floyd Putnam, *The Williston Story* (Essex Junction, Vermont: 1961), pp. 35-36.

21.The identity of Charles Lewis is not known.

22. "Ben Bolt" or "Ah! You Don't Remember" by Thoms Dunn English in Ralph L. Woods, *A Treasury of Familiar Verse* (New York: Macmillan Co.,1955) p. 473.

23. Captain Harry George was born in England in 1827. According to the *8th U. S. Census*, Houghton County, 1860, he and his wife, Jane, age 30, had three children, Henry, age 9, Thomas, age 6, and Jane, age 2.

24. Mr. Chapman probably was George R. Chapman, a teamster who was cited in the *9th U. S. Census*, Keweenaw County, Clifton, 1870.

March—April 1863

The stacks at Cliff Mine remained after the mine closed. Hobart lived in the home of Joseph Rawlings (inset) and described him as a "smart, witty genius."

Mine officials and miners pose for this 1862 photograph. Seated (left to right): John Slauson, William Van Orden, Solomon Cundy. Standing: Charles Cormley and Alex McInyre.

March 2, 1863

We are now having very cool weather & considerable wind. It snows a little occasionally & drifts some. It is very evident that we shall not have severe weather this winter. Lake Superior is still open and we may expect a boat up very early. Mr. Percival Updegraff, clerk of the mine, started for below overland this morning.[1] He is to order goods for the store.

March 4, 1863

It is very cold today & there is no wind. The spelling school in the evening was well attended. Whipped the [Eagle] River School again. Seventy-five scholars spelt.

March 8, 1863

It is Sunday today & sitting in my sunny little room my mind wanders to home and home scenes, and I long to be there, long to enjoy the comforts of the dearest spot on earth, *home*. But this is an impossibility at present. I am living where I should be unable to reach Vermont with my present means. I am not homesick, far from it. I am contented and happy. I have been up this morning & attended the Methodist Sunday School! Taught a class of boys at their earnest request. This afternoon intend going to the Episcopal Sunday School where I have a class to instruct.

We are blessed here with the very best preaching. Rev. Mr. Baughman, the Methodist preacher, is a man of superior talents.[2] [He] takes a great interest in my school. Has held the highest position as a divine Presiding Elder Agent of the American Bible Society etc. He is now sixty-one years of age, weighs 251 pounds [and] has never taken intoxicating drink in any form or tobacco. Would that every man might say the same.

No man possesses correct knowledge and information unless it be founded on religion. It is the correct basis of all genuine character and the source of true wisdom. If a young man would go forth in the world or try and store his mind with wisdom, if he would lay a sure foundation for a character pure & perfect; he must settle his religious principles first. It is not a question of minor importance,but it is the first thing a young man should do is to settle firmly his religious habits. He is then prepared to battle with life's trails & make himself useful. The most noted men the world ever saw were men of religious principles. The greatest philosophers were strongly imbued with religious sentiments. Would that every young man would base his actions on the great truths of Christianity.

March 9, 1863

The Rev. Mr. Baughman delivered a temperance lecture last night which I had the privilege of listening to. The following is a summary of the expense per year to the United States for the sale of Gin etc. as near as I can recollect.

United States

100,000,000 gallons of whisky sold per year placed at the lowest estimate will amount to $75,000,000;

50,000,000 gallons fermented Liqours at low estimate champagne [will amount to] $50,000,000;

For sale of Beer, champagne etc. [will amount to] $100,000,000;

30,000 deaths by drink in which each man loses at least 10 years of his life which will equal 300,00 years lost which will equal 90,000,000 days, calling 300 in a year at $.50 per day [will amount to] $45,000,000;

The prosecution of crime caused by its sale, jail fees etc. [will amount to] $50,000,000;

Accidents on railroads steamboats carriages etc. [will amount to] $30,000,000;

Total Expenses for intemperance [will amount to] $350,000,000;

Now for the death of 30,000 of our best men 50,000 hard drinkers and 500,000 moderate drinkers & all the suffering caused beside the United States pays over $350,000,000 per year at the lowest estimate By careful research it is found that the annual expense placed out a compound interest will amount to in ten years $4,000,000,000 . Take all causes war, famine pestilence etc.; they do not cause so many deaths as intemperance, and the present war not excepted.

Then draw the picture of 20,000 men passing to the grave; see them, swollen eyes, haggard looks, swearing, singing, jesting etc., & the train of famished widows & orphans close behind. Then comes 50,000 hard drinkers on the same road with the whisky buds on their cheeks. 100,000 moderate drinkers next, look at the picture. What a scene. Who are these men that are thus on the road to ruin? Are they the scum of society? No. Lawyers, doctors, Statesmen etc. The brightest minds of the lands. The very bone and sinew of the country.

Man is so constituted that his system does not require any stimulants. Proper food taken at proper times is sufficient to supply all of nature's demands in relation to the body. There is a certain amount of excitability in man that must not be destroyed. And stimulants taken into the stomach draw upon this excitability it produces an unnatural state, contrary to nature, causes the blood to flow faster consequently the flush of face that may be seen after taking a good horn. It requires the severest exertions of nature [to] throw off its evil effects—consequently the low spirits it produces after the effect. The excitability is destroyed by overworking & nervous diseases ensue of a horrid nature thus "Delirium Tremens." The person thinks he had snakes in his hair & boots, everything is a terrible thing. The hand trembles indicating that the nerves are diseased the rum buds appear on the cheek & nose indicating that the liver is affected.

Persons of a nervous Temperament are the ones to get drunk. Another person can drink it by the quart and he will not get tight, he is like an ox; you cannot excite him. He has not brain enough to get drunk & if I were to measure the capacity of such a man I would say that "He is a whisky barrel in the morning & a barrel of whisky at night."

It is false to say that alcohol is one of the things of God. It cannot be found in a natural state in nature. Take corn [and] grind it, soak it in water, boil it, make mush of it if you please & you cannot get alcohol enough to kill a mosquito. The juice of the grape or apple in its natural state does not contain a particle. It has to go through a state of fermentation or decomposition in which it throws off certain gases and takes some from the air. The grain from which it is taken has to rot in common language. It has to go through a process of decomposition and take certain gases from the air & throw off certain gases. Therefore, it is not found in nature; it is produced by the ingenuity of man by taking advantage of the appetites of men; and will it has succeeded if we are to judge by the quantity sold & the misery it has caused.

In its effects it is like Tobacco. If a person will carefully study the force of habit in man they will account for the reason why a man that uses any stimulant is not at home without it. When first used, it creates a longing or desire for more & this habit becomes stronger, until it becomes a demand that cannot be resisted. The person dreads the effects produced by stopping, longs to have enough down to feel like the boy who was all "Teter" all over.

Alcohol is never taken up in the system; it rejects it. There is a class of muscles in all parts of the body whose office it is to throw off whatever comes in the way the blood that is not required for the healthy nutriment of the body, & when alcohol is taken constantly these muscles are overtaxed and becoming weakened [and] refuse to perform their office. Disease is the result.

A drunkard after death shows that it is not taken up—alcohol may be found in the cavities of the brain and all through the system just as it was when taken into the stomach. It will not enter into the system as nutriment like food. The blood of a drunkard will [be] like alcohol. The alcohol is in its natural state. Therefore it is evident that a foreign substance that will not be taken up as nutriment must when taken often destroy the life for it cannot be thrown off as the muscles become weakened.

It matters not what you give it; it is all the same. In this place it goes by the name of "cabbage." The last name that I heard it called was "Paddy's eye water" and this name was actually given by a paddy. There is nothing in the United States or world that has so much fraud about it as the making & selling of Strong drink. Talk about a pure article of brandy. "The best Madeira." It never saw Madeira. It is made of whiskey etc. in our large cities & colored up & stamped off in fine style. This is a fact. The trash that is sold here under the name of Champagne is nothing but New Jersey cider that is put through a certain process & then comes out real sparkling Champagne. A good name. A great deal of "Cham" about it but the (pagne) pain is real.

And all over the United States barrels of beer and ale are guzzled down by the young & old. Made out of the water from the sewers of cities etc. In one of the cities of New York there was a large beer brewery & they took the water to make it from a pond near by which was used to throw dead horses, cats, dogs, calves & all species of carrion. A temperance Editor exposed the crime & was sued for damage. The trial came off & he proved the fact & brought up an old brewery man who said they put carrion in it to clarify it. Guzzle down the filthy stuff, ye drunkards.

In relation to the fraud here is a case. An old whisky dealer in New York wishing to exchange a load of whisky for the best brandy went to an establishment when the "boss" told him that he had sold his stock but he expected a large quantity in that night, in a ship. And if he would leave his whisky he could have the brandy in the morning which he agreed to & left his whisky which the brandy dealer made into brandy & had it all marked off in the morning & the whisky dealer drives up & gets his own whisky now made into the best brandy. Very honest traffic.

An Incident

Showing that the rum seller despises the drinker & only wants his coppers. He calls the drinker a fool & other mean names. The drinker in the bar room of a city hotel was left drunk on the floor at night & in the morning rising from his hard bed he sees the landlady cooking some nice beef in the kitchen and he longs for a slice well knowing that he had not got it at home where his family w[as] suffering. So he calls for some meat & the lady replies, "So long you dirty brute," throwing him an old dry crust of bread. He asks if he may soak it in the nice beef gravy & for a reply she says, "Get out, you filthy wretch, go home & soak your bread in your own gravy." This starts him & he goes home resolved to reform.

Works like a good fellow through the week receives his money. It looks good & he goes & buys some nice beef Steak, flour & things sufficient for several fine meals. Puts his articles in a wheelbarrow & starts for home feeling happy & proud; goes a mile out of his way so as to drive by the old tavern stand, & as he rolls his load along by the tavern proud as a king, the landlady standing in the door hails him. "Why John! Why haven't you visited us this week?" John replies, "I am soaking my bread in my own gravy."

The man who offers you strong drink is your worst enemy. The seller has no pity for the drunkard. It is the improper love of money that causes man to take advantage of the appetites of men & make & sell the poison stuff. It is an improper love that will cause a man to sell it when he knows what suffering & misery it causes. Touch it not & then the seller may take care of himself.

An Incident among a thousand

Related by the Rev. Mr. Baughman. At the foot of Woodward Avenue in the city of Detroit near the river stands an old French tavern stand, one end of which projects over the river. One spring the water was quite high and [the] floor being full of cracks the water dashed up through the floor. It was a wretched place. The speaker was requested to visit the place where he found two children dead and one in the corner on a pile of filthy rags dying. The wife of the man was there in a wretched state. The husband was taken to jail drunk for abusing his family. The speaker promised to attend the funeral next day & doing so found the three children dead. They were placed in coffins in the city hearse & when they started for the graveyard, sad to tell, the mother lay in one corner of the room in a state of beastly intoxication. What a scene, two bright little boys, one ten & the other eight, and a little girl of six, carried to the grave in consequence of abuse from drunken parents who both died drunk after this.

The speaker was lecturing in Ohio after & related this fact in his lecture & on closing a man came to him hardly able to speak in consequence of his feelings & said, "It was my brother." When young he was a man of superior promise, but taking to strong [drink], he thus ended his miserable life & that of his family.

The true source of a nation's wealth is the industry of the people, with this borne in mind we can see the cost of drunkenness. Time lost, crime committed, keeping poor, prosecution of crime, expense of jails etc., money expended for drink & many other items, makes the handsome sum, when placed at compound interest at six percent for ten years [equals] $4,000,000,000.

An Incident

A good priest was compelled by circumstances and authority to commit one of three things—Get drunk, Commit Adultery or Murder. He concluded to get drunk as the least sin & then he committed the other two while drunk. Drunkenness causes all sins.

March 10, 1863

The weather yesterday was very severe. The wind blew very strong from the west and north filling the air full of snow. My school was small and the wind howled about the old house in a lively manner. In the evening I met some of my scholars at Mr. McDonald's and spent the time in spelling.[3] Mr. Rawlings is at home now. He is a smart, witty genius. Is the best engineer and draftsman on the Lake.

Today it is cold and has the appearance of snowing. It has been quite pleasant although indications were unfavorable in the morning.

As I am now writing, two of my boys, Josiah Penberthy and Horatio Halls, are putting out words from Town's speller.[4] They are fine boys and are learning quite fast. I wish I had a school of such scholars. I finish a letter from home today and wish I might make a visit to Vermont. I learn that a conscription act has passed Congress requiring all between eighteen and thirty five to join the army. A good thing I think and I am ready at any time. There is no news worthy of note.

The Human Will

The celebrated Dr. Edwards has compared the action of the viz "Will" to a pair of scales or balances.[5] It moves in the direction of the stronger motive. This is a fine comparison although there are two good reasons against it viz. The action of the mind should not be compared to matter. The mind is capable of expansion and has intelligence therefore it cannot be compared to the action of matter. Again if the will acts like a balance or scales and acts in the direction of the stronger motive then it may be made to assume an equilibrium, when the motives are equal. A pair of scales assumes the same position when the weights are equal. Place a hungry man between two tables at an equal distance from each and have each one loaded with the same kind of equal quantities of good food. The man is hungry and he looks both ways and the motive to go to either table is the same; he is set and will remain and starve as the motives are the same and there is no greater motive to incline his Will. But you cannot set the will in that way; therefore we conclude that the mind does not act in that way. It does not act like a pair of scales and cannot be compared to matter in its action.

Aour Blockade

The owner of the steamer Princess Royal and cargo was an "M.P."
when last year wanted England to disregard aour blockade cawse it
warn't effishent. I ges he's faound aout —its his block-hed that is in-
effeshent
What d'ye think ou aour blockade naow, old feller?
Dont it make yure hed feel kind o meller
Soft, I mean - when yu reed
Of cute Jonathans deed.
Took yure ship in es the "took" old Weller.
We hev warned yu thet trubble was a brewin
Fur folks thet would do es you was duin—
Tat theres menny a slip Twixt the Port and the Ship—

But you would cum aout tu far tu yure reuin.
I swanny its the best joke ov the season
Though yu might expected it, in reeson
Yu have shown plaine enuf —
You aint quite "up to snuff"
Takes a smarter chap then yu tu thrive on treeson
Aour Blockade is made of paper is it? du tell!
Gess yu've bin made the "victum of a sell,"
Jess keep on es yu've begun
And aour Sailors will nev run,
Prises, Jonny Ball has furnished, suit emwell.

It is now most time for me to retire so I will lay aside the pen
and after reading a few pages from *Astoria* by Washington Irving
which gives an account of Jacob Astor's effort in Establishing a
trading post at the mouth of the Columbia river & engaging in the
fur trade, I will take the needful rest.[6]

March 11, 1863

We have been favored with a pleasant day and much sunshine
although it has been quite cool. A young man had his leg broke in
the mine today. It has been broken twice in the same place and he
is suffering much with severe pain. His friends have sent for Dr.
Heaton of the Portage....[7]

March 12, 1863

As I take a seat in my little room to write a few lines before
school time , the bright sun shines brightly through the window to
cheer me & I think of home & hope that its bright beams also shine
upon the home circle who I trust are enjoying health and happiness. We are separated by a great distance and it takes many days
for a letter to reach home and if any serious accident should befall
any one at home I should not know it for a long time. I hope no
such accident may happen.

I must now commence my hard day's work. My school was
quite large and I have had a severe day's work. In the evening I
had a good spelling school. Mr. Northmore and his best spellers

were present. He put out the words first and my school spelt down. I put out next & my school spelt down. Had two declamations by Josiah [Penberthy] & Horatio [Halls]. Everything passed off pleasantly. Quite a number of the parents in & took an interest in the exercises.

Received of the Treasurer of the district the balance of my pay $180.00. Paid Mrs. Rawlings $20.00 & deposited $160.00 in the Cliff office for safe keeping. Lately, Mrs. Harris, wife of the murderer, was caught in bed with a miner by her son, who had a witness with him. This confirms the fact that she is a woman of low principles & habits. This fact will aid in clearing Harris from Eagle River jail where he is confined for killing a man while with his wife in unlawful business.

Provisions are now getting very short and we cannot have a full allowance or much variety. I have bought two or three quarts of milk when feeling rather unwell.

March 15, 1863

It is Sunday today and is very warm and pleasant, although it is cloudy. The snow is soft enough for some of the coarse mining boys to engage in snowballing which I see them do from my window. I got up this morning quite late and after partaking of a breakfast of salt mackerel & wheat bread; by the way wheat bread is the main stay. It constitutes the breakfast & I get very sick of it. Potatoes are seldom used. As I was saying, after my morning meal I took a seat in my cozy room and commenced reading *Astoria* & was tracing the difficult and dangerous journey of the party headed by Captain Hunt overland to the mouth of the Columbia River where the trading post was built called "Astoria." Founded by J. J. Astor.

All at once the whistle blows long & loud there is a fire somewhere & I pull on my boots & out for the scene of conflict. The back part of the Engineer's house was on fire. Men came from all directions and a brook running nearby [and] we went to work & after a half hour's hard work succeed[ed] in putting it out. Most of the kitchen was burnt. I passed water from the brook to a line of men from the brook to the house in pails. Almost everything was removed from the place before the fire was out. The fire originated from a stove pipe burning out & setting the roof on fire. All the houses have stovepipes running up through the roof and they often burn out. The pipe in this house has been on fire three times. They are very dangerous and as there are no ladders, it is difficult to get at a fire on the roof. If it had been a weekday, there would not have been men enough above ground to put it out.

It is almost time to go to Sabbath School so I will lay aside my pen at present. Listened to Mr. Baughman in the evening. He had a fine sermon. I take pleasure in listening to the sound reasoning of this fine old man and visit him once in a while for the purpose of having a chat.

He made an explanation after the sermon. It seems some of the Catholics took offence in relation to the anecdote Mr. B[aughman] related in his temperance address about a certain priest. He did not say that it was a Catholic priest & had no intention of casting a slur on any sect. He said, "I am too old & have too much manhood for that too much *self-respect*." I related it as it was given to me & was trying to illustrate the fact that intemperance is the parent of crime. A man will commit a crime while drunk that he would shudder to do while sober. The Catholics have a priest who leads them on against Protestants & they even threatened our gray- headed minister. Says Mr. B[aughman]: they would kill an old man like me; I shall die soon. And to tell the truth the trouble was somewhere else. To use a common phase it pinched them where the nigger's shoe pinched him—"Across the Stomach." I have no respect for drunkards in any church or denomination.

There seems to be a mystery to many in the idea of a trinity in one. And to overcome this mystery it must be borne in mind that it is not in the same sense. Take an equilateral triangle or one with three equal sides. Now there are three equal sides making one triangle. There must be three sides or no triangle. In a perfect stalk of clover there are three leaves & it could not be a perfect stalk without three leaves. Three in one; one in three. I must not remain up any longer. *Il est minuit "a le Francais."*

March 17, 1863

I have no news to write this evening only that the weather was a little cooler this morning and some wind from the north. The days are now quite lengthy and the brunt of the winter has passed being remarkable here for its mildness and want of severe weather. The waters of Lake Superior are still free. This week many of my scholars who have been detained by rough weather have returned to school and yesterday there was 115 present. Today being St. Patrick's Day I have only 105.[8] With severe exertion for two of us we can only close at five o'clock. When the house is repaired and two apartments for the school it will be pleasant I hope. It is far from it now.

Visited Mr. Bergan's last evening. He sharpens the drills and chisels for the miners. He has a case of small miner's tools that he made for show. They are very handsome. I feel the want of home living very much and long to taste of corn bread and some mush and milk. I have bought two or three quarts but it does not satisfy me yet. We have not received any war news here for some time & expect a large mail tomorrow night. I have labored very hard and will now read awhile & then retire.

An Incident

One of our noble Union soldiers was arrested for stealing a goose from a Rebel and he gave the following reply when asked why he done it. "I found the goose hissing at the 'Stars & Stripes' and I arrested it for treason."

A man having a fractious horse that had thrown off his wife & killed her would not sell it as he intended to get married again. Funny.

March 19, 1863

The sky is very clear this morning and the sun shines very bright giving promise of a fine day. The clear healthy atmosphere that surrounds this point of land whose shores are washed by the pure waters of Lake Superior cannot be surpassed in the Green Mountain State. This is a healthy country, the air is pure and bracing and this is one of the most beautiful mornings I ever saw in my life. Yesterday was the same.

It is said that there is very little sickness here there are very few cases except those who come here sick and at the "Portage" twenty miles distant it is quite unhealthy there being many cases of "typhoid fever" which is attributed to the bad water and muddy little lake on which the village is situated. At the mines near Ontonagon it is healthier than it is here. Before night the wind breezes up from the south and there are indications of an approaching storm. The snow is settling some and it looks like spring.

Mr. Rawlings and Edward returned from the Portage this afternoon. William, a brother of Edward's, also came from Ontonagon where he has been fitting and running an "Engine."[9] He is going to school.

The air, A Bachelor

The air is a bachelor, merry and free
He roves at his pleasure o'er land o'er sea;
He ruffles the Lake, & kisses the flower
And sleeps when he lists in a jessamine bower.
He gives to the cheek of the maiden its bloom,
He tastes her warm kisses & Breathes their perfume;
But truant like often the sweets that he sips
Are lavished next moment on livelier lips.

Henri. [10]

March 20, 1863

We have had a pleasant day although there has been some wind from the south. Last night the wind was very strong and the waves on Lake Superior I could hear dashing against the rocky shores three miles distant. It reminded me of the times when I crossed the sandbar that connected Grand Isle in Lake Champlain with the main land [and] also of some of the nights I spent on that Isle engaged in teaching and while boarding around sleeping in some cold chamber near the shore listening to the music of the waves. I went down to Captain Paull's last night and passed the evening very pleasantly in their comfortable sitting room engaged in conversation with the family. They are fine people and have three bright little girls and two little boys. Two of the girls and one boy come to my school. Today I had over 115 scholars; the house was crowded full and I am very tired tonight.

Le vent est tres oit; Il est tres bean temps maintment. Il n'est pas tres froir in tres chaud.

Goldsmith's Pedagogue.

A man severe he was and stern to view
I knew him well and every truant knew:
Well had the boding tremblers learned to trace

The days disasters in his morning face;
Full well they laughed with counterfeited glee
At all his jokes for many a joke had he.
Full well the busy whisper circling round,
Conveyed the dismal tidings when he frowned.

The world is God's seed bed. He has planted deep and multitudinously, and many things there are which have not yet come up.

H. Beecher.[11]

March 22, 1863

I have passed the time very pleasantly today in reading and attending the Sabbath School where we had a good discussion about the lesson. Young Thomas P. Williams acted as our teacher.[12] This school is in a very flourishing condition, while the Episcopal school where I have a class does not prosper well. The people here all like the old white headed preacher "Mr. Baughman." I shall go & listen to him tonight.

The weather is quite stormy and there are many indications that summer will return soon. It is raining and hailing today. The wind blew quite hard yesterday from the south. The provision is scarce now & all will have short allowance. We have had no good butter this winter. It is stinking stuff from old warehouses & would make a good soap grease. I do not think it could be sold below. I mean no disrespect to the men here who have the charge of the business of furnishing provisions. Men have different spheres. It is for some to evolve great moral truths as the heavens evolve stars, to guide the sailor on the sea and the traveller on the desert. And it is for some like the sailor & the traveller simply to be guided. "There is truth in the above." "For truth is as impossible to be soiled by any outward touch as a sunbeam." "One of the rarest powers possessed by man is the power to state a fact."

Two good verses
That man true dignity will find,
Who tries the matrimonial estate,
Who pours contempt on woman kind,
Will mourn his folly when too late.

> *Stop a minute, in your ear*
> *A word I'd whisper, hark ye,*
> *May I come on Sunday night,*
> *And by the fireplace spark you.*

March 23, 1863

It has been a very wet drizzling kind of a reminding me of the sugar season in Vermont. There has not been much rain but it is misty & foggy and the snow is getting soft, under foot. We shall soon have a general break up and boats from below. There is very little ice on the shores of the Lake & when the wind blows I can hear the roar of the waves beating against the rich shores of Lake Superior. This country will be a place where many men will make their fortune. The mines are all going to work in the spring and wages will be very high. Went to the town hall and witnessed the nomination of town officers. The meeting was short and passed off finely.

March 30, 1863

It is cloudy this morning and very mild and has the appearance of a storm. For the past two or three days it has been very cold making a good crust & in the evenings the ladies of the place may be seen out sleigh-riding downhill. Any amusement of this kind all engage in without any regard to age. I saw an old lady out the other evening who has a family of six or eight children enjoying the sport with the others. My school last week passed off pleasantly, with the exception of one thing viz I accidentally hit a little boy on the nose with a book & as he was accustomed to the nose bleed it bled a little. It was an accident and was not a blow.... He was sitting behind me & I was hearing a class & swinging my hand back it hit his nose slightly causing it to bleed some. The next day I received the following note from the father.

Dear Schoolmaster

What for business you have, that you *streick* my boy wiht a book on the *nos* I *sch'and* kall you for a *school* mister. You bein a rekler foll I want tell you I wont you si bout to morre after noon 5 glock in my House, if you not I sent the Constabler after you that little boys lost bout five quart of *blot*. The whol way *ei* fount em on the *road ei kowtten stoppet*.Sham your self.

Daniel Metsger

The next morning after the little boy had the nose bleed I received the above epistle. I shall make no comments on it. I sent word to him that if he wanted to see [me] to come where I was. The Constable has not visited me yet.

Napoleon Boneparte has been compared to a sponge dipped in the regions of hell & squeezed out all over Europe.

Some persons here cannot see the propriety of building a new church; they must always be talking about the matter and making remarks against every reform.

Some persons claim that the distinguished personage Christ was nothing but an apparition; that the history of his career was a mere story that had gained remarkable credence among the Jews. That it was a spiritual apparition who appeared to suffer; to rise from the dead. If it is right to deny that there was such a person, it is also correct to deny the other facts of history. Why not say that there was no such personage as Alexander. It is just as reasonable. There is no reason for denying the facts of history. Another doctrine is this: That Christ was meant to represent the sun & the twelve apostles the twelve signs of the Zodiac. This is a foolish doctrine that needs no arguments to show or prove it false. It is not right for anyone to take some particular event that may be taken from the history of the past & construe it to suit the bigoted notions of some hypocritical fools. Why not say that Alexander the Great was intended to represent one of the pyramids of Egypt. Why not deny all past history. It is just as reasonable.

The history of the past is for us to accept we have no way of denying any of its facts; if one is objected to the others may be also and there would be no end to these objections until the past would become an entire blank.

There was such a personage as Christ; he was crucified & rose from the dead. For he says: "I am he that liveth; I was dead and am alive forever." Now if he was dead and is alive he must have risen from the dead. He died between two thiefs on the cross; for the earth quaked & the sun was covered in darkness. His executioners pronounced him dead. When his side was pierced with the soldiers' spear blood & water came out & it is a physiological fact & may be proved that death had taken place. They were so sure that his legs were not broken as was the custom with criminals. He was laid in the tomb & it was locked with the Government seal that must not be broken under penalty of death & a guard of sixty Roman soldiers placed there under a Roman law that required that if he slept on his post he should be put to death. Every precaution was taken. The soldiers were taken from a fortress near by as it was the time of the annual feasts & 120 were stationed there to prevent an outbreak. Sixty standing on guard half of the time.

Now one of three things took place. He either rose from the dead, or was stolen by his disciples or carried away by his enemies. Now if it had been conveyed away by his enemies when his disciples declared that he had risen, they would brought the body forth & put a stop to the thing. They did not bring it forth and that is conclusive evidence that it was not in their possession. His friends would never think of breaking through a guard of sixty men armed to the teeth, and then run the risk of breaking the seal which was punished by death. We conclude that he rose.

Strange to say the guard to a man fell asleep when the law punish them with death. And they said he was stolen, strange, all of them fast asleep & they knew he was stolen. But he was seen by a sufficient number after to prove that he rose. Under a sermon immediately after in sight of Calvary 3000 persons whose hands were stained with is blood were converted & 5000 the next day. The history of Christ is worthy of careful study. We might bring up the history of Christianity and of those who have finished their career with their blood in defence of Christianity. If Christ is rejected, on what ground can we base our conduct & course of action.

April 6, 1863

Election for Houghton Township

The election of town officers came off today in the town hall of this place.[13] The general feeling is in favor of union and liberty; but the strife that caused so much excitement this time was not a strife in relation to the great question that is now agitating our country causing the expenditure of treasure and the sacrifice of thousands of precious lives; neither was it party feeling but a strife between two places viz Cliff Mine & Eagle River, both wishing to select their own officers. The contention between the places was not an idle one. It has been brewing for some time and the leading man in both parties put their best jumps for the stakes. Men who are unable to read & write and who were born with a natural love for the beer and whiskey are very easily influenced to vote for certain parties or those who are liberal with a "drop of the critter." Many a "quert" (Cornish) was taken and no man was dry that day. The captains here raised a pole Saturday night & the men were treated with plenty of beer or to use the name that it goes by here, "a drop or quert of cabbage."

An election in any community draws together all class of men but in no place is there so much of the ridiculous and so much that exhibits the different phases of society as in a mining country where water is looked upon as only fit to wash copper. Here you see collected together Cornishmen, men from all parts of England & Ireland, Germans, Scotchmen, Welchmen & occasionally an American & Yankee. The last named class I had the honor to represent. I taught school until five & was there only one hour so I failed to witness many amusing sights. But the excitement was off the greatest kind, and such fights, betting, bragging, dancing, working for votes *I never saw.*

Election Concluded

After closing school, I went down to cast my vote in favor of the Cliff. When I arrived near the town hall five or six men had a fellow trying to persuade him to vote one way & as many were trying in favor of their ticket. Some splendid arguments were brought forth by both parties but the Cliff boys had put him all right the previous day with beer etc.

Marched into the hall, cast my vote, got away with injury etc. Captains etc. standing round the box watching every vote.

"Vote this ticket." "No take this one." "Come let us have a glass of beer now you." "How Gets you now." "I challenge that vote."

Squire Vivian looks solemn; turns over the law book etc., fills his pipe & finally decided the case in favor of Cliff & the general exclamation is "bully for you, Touch the pipe a bit" or "tapir off a bit, squire." Old gray-haired man gets up in the pulpit, "for the place [was] used as a church," & leaning on his cane he dances a jig. "Bully for you old man come & have a quert of beer you." Squire rises, removes his specs & says "hear, hear, hear." Box turned in ten minutes; betting, the oysters, beer etc. Box turned & votes counted. Eagle River gets the most important officer; Cliff has the others. All hands for the Ale and then take a touch of the pipe. Thus election closed.

Everyone well soaked before morning. It is amusing to see how every will stick up for his rights at election. The biggest men there are the ignorant fools that know nothing. There is much instruction to be gained by witnessing the actions of all to hear their conversation etc. If I had been present during the day I should try & give a good description of the Cliff Election.

April 9, 1863

The pleasant weather that we are now having would be very remarkable for old Vermont. It is very warm every day and cold nights making a very hard crust. The snow is melting away quite fast. And the rocks & stumps begin to show themselves. The atmosphere is very pure and clear and I am confident that this pleasant place in summer. My school is quite large and there are a number of large ones. Mr. Mc'Grah attends & all appearance he is twenty-two years old. I am now having very pleasant times enjoying Mr. Rawlings' jokes etc.

April 14, 1863

I am aware that I am sadly neglecting this Journal for the month of April and I do not know as I can do otherwise. My time seems to be taken up in some useful employment. I was intending to read one of Washington Irving's works this week but shall fail for want of time. Two of my evenings are taken up in trying to learn the rudiments of singing for be it known I shall learn to sing if I can. Wednesday evening is taken up in spelling exercises at the school house. I have also agreed to train the scholars of the Methodist Sunday School preparatory to the anniversary the first of May. This will of course take most of my time.

We are now enjoying very fine weather and the snow is melting away very fast. It will soon all be gone. The weather reminds me of last spring in Vermont; the nights are cold enough to make a hard crust but the days are very warm and pleasant. There is nothing to prevent a boat from coming up now and we expect one every day.

There is no meat to be had in the place and we are on very short allowance.

My school passes off quietly. Miss Cundy is very busy with the small ones and is getting them along quite fast. Captains Halls, Souden, & Mr. Trewarther were down yesterday to see about putting on an addition of thirty feet on the school house and making the house seventy-five feet long and making two large rooms.[14] It does not stand in a very pleasant spot but the District is not willing to incur the expense of placing it in a better place. This is wrong as this mine is growing better & there will be an increase of scholars and soon it will be necessary to have a better house. It is very wet where it is now and should be moved to a dry pleasant place.

April 15, 1863

It has been a warm day and cloudy part of the time. Still it has thawed very fast and the snow is disappearing rapidly. The rocky sides of the old bluff are free from snow and ice and occasionally a hillock is bare. There is very little snow in the road and the wood for the Engines of the mine is drawn up on wheels from the piles on the flat. Some places the water & snow is very deep. A part of the sidewalk that leads to the schoolhouse is bare. Everything indicates that the snow will pass away without the necessity of a severe storm! It reminds me of last spring at home. There has been quite an excitement here in consequence of the report that a boat had come up. I think the report was not true but all were talking about eggs, oranges, and the little luxuries that we have been deprived of for a long winter. I bet one dozen eggs that there would not be one for a week. I expect to lose it & *it will not make much difference.*

A very fine verse.

Then why should we quarrel for riches,
Or any such glittering toys;
A light heart and thin pair of breeches
Will go through the world my brave boys.

Mr. Thomas P. Williams is going to deliver a lecture here on the beautiful. He is a miner here and quite a smart little fellow, although he tries to show off quite too much to suit everyone.

He has put up his notices and on the top may be seen the following sentence. "A thing of beauty is a joy forever."[15] I must go to bed as all the dogs in the town are yelling & barking & I dislike the miserable noise.

April 16, 1863

I rise from my comfortable bed this morning at six o'clock: the sun is shining brightly giving promise of a fine day; the wind does not disturb the pleasantness of the morning and I am almost ready to declare that I have not seen a place with so pure and embracing an atmosphere as we are blessed with here. The few roosters of the place are making music by their ceaseless crowing reminding one of farm scenes at home & I long to see home again.

John and I took a ramble over the bluff with the blue waters in full view at the north stretching away to the Canada shore just discernable in the distance. All other sides present a dense wilderness except one or two small farms. The little ground bird and striped squirrel were to be seen once in a while also the rook resembling the Vermont crow although it makes a different noise. I find that a walk in the morning does me some good & I shall continue the practice as I do not get much exercise. I must now go to school.

Good

A gentleman who had lost his wife, whose maiden name was Little, addressed the following to Miss More, a lady of diminutive stature:

I've lost the little once I had
My heart now is sad and sore,
So now I should be very glad
To have a little More.

To which the lady sent the following answer:

I pity much the loss you've had
The grief you must endure;
A heart by 'Little' made so sad
A little 'More' won't cure.

The snow has thawed away very fast & the water was so deep one side of the house that I had to wade through & carry the small girls across.

The news from all quarters or sources speaks of the despairing condition of the rebels while there is an indication that confidence is being restored throughout the north. The Copperhead demonstration is a failure. Gold has fallen twenty percent etc. Starvation is reigning in many places in the south in the cities of Richmond, Charleston, Mobile etc. Flour is worth from sixty to one hundred dollars per barrel and rebel currency the only money current is so worthless that gold is worth six hundred per cent premium. Traffic is stopped & Agriculture has been ruined by the conscription act. Everyone lives from hand to mouth. Bands of guerrillas scour the country impressing young men into the service, hanging those who differ from them, burning cotton, stealing property & making the country a desolate waste. Such is the picture of the once sunny south as given by Southern papers & Southern refugees. With the whole power in their possession to commence with, they have been reduced to this condition in two years. The armies will feed themselves if all others starve & the leaders will continue as long as they can keep their armies together. I hope it will soon fall and its authors and supporters receive the punishment that they deserve.

True I think

A law is good for nothing if the penalty is not attached to it. It has no binding force without the penalty. Why is it that severe penalties are attached to laws. Law is made to prevent crime and therefore the penalty is severe so that crime may not be committed. It is not the intention of law only to punish crime. Its main object is to prevent it therefore the penalty is severe. Persons will have to suffer the penalties attached to laws as they are liable to sin & violate them & must therefore suffer the penalty. The penalty is not too severe if a person lives such a way as not to infringe or violate its principles or decrees.

April 19, 1863

Saturday morning John and I took a walk down the road before breakfast. The road was quite dry in places. It was a warm sultry morning and cloudy and I was taken very much by surprise on hearing the sound of thunder every few minutes and occasionally a flash of lightning could be seen. I was surprised on hearing thunder on the eighteenth of April. I expected very different weather. We came home and partook of a scanty meal for there is no meat here now and very many are reduced to an uncommon short allowance. William and I then went to the river, and spent the day. Took dinner at our Friend's viz "Joe Rectallick."[16] The old Indian called "Jack" who was the oldest man on the Lake died in his little hut on the Lake shore. He was an old fisherman and sold trout round at different villages. Very many were expecting a boat in but there is no boat yet.

Mr. Leopold had an auction at his store.[17] He is an old German Trader who has made himself immensely rich selling Goods here. Merchants make a great deal of money here. And wherever there is money to be made there "Jews and Germans" may be found getting rich. As a class they will make money with very little hard labor. At four we started for home where we arrived in two hours tired enough and with the Solemncholy consolation of having walked two miles with boots full of water as the brooks were over the road in many places.

In the evening I went to hear Mr. Williams deliver a Lecture on the beautiful. It was a rambling description of everything and there were only a few sound ideas in the whole piece. Mr. Williams is a young miner who studies quite hard and has a remarkable memory and flow of language. He closed by saying in his ramblings after the beautiful he had not yet reached the connubial state of matrimoney. Mr. Baughman said it was because the ladies did not appreciate the beautiful: Says he, Ladies there is a candidate in the market. I then presented a resolution of thanks which was unanimously passed. I hope Mr. Williams will reach that state of happiness for which he so much longs.

April 19, 1863 (evening)

It is a damp, wet day and rains quite hard at times. The snow is all off except the large drifts and in the woods. The small birds are plenty everything looks like spring. I am reminded of home as I sit in my room and listen to the rain as it falls on the roof of the house. It has a sound that reminds me of the room upstairs at home or boiling sap in the sugar works some rainy day with one or two boards over my head & my back to the fire or to use a Cornish style of Speaking with my "dear little tail" to the fire. I finished yesterday a set of rules for [a] Young Men's Temperance Society.

This forenoon I went up to the Methodist Sabbath School. Captain Souden is teacher of our class and we had a very pleasant time. Some of the scholars rehearsed their pieces after school that they intend to speak the first of next May.

There was a man hurt last Saturday in the mine not seriously however. The rock fell on him. Many are the cuts and bruises that men receive in mining which is very dangerous business and an old miner has a great antipathy to working above ground. They are willing to run through all the dangers attending mining rather than work in the light of the sun.

This mine is rich in very curious specimens of copper & silver. Mr. Watson has a great many.[18] I shall try & procure a few to take home if I can. It is very expensive buying them as they are sought for by strangers & visitors from below.

Is it true?—"A thing of Beauty is joy for ever."

April 20, 1863

It is a cloudy damp morning and the county around presents an agreeable mixture of water, mud, stumps, and a few snow drifts. For variety of articles or things the scene may well be compared to a Cornish Soup. And its rough dirty appearance may be compared to many a kitchen that I have seen in our little mining city. This would be a fine scene for an artist; to take his station on the Bluff while below him the little log city looms up among the stumps like a boat on a goose pond. Before each hut stands a high pile of wood and in the streets may be seen the very smart intellectual-looking animal, the "Hog", nor is he alone in his migrations through the streets and in the kitchens. The "Dog" still claims a share as an inhabitant of our city, and often vying with that Solemncholy looking specimen of humanity, man. To compare the three in point of intelligence would involve great difficulty. There are noble specimens in both classes. In point of cleanliness there is a variety of opinion; in many localities the Dog takes the lead; and in many others the Hog and I attribute this fact to his being outdoors much of the time while the other specimens are confined. Well, our Artist on finishing his sketch would find it well diversified and shaded with those charming and pleasant colors that proceed only from the Hog and Stump. Perhaps there is not another spot where these colors are so finely blended as at the cliff. The School house too would form a pleasant contrast, situated among stumps, and water on all sides, and a stranger might get the idea that the old system of teaching had been long discarded and a plan adopted and carried on by water. An agreeable place for young minds to receive ideas of beauty and grandeur for they have only to look on the pure waters and majestic and awfully grand appearance of the stumps. They may realize these truths by taking a short trip in a dark night. They would receive correct ideas of stumps & water. Judging from Experience.

An Incident

As the Methodist conference[s] were in session in the State of Maryland, a gray haired old gentleman entered the room with evidences of the deepest sorrow and anguish depicted on his countenance. He proceeded to scatter slips of paper among the members asking them to sign a petition to the governor to release his son who was soon to be hung. The father had been very strict and the son ran away and getting short of money he was led to engage in robbing the mail in company with a notorious robber by the name of Hare.

The road led through a dark woods and the mail was to pass at midnight. The robbers built a fence across the road and waited until the stage came along. There were no passengers and they took the driver and tied him to a tree and robbed the mail of several thousand dollars. Hare then told the young man his accomplice that he must kill the driver. The young begged that he could not do it but Hare told him he would kill them both if he did not. The young man little expected it would come to this but he was in the hands of a desperate robber and must forfeit his own life if he did not do it. The driver prayed that they would not kill him, the young man was so excited that he inflicted only a partial wound & Hare finished the work. They mounted a couple of horses and rode away. They were soon taken. Hare escaped and the young man was hung.

Moral: " Young Men avoid Evil Company."

If a person commences a course of evil and continues to pursue it they go on from one thing to another increasing their speed. For instance, an intemperate man continues drinking more and more. He is like the little boy who slid down hill and broke his leg against a stump. Says he, I got my sled started and could not stop. "A drunken man or one pursuing an evil course rushes on with greater speed to ruin."

A Man will give more to have his 'will' than anything else.

A minister of the gospel of the Methodist persuasion gave up his preaching and commenced the practice of medicine. A friend asked him why he pursued so strange a course. "Why," said he, "I found that people thought more of their bodies than of their souls and would therefore pay the Doctor more than the minister." He practiced medicine for a short time and then took up the practice of law. "Why Sir did you change your profession this time.?" "Why I found that people would give more to have their will than they would for body and soul and therefore I thought the profession of the law was the place for me to work." This is true with a great many individuals.

My school was quite small as the roads are very bad. It had one hundred today and everything passed off very pleasantly. It has not rained much today. There is joy in our place as we have bought some beef. Fresh sells here now for fourteen cents per pound. In some places it is worth one shilling.

I went up to the mine last night. The boss of the copper yard said that they raised one hundred and fifty tons of copper per month and some months as high as two hundred tons. I am now reading Irving's *Knickerbocker*, which gives an account of the early history of New York City.[19] Irving was a very popular writer. His works are very interesting.

Our class met last night to practice singing. We are making some progress and can read the notes in the natural key quite readily. I am in hopes to learn something about Singing; I have no idea of making a splendid singer but I would like to understand music. Mr. Rawlings is taking great pains to train us and we pass our singing evenings very pleasantly. Mr. Rawlings has drawn with a steel pen a map of this point. He is now building a machine for washing copper and putting it up in the wash. Mr. Watson employs him for a difficult job instead of Mr. Theulier, the engineer of the mine.

April 22, 1863

I rise this morning from my couch with the firm belief that bedbugs are a nuisance any way. This place is infected with vermin of many kinds. Some of the houses are well filled with bedbugs. And strange to tell the mine is swarming with rats but I will wind up on this subject by saying that I took a pleasant walk this morning There is a strong wind from the south and warm. It is very cloudy and occasionally the sun shines out brightly as perhaps an evidence that we shall soon enjoy its cheering beams in their full splendor. It seems very uncomfortable to be confined to the house this warm weather. Former springs always brought liberty from confinement to me but now I must keep the house. It is all right as I am contented and happy and enjoying myself quite well in my labors.

Yesterday evening I met the Sabbath School Scholars and drilled them in speaking and rehearsing pieces. They are very much interested in this exercise and are getting along nicely. I will have them well trained in a short time.

The news received yesterday that our forces had taken Charleston and last night there was quite an exciting time trying to climb the liberty pole so as to fasten the rope so as to hoist the Flag. The pole was one hundred feet high. Ladders were run up about two-thirds of the way and a young miner went up and put the rope into the pulley. The man who done it was to receive ten dollars. I would not think of risking my neck for ten dollars. It is an amusing sight to see a miner climb a ladder. They go up easily and handsomely. There is no one that can compete with them in this exercise. I had an idea that I could go down a ladder very well but to go down six hundred feet a miner will go down twice as fast as a man who never worked underground. I found this to be true when I went down.

"Taper off, boy, a bit" [and] *"Touch pipe bit now."*

The above expressions are commonly used by that class of individuals who live underground and are called miners. Where or how they originated or when I cannot tell but I have no hesitancy in declaring that [they] must have been used first by miners and no doubt Cornish miners have the honor of claiming the phrase. They are doubtless used with the same meaning although I should judge from observation that "Taper off a bit" has a more general meaning. What the true meaning of these terms are when used by miners it would puzzle a Philadelphia lawyer to tell. Its general meaning is to gradually ease away or slacken. For instance, a party are enjoying a comfortable chat when one rises to go away another speaks thus. "Taper off a bit old countryman" here means to wait awhile or not be in a hurry. Another instance. A man gets tight for awhile and soaks himself up a week or so, and then he must Taper off a bit or take a Small drop now & then to ease away on. This is tapering off in mining style.

The miners go into the mines mornings and evenings in parties of two or three hundred. The first thing on rearching the bottom is to sit down and smoke or "Touch pipe a bit." Miners all smoke and I think that is a very good plan for them in many respects for the mine is filled with powder smoke etc. If you go to the top of the shafts in the afternoon the powder smoke is coming up like smoke out of a chimney and in a long drift at the bottom there is no circulation of air only as it is driven in by hand etc. The miners work in this smoke and of course their lungs are filled with dust etc. Smoking causes them to spit & throw off this foul matter in the throat and lungs. It may be seen that "Touch pipe bit" not only means to smoke but at the same time to enjoy a short talk so as it has a double meaning it must answer two purposes. After a man had killed another in a fit of drunkeness it was remarked that "he tapered off a bit." This expression has a general meaning. They are both fine terms for general use.

This evening Mr. Rawlings and a numbers of others were out in front of our quiet home playing marbles. This is an exciting little game and it is played with much skill by all classes young and small. The people of England are great for games especially in mining districts where they quit work and go to work when the whistle blows and on a sunny afternoon they get out together and engage in playing ball or marbles. Anything in the reading line they cannot engage in as they are generally unable to read or write. To think of men playing marbles in Vermont would be too small for boys play. There are many amusing and curious practices among the miners and I will try and speak of them as I have time.

A curious notion

The assistant clerk of this Mine, Mr. John Penberthy, is a believer in a very strange notion to me. The former history of his conduct and actions would lead one to suppose that he was a monomaniac at times.

Severe study or labor of the mind brings on what he terms a nervous attack. He has a strange feeling that runs through him causing him to rave and press his head with his hands and exclaim, "O, it is coming now, Oh," etc. Dr. Heaton, formerly surgeon of this mine, used to laugh at him and tell him to keep his hands down and then he would get over it at once. It is a fancy of the mind. This same John has an idea that some persons cannot live without a stimulant and that he is one of those fortunate persons. Stimulants have a very great tendency to make him fat and strong. This is a false notion. There is no truth in it. A healthy person requires no stimulants which excite the body beyond his natural strength and when it falls back to a state much weaker than it was before. A false strength is not what a person requires. Nature has provided ample means to supply the wants of the body. This notion is intended to hid the taking of intoxicating drink. A very good notion for a toper to preach.

April 23, 1863

I rise from sweet slumber as the bright sun lights up the purple-blue of the sky and sends his cheering rays into the window of my cozy little room. It is now approaching the delicious season of the year when nature breaks the thraldom of winter, like a blooming damsel from the tyranny of a sordid old father, throws herself blushing with ten thousand charms, into the arms of youthful spring. The slight and gentle touches of last night's frost disappears as the sun mounts the sky and I am ready to declare that this will prove the finest day I have enjoyed on Lake Superior little village is all life and animation, roosters crowing, ducks quacking, children playing, babies squalling and various other noises meet the ear. Of course our streets are not crowded with grown up people as the day shift men are in the mine and the night shift men are now seeking repose preparatory to going to work at six o'clock this evening. After four in the afternoon the men may be seen on the store steps basking in the sun and "Tapering off a bit." Occasionally they engage in a game of marbles etc. It is now time for me to attend to the labors of the day. So I will lay aside my pen and put on the dignity of a Pedagogue. "What a change." School passed off pleasantly with about 110 scholars. A mail in at five o'clock bringing a welcome letter from my firm friend Jesse Bushnell.

I took a walk this evening with William on the bluff. The Lake lay in the distance with its dark blue surface very smooth and not disturbed by the wind. The sun was just sinking in the western sky giving a golden appearance to the waters and sky where they seem to meet in the distance. The outline of Isle Royale can just be distinguished about forty miles distant. As I sit upon this high bluff and look upon the clear waters below streching far beyond the reach of sight, I think how pleasant this scene would be if a steamer from Detroit should loom up in the distance with fresh things from below and perhaps letters from parents, sisters & friends in Vermont. A boat is expected soon.

April 24, 1863

We have another fine morning although there is a breeze rising from the north, which will blow quite strong, I think before night. It is very warm and the ground is drying up very fast. There is very little snow in sight although it was more than four feet deep a week or two since.

Took a walk this morning on the farm among the stumps a cheering prospect for one who is inclined to a farmer's life to see. An inclination for agriculture would soon be used up in view of this rough place, and it will be a long time before this will be like the garden of Eden. This would be a good place to place a city man whose mind is filled with theories about farming and let him put his knowledge in practice. I would give him the first lesson in plowing by letting him hold his model of a subsoil digger among the roots and the stumps. Give him another lesson on digging ditch and laying wall. Also put him to shovel manure and he would have very little sympathy for some of the theories that come from them who are unacquainted with the *modus operandi* of a farmer's life. It is well enough to speculate about theory when they are put in practice and made effective. But I dislike to see a man filled with foolish and simple theories when he knows nothing about the practical part of a businessman's life and labors. I like to see a man try his hand at the business and if he can make an improvement and put it into practical operation he is the man whose inventions will prove beneficial.

I have been at work this morning with the shovel preparing a little garden and I am aware that my hands are very tender by the blood blisters etc. If I engage in teaching this summer it will be quite a change from former summers' work. I have always spent summer working hard on the old farm. Drilled the scholars in speaking this evening.

April 25, 1863

We are now in full enjoyment of very fine weather. Every day is warm and pleasant. Last night it very cold, but the sun shines with increased brightness and warmth. I cannot avoid noticing the pureness of the atmosphere here and how healthy the climate is. I take my walk this morning as usual and partake of a good hearty breakfast. Mr. Rawlings has gone down to the North Western, a small new mine belonging to the Cliff company, to put up an engine. While at home he spends his time drawing. His drawings cannot be surpassed in this region of country.

I have very little to do today as I do not teach. It is James' birthday and he is going to have a small party tonight.[20] Think I will answer one or two letters soon. It is a long time since I last wrote. I do not receive many letters and we do not get any mail now. I hope I may soon receive some news from friends & the war. I will now lay aside my pen and go to supper where I shall prove an able man without doubt.

As I sit writing at the window in my sanctum I think of home and wonder how things are looking there and how everything prospers. I suspect that they have some severe labor to perform and will doubtless miss my help. I sincerely hope and trust they will succeed and be prospered with health and happiness. I must live here at present and labor among the young. I think I can earn good wages here for a while and am having good success in teaching. The scholars and parents all have a great interest in my labors and efforts as a teacher. I do not say this as self praise for I always dislike to speak in praise of myself. A number of large boys have now gone to work and I shall not have so many scholars to instruct until the summer term commences when I shall have enough to contend with for comfort.

April 26, 1863

This is a very warm, cheering day and everything speaks of spring. The birds are singing. The men sit out in front of their houses enjoying the bright sunshine. What comfort it is to thus enjoy the beautiful weather of spring after a long cold winter. And it would be much more cheering if the boat would come up and we could get some of the luxuries of life.

I went up to the Sabbath school and taught a class. Mr. Baughman gave the boys a lecture on a practice that they have here of shivereeing new married couples—a practice that is unlawful, that is a riot, [and] that is upheld by the older citizens of the place. The boys have all agreed to abandon the practice.

In the afternoon and evening I attended Mr. Baughman's meeting. Had an excellent side course in the evening on this subject. "Quench not the Spirit." This subject reminds us of fire and the English word. "Quench" means to put out, to hinder, to scatter. Many have an idea that when we stop the action of fire it is destroyed. This is not the case. There is just as much fire in the world today as when New York or Moscow were burned. It is impossible to annihilate a single particle of Matter.

Fire is produced by the concentrated action of heat on combustible matter, and wherever there is heat enough to produce fire there is light. It is produced by various means and doubtless the principle cause of fire is Electricity. It is said that the refiner of silver puts the metal in the crucible and sits directly over it and lets on the heat. When the precious metal reflects his face the metal is pure. So the Lord puts man in the crucible of the gospel and when he reflects his image he says it is enough. He goes through the refining process, is afflicted at times and refined by various means. There are various ways of quenching fire. The common way is to pour water on it. In this process the fire or concentrated calorie is scattered water is a direct antagonist of flame although one of the gases of which it is composed is inflamable. Being an antagonist it scatters the calorie. The direct way of quenching the spirit is to engage in sin the direct antagonist of all that is pure and holy.

Another way of quenching the spirit is to put earth on it or anything to smother it or prevent the oxygen its support from reaching it. So Christians do not heed the warning of the spirit. They allow themselves to be separated by petty things etc. When a fire is going well if you throw the sticks one way and another it prevents the action of the calorie and destroys the further progress of the fire. These old blackened chunks or sticks may be compared to backsliders scattered everywhere, blackened, burnt soaked and good for nothing. Quench not the spirit. Heed its admonitions and be led into the path of virtue and truth.

An Instance

There is no position that man may be placed in so terrible as a state of hopeless despair and to witness one in this place is an awful scene. Says Mr. Baughman:

> When I left the state of Ohio for Michigan...there was a young man of fine principle there who was led into sin etc. On returning to Cincinnati, I thought I would visit the lunatic asylum in company with my amiable wife. And as we were passing through, I saw a young man chained in a cell who was my former friend. He exclaimed: "I am lost, lost," etc. I obtained permission to visit him and with all the arguments and reasoning I could employ, I could not make a single impression on him. "I did not heed the admonitions of the spirit and now there is no hope. Damnation is my portion." It is not in the power of langauge to describe a case of hopeless despair. It is the most wretched sight one can witness.

April 30, 1863

This is the last day of the month of April which has been very warm and pleasant with the exception of day before yesterday which was quite cool. The President has appointed today as "fast day" which will be generally observed although the work will go on in this mine.

There has not been any very remarkable occurence at this place in this month. And we have not had any late mail so I cannot tell the great event of the war for April. The lastest date that I received contained an account of the marriage of the Prince of Wales, which took place the tenth of March. *Harpers* and Frank Leslie give very beautiful pictures of this event.[21] I take the *Independent*, one of the best papers printed. I notice in that paper an extract of a speech of General Butler's delivered in New York April 2. It is a very good thing and shows that he is deeply imbued with pure love for the Union & Government. He is one of our best generals and should have a high position. But it is evident that General Halleck is opposed to him and Frémont. It is a pity that he does not occupy Halleck's place.

The House & Senate committee have made their report on the conduct of the ware in which is plainly shown that many of our leaders were traitors especially [General George] McClellan. This explains why we have not put down the rebellion. It would be but just if the Government would hang all such men as McClellan.

Monday evening Miss Cundy gave a small party to a number. of friends to celebrate her birthday. We had a very pleasant time. I believe that I always celebrated mine with hard work which is a very good way. It is hard to personate and act a part long; for where truth is not at the bottom nature will always be endeavoring to return, and will peep out and betray herself one time or another.

Notes for March-April 1863

1. Percival Updegraff was born in Ohio in 1834, according to the *9th U. S. Census*, Houghton County, 1870. He was chief clerk at the Cliff Mine. His brother, Samuel Updegraff, is listed as storekeeper at Eagle River in the Pittsburgh and Boston Mining Company Annual Report, 1864.

2. John A. Baughman was a well known and highly respected Methodist Church leader. He was born in Hereford County, Maryland in 1802 and appointed to the Detroit Methodist Circuit in 1825. He had parishes in Ann Arbor, Monroe, Ypsilanti, Pontiac, the Hancock-Houghton area and Lexington, Michigan. During his career he served twelve years in Ohio and thirty-two years in Michigan with total of forty-three different appointments. In 1826 he married Sarah Harvey Baker, the widow of a Methodist preacher. He was described by one contemporary as "a man of extraordinary physical strength, with a loud voice, a cheerful temper an untiring industry." Another described him as "young, handsome, polished and educated . . . refined in character and manners." He died in Detroit on March 1, 1868, at the age of 65. See Lorenzo Davis, "Pioneer Minister of Washtenaw County," *Michigan Pioneer and Historical Collections VIII* (1885), pp. 214-223; Margaret MacMillan, *The Methodist Church in Michigan in the 19th Century* (Grand Rapids: Eerdmans, 1967), p. 71, Elijah H. Pilcher, *Protestantism in Michigan* (Detroit: R. D. S. Tyler & Co., 1878), p.149.

3. Samuel and Ellen McDonald, ages 40 and 42 and born in England and Scotland respectively, were the parents of Mary A. McDonald, born in 1855 in Wisconsin.The *8th U .S. Census*, Houghton County, 1860.

4. Horatio Hall, age 9, was the son of Josiah and Fanny Hall, according to the *8th U. S. Census*, Houghton County, 1860.

5. The reference was probably to Jonathan Edwards (1703-1758), renowned New England theologian.

Copper Country Journal

6. Washington Irving, *Astoria* (New York: G.P. Putnam & Sons, 1860).

7. Dr. Abraham S. Heaton was a physician in Clifton for the Pittsburgh and Boston Mining Company in 1860. He was listed in that year as age 31 and a native of Virginia. His wife Lydia was born in Pennsylvannia in 1836. They had a son James, age 2, born in Michigan, according to the *8th U. S. Census*, Houghton County, 1860 .

8. St. Patrick's Day was celebrated throughout the mining towns in the Upper Peninsula. In Houghton in 1863, 312 Catholic parishoners participated in the celebration, which included a parade, banners, flags and speeches. *Portage Lake Mining Gazette*, March 21, 1863.

9. William Penberthy was born in Ireland in 1848, according to the *8th U.S. Census*, Houghton County, 1860.

10. "Henri " was a name Hobart used for himself.

11. Henry Ward Beecher (1813-1887) was a well-known New England clergyman.

12. Thomas P. Williams was born in England in 1826. In the *9th U.S. Census*, Keweenaw County, 1870, he is listed as married to Sarah , age 39. Their three children were Elizabeth, age 12, Thomas, age 10, and William, age 6.

13. *Portage Lake Mining Gazette*, April 25, 1863.

14. Hobart was referring to Captain Josiah Halls, James Souden and Abraham Trewarther. According to the *8th U.S. Census* , Houghton County, 1860, Trewarther, age 28, was born in England. He was married to Louisa; they had two children. James Souden, whose name was also spelled Sonden and Sawden, was born in England in 1827. He and his wife Phillipa, who was born in England in 1824, had two children as of 1860—John, age 3, and William, age 1. Souden also served as Justice of the Peace in Eagle River in 1863. *Michigan Gazeteer for 1863-64*, p 292; *Michigan Mining Gazette*, January 17, 1849.

15. John Keats, *Endymin*, Book 1, Line 1.

16. Joe Retallick, Sr., age 52, was listed in the *9th U .S. Census*, Keweenaw County, 1870, as a blacksmith and resident of Eagle River. Ten years earlier the Census listed him as a hotel keeper in Eagle River, married to Ann, age 42. Joe Retallick, Jr., is listed as a wagon maker, born in England.

17. The Leopold brothers, Henry F., Samuel F. and Aaron F., were leading merchants of Eagle River in the 1850s and 1860s. Their general store provided service to residents of the Cliff, Central and other mines of the area. Henry Leopold, who was born in Baden, Germany, in 1826, and his wife Ida, born in 1830, had three children, Carolyn, age 7, Mary, age 4, and Albert, age 2, according to the *8th U. S. Census*, Houghton County, 1860. In that same census his real estate was worth $1000 and his personal property $4000. Samuel F. Leopold was born in 1827 in Baden, Germany.

18. James Watson served a number of years as superintendent of the Cliff Mine. In 1863 he assumed the superintendency of the North Cliff

132

Mining Company. *History of the Upper Peninsula of Michigan* (Chicago: Western Publishing Company, 1883), p. 333.

19. Washington Irving, *Knickerbocker's History of New York* (New York: Inskeep and Bradford, 1809).

20. James Penberthy was born in Ireland, April 25, 1846. The Penberthy genealogy was provided by S. Joseph Penberthy.

21. "The Princess of Wales and Her Bridesmaids," *Harpers Weekly Magazine* (April 18, 1863),pp. 241, 253.

While fishing and camping, Hobart enjoyed scenes like that above. On the following page is the ice breaking up at Marquette, a harbor on Lake Superior, fifty miles from Copper Harbor, thus allowing vessels to bring supplies.

May—June 1863

May 2 , 1863

It is a very cold windy day and the sky is overcast with dark heavy cloud. It is a great change from the former clear warm days of our Lake Superior Spring. The cheering face of the bright old sun breaks out for a moment, now and then, with all its splendor and brightness, lighting up any cozy room and reminding me that the chilly winds of spring will soon be no more, and pleasant summer breezes from the beautiful Lake will sweep over our point imparting beauty to the green growth of Spring and health to all who live here. I am confident that a summer here would be very pleasant for one to enjoy. Consumption is unknown here only as it is brought from below.

Yesterday was a day of great rejoicing with the people of our village for the following reason. We have been in a very starving condition or deprived of meat and almost everything else except bread and yesterday a boat came in at the River with cattle and many fresh articles from below necessary to supply our physical wants. Of course, the majority of the miners would take a drop of Beer and paddy's eye water "to taper off" on. I celebrate the event by taking a half dozen eggs and ham, which caused me to have the pleasing satisfaction of believing that I was all right and had taken a very good way to enjoy the event. I witnessed several who used the "eye water" and were *hors de combat*, or in other words tight as Nooies (Cornish) raving mad under the influence of Gin. What a disgraceful scenes for men to enact. I have seen them abuse their wives and kick them & beat them pursue them from one place to another until they would hide in some house until the man was no longer drunk. I can witness such scenes from my window now and then. To see these poor women cry and lament their fate is very sad indeed.

I receive from home a welcome letter conveying the good news that parents and sisters are all well and the sad news of Uncle Carpenter's death and burial the first of last April. I am greatly surprised for I had no idea of receiving news of that kind. The last time I saw him he was healthy and enjoying life— full of his jokes and fun. I had a very pleasant visit there but now I can see him no more in this world. How unexpectedly death takes away a friend or relative. Who will be next? It should be the aim of all to live a virtuous and holy life and think seriously on the future. "So live that when summoned to join the innumerable caravan that is moving to the pale realms of shade: Thou go not like the quarry slave scourged to his dungeon, but approach thy grave with an unfaltering trust and a unshaken confidence." A life in accordance with virtue, truth and Christianity will enable one to meet the shock of death with composure. I hope I may live a virtuous life.

Everything seems to prosper after the old style at home as father writes. I am glad that they have a good man & woman to help about the work. If they are not taken sick they will get along well.

The mail came overland. The mail that came up on the boat was not left as the wind blew hard and the boat could not come in to the dock. The sand has washed in around the dock as it is built at the mouth of Eagle River. This will hinder us from receiving mail this summer. One of the boats, the *Cleveland*, on her way down ran on a reef at Eagle Harbor and is rendered useless.[1] This is a very discouraging beginning for the season. The first boat sunk on her first trip. No one was hurt probably as the water was quite shallow I have not seen any of the boats yet. We have provisions of all kinds, on the way here. Eggs are now plenty.

May 5, 1863

Went to work this morning feeling quite unwell. Worked hard all day and now and quite well. Had a half dozen new scholars today. There was more than one hundred there. Things are prospering very finely in my school. Miss Cundy has quite a number of small ones to hear read. And we have hard labor to perform. The weather is cooler and cloudy. Had to keep a fire in the schoolhouse today. It looks very much like rain. I think we shall get some severe weather soon.

Teach the Bible to Children Early

Man has a nature so constituted as to demand an education of some kind. It is a peculiarity of the mind to develop itself in some form or other. It must expand and herein lies our superiority over the brute creation. And this mind is the gift of God. Philosophers reason that man sprung from a lower order of creation. They commence with a mushroom and reason from one stage to another up to the Baboon & then on to man. Trace this thought. A cause can never be less than the effect or in other words the effect cannot be greater than the cause. Now if you go up from a mushroom, you make the effect greater than the cause, which is an impossibility; therefore, what was a mushroom first is one still. What was a Baboon first is one now. This wonderful nature of ours that can by thought traverse the regions of space is the gift of God and it is for us to train and educate it properly. Youth is the time to cultivate this mind. The impressions made then are more durable and lasting than any succeeding impressions. The more the young mind is trained in any course the more is its capacity increased for good or evil. Now since the first impressions of youth are lasting, these impressions should be of a good moral nature thus giving a right impetus to the individual, or directing his conduct toward good.

The child should then receive moral instruction while young; for if his proper training is neglected his mind will receive evil impressions and his life will be spent in ignorance or sin. If he secures a thorough education and has not received proper religious instruction while young, he has a greater capacity for doing evil and displeasing everyone, causing his parents trouble and injuring society. Lord Byron had a cross crabid mother and he was brought up in sin and evil. He had a powerful intellect and perhaps the world has never seen his equal. His religious instruction while young was wholly neglected. He became a man of evil. His mind was completely warped from all good. He wielded his pen as no other man could scattering his productions everywhere to the great injury of society etc. What a vast amount of good might have been accomplished by his superior talents if directed right. His youthful instruction was wrong. "Train up a child in the way he should go and when he is old he will not depart therefrom." The principles of the Bible, morality, and truth should be firmly implanted in his mind giving stability to his character and fitting him to meet the storm of life manfully and contribute to the growth and welfare of Society. Judge McLean while sitting on the bench taught a class of boys in Sunday School. This was one of the noblest acts of his life. The Governor of Indiana was found regularly at the Sabbath School to instruct a class. The smartest men the world has ever known are men of religious principles. It is the basis of all correct knowledge, all correct character.

Misses Cundy, Souden, Hales, & Mrs. Burrows & myself took a walk over the bluff the other morning. We go out on a walk quite frequently in the morning.

May 7, 1863

It is a warm pleasant morning and promises to be warmer than it was yesterday. The weather is beautiful. The grass is springing up covering the hills and valleys with a beautiful coat of green. Some of the trees are putting forth their buds and the immense forests that surround our place will soon be arrayed in their summer garb. The gentle breezes of spring give a refreshing and invigorating feeling to the atmosphere such as is not enjoyed in the dusty streets of our great cities. The birds are singing this morning, roosters all crowing. Everything is joyous with the music of Spring. At home I suppose the cows make music enough. I wonder how things look there now. The same as formerly I suppose. Success to the business at home.

We have just received a heavy mail from below with dates as late as the first of May. *Frank Leslie's* has several pictures of the bombardment of Fort Sumter by our ironclads which was a failure, or we could not reach the city of Charleston owning to obstructions in the river. The month of April has been one of the most eventful in our nation's history. The rebellion culminated into open war two years ago & Fort Sumter was taken by the rebels after fighting with only seventy men to defend her against thousands. The rebels have been strengthening her defences ever since and the battle on the afternoon of April 7th proves that she is strongly fortified & monitors can stand a terrific fire of shells & conical shot at short range. If the obstructions could be removed the monitors could pass the batteries & reach the city & take it. There was one break in the obstructions where a torpedo with five thousand pounds of powder was waiting to blow up the first boat that should pass over it. Fort Sumter is not taken yet.

There is a report that Hooker has advanced. I do not know as this is true yet. General Foster with two thousand men went to Washington, North Carolina & has doubtless had to surrender as he was surrounded by twenty thousand troops. The time of one-third of the army soon expires. On the whole things are very discouraging. Still there seems to be truth in the reports that the rebels are in a destitute condition. Jeff[erson Davis] & his war secretary have appealed to the people to keep the army from starvation. We are enlisting negroes very fast and & hope there will soon be an end to rebellion. I must now go to school.

> *Thou vampire Slavery own that thou art dead ;Yield to us*
> *The wealth thy spectral fingers cannot hold;*
> *Bless us and so depart to lie in state,*
> *Embalmed they lifeless body, and thy shade*
> *So clamorous now for bloddy holocausts*
> *Hallowed to peace by pious festivals.*
> *Then hail the day when o'er our land*
> *The sun of freedom shone;*
> *When, dimmed and sunk in eastern skies*
> *He rose upon our own,*
> *To chase the night of Slavery*
> *And wake the slumbering free!*
> *May his light shine more bright*
> *May his orb roll sublime*
> *Till it warm every clime*
> *And Illume from sea to sea.*
> *"I am an abolitionist,*
> *I glory in the name*
> *Though now by slavery's minions hissed,*

A covered o'er with shame.
It is a spell of light and power
The watchword of the free
Who spurns it in the trail hour
A craven soul is he."

May 8, 1863

A beautiful, pleasant morning. The old sun shines out bright and cheeringly, warming the green, growing grass with the heat of its rays. The wind is quite strong from the south which perhaps is an indication of rain before many days. The boats come up now quite regular. Mr. Betzing brought up a drove of cows yesterday.[2] Mrs. Rawlings did not buy one as they were a poor lot and he wanted $55.00 per head. A good cow will cost sixty dollars. A miner had a leg broke the other night in the mine.

Something about Friday

On Friday August 21, 1492, C. Columbus sailed on his voyage of discovery. October 12th, 1492, He first discovered Land. January 4th, 1493, he sailed on his return to Spain, which if he had not reached in safety, the happy result never would have been known which led to the discovery of this vast continent. On Friday March 19th 1493, he arrived at Palos in safety. Nov 22nd, 1493, he arrived at Hispaniola on his second voyage to America.

On Friday, June 13th, 1494 he discovered the continent of America though unknown to himself. On Friday, March 6th, 1496, Henry 7th of England gave to John Cabot his commission which led to the discovery of North America. This is the first American state paper in England. On Friday, Sept. 7th, 1563, Melendez founded St. Augustine, the oldest town in the United States by more than forty years. On Friday, November 10th, 1620, the *Mayflower* with the Pilgrims made the harbor of Provincetown and on the same day they signed the August Compact, the forerunner of our present glorious constitution. On Friday, December 22nd, 1620, the Pilgrims made their final landing at Plymouth Rock. On Friday, February 22nd, 1732, George Washington, the father of American freedom, was born. On Friday, October 17, 1777, the surrender of Saratoga was made which had such power and influence in inducing France to declare for our cause.

About Friday

On Friday September 22nd, 1780, the treason of Arnold was laid bare, which saved us from destruction. On Friday, October 10th, 1781, the surrender of Yorktown, the crowning glory of the American arms, occured. On Friday, July 1st, 1776, the motion in Congress was made by John Adams seconded by Richard Henry Lee that the United Colonies were and of right ought to be free and independent.

May 10, 1863

Very pleasant and agreeable weather in the afternoon but rained last night & in the morning some. It was cloudy in the morning and quite cool. I did not go to meeting today and spent the day in reading and writing. Went up in the afternoon and took charge of the Episcopal Sunday School in the absence of Mr. Johnson.[3] The school is not in a very flourishing condition at present. Mr. Baughman goes to Detroit after his wife, this week. I have sent by him for singing books for my school. I intend to introduce singing books for my school. I intend to introduce singing and hoped I may succeed well in the good world. To have singing would render it quite pleasant and attractive. Hope I may receive earnest support in my labors for the improvement of the young in Clifton.

Wisdom

Very many are the definitions given to the word wisdom but there is no defintion perhaps so comprehensive and beautiful as the following: "Wisdom is the correct use of knowledge." A wise man will always put into practice what he knows to his own benefit and comfort. Put his knowledge to such a use as will direct him in the right path and to avoid the wrong. How few of the old and the young are truly wise. How few put in practice their knowledge for any good purpose or for their own benefit.

A Fishing Excursion

Very many have gone out on excursions of this kind anticipating fun and pleasure and alas have met the fisherman's luck: "A weary leg and hungry gut." I am now very strikingly impressed with the truth of this passage, for yesterday I enjoyed one of these excursions up Silver Creek which flows through the wilds of Lake Superior.[4] Saturday morning I was up at half past five making preparations for my trip in the bush. Line, hooks, lunch etc. ready & in company with six of the boys of my school. We started on the road for the place where Tom Paull lives about three miles distant toward the Portage. We pass the Albion Mine which is just commencing business. Many predict that it will equal the Cliff. We reached the mill pond near Mr. Paull's which is said to be filled with large speckled trout. This pond is on Silver Creek, a stream as large as the one that flows through the New Hampshire corner in Vermont. I am obliged to use beef as fishworms cannot be found here. I commenced work by hauling out a fine trout. For want of a boat I did not succeed in catching any in the pond. So I determined to go up the stream in the wilderness. Sending all the boys home except William Penberthy we ascended the stream through immense forests of heavy vine & hard wood on all sides and quite a heavy growth of underwood also. There were a number of snow banks & the water in the stream is very cold. I caught nineteen nice trout and am confident that a person can catch a nice string in warm weather. Now and then we come to where some one has explored for copper by drifting or sinking a shaft in the rock a short distance. Again we come to a large beaver's dam & houses, a curiosity and I secured one of the chips that they cut out as they cut the trees down. Reached home in safety resolved to try it again.

When I came in sight of the Cliff on my return from fishing—lo and behold the "Stars and Stripes" were waving in the wind from the top of the flagstaff. There must be good news as Mr. Watson had prepared the flagpole ready for good news. On arriving at the store, I learn that the *Iron City* had arrived bringing Mr. P. Updegraff the clerk & the news that F. J. Hooker had surrounded & taken part of the rebel army.[5] He has cut off their communication from Richmond. I hope it may prove true and Hooker may succeed in capturing the main army. Rosencrans is confident of victory in the West & expects an engagement soon. Everything appears better now than it did three weeks since.

Obstinacy

An obstinate man does not hold opinions but they hold him: for when he is once possessed of an error it is like a devil only cast out with great difficulty. Whatsoever he lays hold on the never loses, but clings like a drowning man though it sink him the sooner. His ignorance is impregnable or abrupt: no argument can make the least impression on his mind. It is impregnable to nature and art and will maintain its ground against every fact & argument if it have nothing

142

but rubbish to defend. The slighter & the more inconsistent his opinions the more firmly will he defend them and tries to understand no man's reason but his own. His skull is so thick that it is proof against any reason & never cracks only on the wrong side opposite to where the impression is given which, surgeons say, happens frequently. Such is always self conceited and grossly ignorant and are of no benefit. They are willful to seek any instruction or listen to any. It is the pleasant man who listens to instruction allows errors to be corrected who stores his mind with knowledge.

May 11, 1863

The sun this morning breaks from the clouds warm and pleasant. There is no wind stirring; all is still except the music of the birds cheering all. I hope the fine weather that we are now enjoying will continue.

School Houses

The school houses throughout the country are poorly adapted for the grand object for which they are made. It is a rare thing to find a good well-ventilated, well-arranged well-furnished school room. There is enterprise enough in some snug little village to build a fine school house for their children, but most of the houses are fitted to torture the children rather than to add to the comfort and ease. Under such circumstances they dislike to go to school or when there are so uncomfortable that they cannot learn or improve at all. People are very indifferent to the education of their children as a general thing while they should devote everything to accomplish this improvement. Instead of hoarding up their money to leave behind, they should spend it giving a good education to their children and thus fit for usefulness and property in life. Build good schoolhouses etc.

The Cliff people have decided on putting an addition on the school house here making it about eighty feet long. This would be very well if the present house were wide enough, but it is not. If they were willing, we should have a new house sixty by forty & two stories high but the tight-heads are not willing to pay one cent. As a carpenter truly remarked, "they are too stingy to have any thing decent." There is money enough here and it could not be put to any better purpose than building a fine school house for the accomodation of the three hundred children who are here wanting schooling. A teacher has some idea of a schoolhouse & what it should be although people may not believe it while it costs money.

May 12, 1863

It is quite a clear pleasant morning although somewhat smoky and cloudy about the horizon. The wind breezes up gently from the south rending it very comfortable and refreshing. I went up last night after school on the farm to clear the brush off from a piece of burnt ground so as to plant a few potatoes for Mrs. Rawlings. The fire has burnt over a large piece and about fifteen hundred cords of wood for the Company that had not been removed. Mr. Rawlings, now Engineer of the Mine, starts for the North Western about six miles distant where the Cliff Company . . . [is] sinking a shaft. It is near the Central Mine. Mr. Theulier left for below last week. Captain Halls is now at the North Western, sinking a shaft. The new goods are now being opening at the store. Mr. Henry Williams, a relative of Mrs. Rawlings, is here from Portage. He has enlisted in the cavalry and starts this morning for below.

Mrs. Carter

This lady lives in a house opposite to us. She is of a very high family in Ireland. Her father is the head astronomer in the Royal Observatory, Dublin. She received a thorough education in Music, French, Fancy work & everything she is well skilled in. I suspect that she was unfortunate while young & sent to this country to prevent the thing being known. On her way here she fell in with one Dick Carter, a thorough Irishman without education and inclined to drink, also passionate.[6] She married him and moved to this place. He is a carpenter and has his drunken sprees when he is very abusive; this often causes her to drink to her injury. She was drunk the other evening using very disgraceful language and is now very sick from its effects. If she had married an educated man she would adorn the finest society

May 13, 1863

There is a perfect sameness in the weather we are now enjoying from day to day. Very bright and pleasant except some smoke now and then on account of the great fires that sweep over a new country. There are a few clouds to be seen this morning and a brisk little breeze from the south makes it very pleasant. Our little village is lively as usual with the noise of children at play, and roosters crowing. There has no unusual thing transpired yet. I went last night to clear out [the] little potato patch. It has all been burnt over but we have cleared it of brush, roots, blackened logs etc. It is quite amusing to see men up there in all directions preparing a small patch of potatoes. I have as fine a piece as any containing thirty-six square rods very tough and rooty and shall have to use a big hoe to plant with. As I am writing here, William brings me a letter from my good friend, John M. Fay.[7] It brings very sad news. Mr. John Yale has returned from the war.[8] He resigned. Rev. Mr. Sargent, who volunteered as a common soldier from Williston and was made captain, died of Fever in camp.[9] He was a true patriot and I well remember about his discussion of the war in lyceum and elsewhere, but when men were wanted he offered his services although having a good place to labor in. I was at a war meeting in Underhill & heard him speak about his volunteering and urging others to follow his example. He spoke about sneaking traitors etc. in such a way as to cause the people to cheer finely. This speech was full of genuine courage and patriotism and he had already enlisted. It is sad to look at the many noble minds who have fallen in defense of the Government. All sections of the country mourn the loss of brave men. The struggle is not ended; many more must fall on the field of battle & by disease.

May 15 , 1863

It was quite warm last night and left the window to my room up and in the night the wind was blowing so hard that it waked me & this morning it was very cloudy with a fair propect of rain. Had quite a large school today and got along very well. It rained very hard in the afternoon and was quite dark and unpleasant.

I will now speak of a scene enacted by Mrs. Carter of whom I spoke last Tuesday. The scene transpired in front of our door. She has now been sick for one week and had the doctor and the truth is she is drunk & taking the poison stuff all of the time. Her husband is away. Yesterday a nigger employed by the company to whitewash the houses was at work on Mr. Kunkle's only one rod distant

& while working he had occasion to sneeze and cough. Mrs. Carter happened to be at her door on the other side of the street & being drunk she at once concluded that he done it to insult her & over she came raving mad. The Darky had not seen her & did not know that she was there. I was rolling in a barrel of eggs just brought to the door & she goes over to the Darky & talks to him as I never heard man or woman talk. The most obscene and vulgar language that it is possible to conceive. Nigger was surprised, but saw at once that she was tight. He was very cool and told her that he would respect her and consider her a lady if she would go into the house. She then came over to me & took me off in worse style calling me all the Damn Yankee names she could think & concluded that I was worse than the Nigger. She was always talking against niggers and I always spoke in their favor. A large number of women & men saw the performance. A drunken woman is the nastiest thing that can be found. I have seen many awful scenes here caused by gin etc. "Touch not."

May 16, 1863

It is a cloudy windy morning but there is not much appearance of rain. It rained some last night. There is no school today. Mr. Rawlings came home last night. Went out and assisted in opening new goods last evening. Mr. P. Updegraff has brought up a good assortment of goods but they are very dear. A common suit of clothes costs $33.00. Edward brought an everyday coat that cost $26.00. If this is the way things are selling men must receive more wages. Miners have to pay $13.00 for board now. Everything is going up except wages & I think that they will go up soon. Some miners are making $50.00 per month and this reminds me that I must have about $60.00.

"How are you at - all you, ee"

I noticed of late that this is a very common way of salutation or passing the time of day among miners. It is quite as often used as "how gets" and has a very charming sound when spoken by a Cornish man; but it is awful stuff for a Yankee to take. How it originated I do not know; still I would not hesitate in saying that it must have been a Cornish miners' invention. It must be very significant and doubtless means the same as "How gets," "Bully" &

"Midling" are the usual answers to these questions and have full as much music about them as the salutation. I wonder what will next be used when people salute each other. *Fini.*

Lives of great men all remind us
We may make our lives sublime
And departing leave behind us
Footprints on the sands of time .[15]

May 19, 1863

It is quite windy this morning and cloudy yet the sun shines most of the time; it is very warm and pleasant, quite uncomfortable in bed last night, nearly devoured by bed bugs. Every house is filled with them as they are not destroyed. It is not very pleasant to sleep with them. I prefer a different kind of bedfellow, but I will say no more about bedbugs as I hate them. I spend my evenings planting potatoes and find I have very little inclination to write. Miss Emily Edwards, John Penberthy's wife's sister, came up from Detroit on a visit.

An Incident

I took the pledge, said an old man, at the foot of the gallows when I saw a young man hung. The sheriff took out his watch and said, "If you have anything to say, speak now, for you have only five minutes to live." The young man burst into tears and said:

I have to die. I had only one little brother; he had beautiful blue eyes and flaxen hair and I loved him. But one day I got drunk and coming home, found him gathering berries in the garden, and I became angry without cause, and killed him with one blow with a rake. Whisky has done it—it has ruined me! I have only one word to say—never! never! never! touch anything that can intoxicate

When I see a house well furnished with books and papers where I see intelligent and well informed people, but I dislike to see man discuss any subject and especially the war question when he does not take a paper or read a word. Such a man is always willful and set in some foolish opinion. He lacks those qualities that make a true well informed man.

May 20, 1863

Yesterday was the hottest day that I have experienced yet here and it was almost suffocating during the night and to make it more solemcholly the little bedbugs were plenty and very anxious to become acquainted with a person. The wind continues blowing from the south but not much prospect of rain this morning. It sprinkled some last evening and thundered once in awhile. It looked very much like a shower. We shall have a very hot day for the sky is clear and the sun shines very brightly. This evening is very warm, the heat is oppressive and the day has been remarkably hot. I understood the thermometer stood at ninety degrees in the shade. We do not ask for any warmer weather, I did not go up to plant potatoes this afternoon. I will now relate a Cornish incident while William relates it to me.

Captain Tonkin

In many parts of this country it is very wild and thinly settled and preaching is seldom heard and usually some captain or active miner assumes this duty and gives his men good pious instruction. Sometimes very amusing scenes occur especially if some of the men have taken a "quert of beer." The following is true and so amusing when spoken with the Cornish accent that I will write it down. The North Western Mine was once under the charge of a pious old soul by the name of Captain Tonkin.[10] He very frequently preached to his men giving them good advice. One Sunday having a large audience and waxing warm in his discourse he was talking in the following style & giving line upon line, precept upon precept. "Everyone who swears, lies, steals, and does not repent Shall go to hell and be damned." One of the men who was listening with great attention and feeling good & talkative under the soothing influence of an extra glass of grog rose from his seat & addressed the Captain as follows:

Now-ere Captain Tonkin. Take and give a man a chanence wan-est-a. I don't want to go to hell youe. Wast to give a man a chanence.

The Captain orders the men to throw the drunken fellow out doors, when the man says:

Captain Tonkin, Thee cusent put me out nor any man in the House. Thee cusent do it youe, Captain. If thee shust go to put me out I shust give thee a scat in the chops. Thee hast better let this ould boy alone Captain Tonkin.

The Captain went without any further trouble. I will now retire as it is eleven. *Bon jour.*

Self conceit

An observing person who travels will agree with me when I say that this principle is quite universal among people, especially among young men. I have witnessed it among young men in Clifton to a much greater extent than anywhere else. Give a young man a thorough education, and if he is naturally inclined to show himself off in a vain way, it has an influence towards checking a foolish vanity. But let him be brought up with just a touch on an education, promote him a little and if he is born full of self conceit he will make the most ridiculous appearance of any specimen of humanity. I see every day a young man of this description act the ignoramous to perfection. Although unable to read well he would undertake to advise me in everything, causes everyone to hate him on account of his way of showing off putting on airs, ordering & talking to people in a haughty way. Try to reason with him about such foolish ways and you will be insulted & told to mind your business. I think I am not the inclined to assume airs and show off in a foolish manner. I leave it for others to judge.

May 25, 1863

A Pleasure Excursion

I closed my school last Friday for a vacation of one month during which time the school house was to be repaired. Having been confined seven months to my labor I concluded to take a little recreation and decided to go up the Lake fifteen miles in a small boat and look for agates. This was at the mouth of Gratiot River and I took fishing tackle also.[11]

Saturday morning I took one-and-a-half bushels of potatoes on my back and went up three miles to plant them. It was a warm cloudy day and I worked until two in the afternoon. I suffered terribly from the bites of the black fly. They are larger than a mosquito and bite very severe bringing the blood freely. I never saw any of them in Vermont. They are found here in or near the woods. The air was swarming with them in the old hollow where I was planting and they were very ready to test the thickness of my skin, and my face was soon covered with blood. It was difficult to submit to such treatment and I hope that I shall see no more black flies.

I came home & commenced preparation for a trip in a small boat up the one beautiful Lake. Had a small basket of provisions prepared consisting of one loaf of bread, one dozen of biscuits, one dozen of eggs, plenty of beef steak & ham, turnip, salt etc. The party consisted of A. Stoddard, head blacksmith of the mine, C. Barkwell & James Raphson, miners, & myself of course.[12] All had made a good provision as myself & at five we started for Eagle River & got there at six after a four mile walk.

In a half an hour we were on our boat plying the oars with full vigor sending her flying up the Lake. There was a slight breeze but the lake was not very rough. Some white capped waves in sight. Rowing a boat is business that I never tried my hand at before and I found it pleasant and not very tiresome. We met with no accident and got along finely. It was very dark after rowing twelve miles & we came very near to running on a reef. After rowing a mile further we were able to land and pulling well up on the gravel we selected a good place at the site of the dense wilderness that surrounds the lake and piling up the large quantities of flood wood soon had a very large fire.

Found some old boards we arranged them & placed some spruce & cedar boughs on them for our bed. We partook of a part of our lunch & had some of the pure water of the Lake to drink when we laid down in our camp before our great fire which was throwing out its cheering light & heat on everything around. Camp life, fifteen miles away from any habitation, on the coast of Lake Superior, the water extending far out of sight in front & a dense wilderness stretching back for miles.

As I am enjoying my first night in camp, I wonder what friends are doing at home. How strange they must feel if they could see me as I was there in camp. We had a few short doses before morning but the thing was so novel to me that I did not sleep much. Spent most of the time in telling stories.

About three in the morning we arose and took a wash in the Lake and looked around to see what kind of a place we had landed in, and found that it was a good place between two rocky points— the beach was composed of round stones quite small &

mostly of a red color piled up about ten feet high by the waves & extending back about thirty feet to the woods.

The rock is visible on the shores of Lake Superior either on the beach or out in the water a short distance. Every few miles that we passed rocky points extend into the water composed of a round red stones cemented together with a substance like or partaking of the nature of sandstone. It is very curious rock and at a distance one would think it a pebbly shore in many places the rock washes away leaving the cobbles and pebbles or great hollows in the rock. Under this rock the greenstone rock doubtless runs. Same parts of the stone is composed of the reddish sand that composes the soil of the county. It is quite similar to a sandy plain where the pine grows.

After walking around a short time finding an agate or precious stone now and then, we proceeded to cook breakfast. I found an old basin in our boat in which I boiled the eggs & we had a good morning meal. The sky was clear and Lake smooth and we launched our boat and after rowing one half of an hour arrived at the mouth of Gratiot River. This is a small steam of water whose mouth is quite deep and wide. It is filled with small speckled trout some distance up but it is very difficult going up through the brush so we looked for agates. We found very few of them and started down the Lake in a couple of hours. Saw the steamer *Northern Light* going down.[13] We kept along the shore leisurely and landed a number of times for agates and to see the shore etc. Stopped at a little harbor and looked at an Indian's hut which was very comfortable. We went down along the shore within one half of a mile and could see the green rock at the bottom of the water. This rock in places is of different colors and seems to lie in veins. The copper veins were plainly seen in many places. It may be known as it is composed of white spar which is an indication of copper & silver. These veins lead to the copper. They extend directly out into the Lake, and run through the bluff cross ways. We saw the Cliff vein where it reaches the lake. It is very rich looking. It is a grand sight to look down from ten to twenty feet through the pure water and see the rock at the bottom. Almost all colors in different layers etc.

We arrived at Silver Creek, about three miles from Eagle River where we made a landing and took dinner. Had considerable sport at the mouth of the creek. Just above where it enters the Lake is a place about fourteen inches deep quite a number of old logs in it and a dozen suckers about eighteen inches long. I stood at the mouth of the creek and the others caught them with their hands. By slipping the hand down cautiously & tickling their bellies a little, a person can have a good grab at them. And it is necessary to have a good one near the gills in order to hold them. We caught the twelve suckers in a short time and shoving off were soon at the River where we rested for awhile and then returned to the Cliff tired enough. I enjoyed this trip finely as it was a new thing. I did not wish to go Sunday but the others were obliged to so if I would go at all I must then. I met with no accident and can say that I camped out on Lake Superior one night and helped row a boat fifteen miles and back. I found only a few Agates and had no chance to fish. Shall try some future time to take another trip and give a better account of it.

I learn of Captain Souden that the job of repairing the school house is not yet let out and I am ordered to commence school tomorrow & keep until the thing is decided. I hope it may be soon as I am looking for a rest from the severe and perplexing toil of the school room. The scholars are all very anxious to play awhile.

Captain Halls is now managing the sinking of the shaft near the Central mine by the Cliff company. If it opens well it will be called the North Western mine. Mr. S. Bennetts is now working in Captain Halls' place.[14] R. Carter, head carpenter of the mine, has just come to his home beastly drunk. He came home a day or two since & smashed things at home & his wife went away & has not returned.

May 27, 1863

I rise this morning very tired and lame. I went up and planted a bushel of potatoes last night and when I returned had a pain in my side. I do not know the cause but I hope that it will not amount to much for I have felt unwell for one or two weeks. I wish I might enjoy a vacation now. I commenced school yesterday but did not have a great number of scholars.

John & wife have had a quarrel with his mother. This is the second one since they were married. John took sides with his wife and abused his mother shamefully. I did not witness the quarrel. He bought clothes etc. to amount to one hundred dollars and took

Edward's money to pay for them. This was the cause and his silly little tattling wife has been putting him up to it for some time. She is a worthless little-minded thing and is very much inclined to quarrel. Her mother has parted with two husbands and is a worthless jade. It is a shameful thing for a young man to insult and abuse his mother. I hardly think I should stand idly by and witness such a scene.

Cousin Jack

A familiar name for a Cornishman is "Cousin Jack" and the following is a specimen of their talk.[15] Cousin Jack coming from below on the boat took his seat at the table with others at dinner time. Among the luxuries was some green corn boiled on the cob. Cousin Jack took it for peas and taking an ear soon ate the corn off leaving the cob bare & then addresses the waiter thus. "Black man put some more peas on my stick youe. Darnee I've ate them all." At another time he says, "Black man give a boy some more tates (meaning potatoes) wast you, or I'll scat thee on the nudic." Better give a man more tates now. Cousin Jack is a strange fellow at times.

May 28, 1863

It has been a very warm day and not cloudy. No good weather to teach as it is uncomfortable in the schoolroom. Quite a number of Mrs. Carter's scholars came to my school today. She has gone to the Portage with Mr. Carter who has been drunk all of the time and has got his discharge in consequence of his drunkenness. A man that will drink is worthless for any business I care not how able and competent he may be for his business. Drunkenness unfits him for any business and hence he should not be allowed to take charge of it while under the influence of such an evil habit.

I prospered finely in my school with one hundred scholars. Everything passes along each day in the same style. There is nothing new or exciting to change the monotony of teaching.

There is a great difference between prices here and prices below. A common suit of clothes will cost thirty dollars here. Common hats three dollars to four dollars. Maple Sugar twenty-five cents per pound. Southern sugar the same. Oranges ten cents apiece. Eggs from fourteen to eighteen cents per dozen etc. And while things are sold at such an exorbitant price, wages are high enough to leave a person fair wages. Men are very scarce here this spring and will receive great pay for labor done in the mining districts of Lake Superior.

Mr. Rawlings is going to put up a new engine at No. 4 shaft for the purpose of hoisting masses of copper. There is a great amount of work laid out for the summer but I cannot tell where the help is coming from. The boats bring up no working men. I learn that a thousand men are wanted at Marquette in the iron mines and on the railroad that runs to the mines. Hope I may receive large pay this summer.

May 29, 1863

We pass through this day pleasantly without experiencing any change in the fine weather except it be a little warm which is far from being a pleasant change when it is warm enough for comfort and business. I have experienced a series of fine days this spring quite different from what I expected to enjoy. There has been only one fine shower of rain and very little wind which I little expected to find on Lake Superior.

I am confident that this is a good place for a person of slender constitution to live. The air is pure and it is a good place to enjoy camp life with speckled trout for fare. If a person is far advanced in consumption a stay here will hasten his death. The air is too bracing or strong. There is not so much in the pure atmosphere here that produces so favorable change on sickly persons as in the rough manner of living. All city style is abandoned. Fare very coarse etc. Camp life can be enjoyed in its perfection.

I made a visit to the Rev. Mr. Johnson's tonight and had a pleasant chat and tea. He says the spring opened about as early here as in New York. He enjoys this climate very much and although an unhealthy person he is gaining flesh. Mr. Watson has just returned from below. He is constantly looking after the interests of the mine and is a good agent for the company.

The mosquitoes are giving me fits as I am writing in my room this evening and when I retire the bed bugs will be more ravenous. I have killed nearly a pint of these sweet creatures before retiring. The ceiling, the bed ticks and everything in the room would be covered with them at times. O horrors, covered with the little biters, how can one sleep. This is a fine county for bed bugs, mosquitoes, black flies and Cornishmen.

May 30, 1863

This is what is called pay day among miners which occurs at the end of each month. There is no work under ground except measuring the number of feet each man has cut or drifted. Any miner can go to the office today and receive pay not to exceed his wages after deducting his expenses. This is a jolly day among miners as they generally go and visit some beer shop and enjoy a "drop of beer." Very many will return to their homes beastly drunk.

I am to teach school and attend to the library in the afternoon. I must go and take a short walk. The sky is becoming cloudy and threatening rain. It is growing cool and I find it quite uncomfortable in the school room. It sprinkled a very little in the afternoon.

I taught school one-half of the day and in the afternoon went to the River and got a cow for Mr. Rawlings which cost fifty dollars. She is a very good one and I sat down & milked her and found that it gave me pain in the wrists. My muscles are very tender. Confinement softens the flesh and muscles and unfits a person for physical labor

The *Traveller* [with] Captain Miller came in yesterday bringing the news that our armies on the Mississippi had captured a large portion of the Rebel army in that section and the remainder was soon expected to fall into our hands.[16] There are so many false reports in circulation through the country that it is difficult to tell what to believe. There seems to be credit given to this generally and the flag was raised in honor of this important victory over "Secesh." I sincerely hope it may prove true and we may soon hear the full particulars. All honor to the western army and its generals if they have achieved such glorious success.

May 31, 1863

It is very foggy and cloudy this morning and last night was a very cool night. I threw off the heavy feathertick and slept comfortable. The sweet little bugs peculiar to some of the buildings here did not disturb me. I enjoyed a dish of milk this morning for breakfast and went to Sunday School in the forenoon. Taught the first class of boys.

Mr. N[icholas] Vivian, the engineer of the Phoenix mine and Mr. Rawlings' old teacher, is here visiting today. He is one of the best draftsmen in the country and is growing quite gray now. He used to draw for the government.

I went up in the evening and heard Mr. Willis preach.[17] He is a miner and preached a good sermon on the following subject. God forbid that I should glory save in the cross of Christ. He is a man of weakly constitution. The new church is nearly completed and is a fine building. With Mr. Baughman to preach it will be a pleasure to go to church.

Nothing important occurs except a very sad and fatal accident at the mine. The engine driver while oiling was caught in the fly wheel & carried round & round & smashed to a jelly; he still clung to one of the arms of the wheel when found next morning and was going round with it. Many fatal accidents occur in a mining country. James Tretheway is walking without the aid of crutches now. He was hurt underground one year ago. He thinks about going below in a month or so. He went to my school nearly six months and is quite a good scholar. My school is increasing every day, mostly small ones. The large girls are coming after vacation. I shall then have a fine school. Mr. Rawlings is drawing a map of this point on a smaller scale than some of the maps he has drawn. I think I will have one of the same size. *Bon Soir*.

June 2, 1863

It is now the pleasant month of June which is a bust month for farmers. Everything here is clothed in a beautiful coat of green that is the vegetation & scrubs etc. The thick forest looks beautiful with its large leaves and handsome foliage. It would be very pleasant to take a ramble along the outskirts of the forest but the flies so peculiar to this region of country would destroy one's happiness if the day was warm. I find that they work generally in the evenings and are not very troublesome during the heat of the day.

I have looked with admiration on the high bluff near our village showing the bare rock now and then among the green bushes with which it is clothes. If a painting could be taken representing the different colors and shades, it would be a fine thing and I have often wished I might get one.

It is quite cool today so much so that I have kept a fire in the school house. It is cloudy and not very windy. Mr. Baughman has returned and brought singing books for my school. I hope I may be successful in introducing them. His wife has come up with him. I am glad he has returned.

There is a great change going on among the miners here. A large number of men are going away and having their settlement every day. Some go below, some to California, some to Pikes Peak and others to South America. There is a great deal of talk in relation to matching a fortune in the gold region of Pikes Peak. There is a prospect that a great number of men will leave this place for the gold country.

John P[enberthy] is now moving his family or wife & her sister to the house that Mr. Funky left. He has bought new furniture and been to great expense, and is receiving only $35.00 per month. He does not speak to his good old mother who has always treated him well.

June 4, 1863

It is now nearly ten in the evening and I sit down to write a few lines before retiring to secure repose for my weary limbs. Yesterday was a cool pleasant day and nothing alarming took place. School passed along as usual. Some men are making preparations to repair the schoolhouse. I am glad to see it and hope the business will proceed rapidly.

I was agreeably surprised to receive a letter in the evening from E. S. Whitcomb, Jr., who is stopping at Detroit now.[18] He wishes to find business here for awhile. I answered his letter but could not point him to a place. I hope he will have success.

It has not been very cloudy today although it was foggy in the morning. It is a dark night, the frogs are singing, and the roar of the stumps and rock breakers of the mine breaks upon the ear. There can always be heard that same noise night and day except Sundays. I walked down to Captain Paull's after school. He has just come up with a large stock of goods. Van Orden, his clerk, is going to make a visit to Washington and the army.[19] He is a fine young man and belongs to the Society of Odd Fellows.

I had a good spelling school last night. Annie Paull & the large girls were in & we had a fine time. Josiah P. spelt them all down. My scholars are first class spellers and we will having amusing times this summer. I shall defy anyone to spell them down. Samuel James intends to try it. He was inspector of the school a short time and has great faith in his ability to do something handsome. I am confident that he will make an easy antagonist in the spelling line. *Fini.*

June 5, 1863

It is a very pleasant day and there is nothing very exciting to disturb the usual quiet of our village except now and then one may witness a man in that pleasant state of happiness when a common road is too narrow to walk in and the mind is rejoicing in a confusion of ideas of everything. The individual delights in a row or is very ready have been friendly with this semi-conscious individual you will be seized by the hand on coming in contact with him and be obliged to listen to his foolish praises and his disgusting language about some supposed army. Mr. Carter came up from the Phoenix Mine yesterday, where he was working, so drunk as to be able to keep on his feet with difficulty, and calling here I very unexpectedly came in contact with the drunken sot and was compelled to listen to his disgusting talk in relation to the Cliff officers as he was discharged from this mine for being drunk and neglecting his business. I wish every person who uses strong drink might be discharged for they are unworthy of patronage. But we will leave the disgusting subject for a remark or two about the school house.

Preparations are now being made to repair the house and in one month everything will be completed. They are making ready for the foundation. I am still teaching school and shall not close until I am disturbed which will be soon. I have a large school now numbering over one hundred and ten every day. I never supposed that I could succeed as well as I have. Everything moves finely. Everyone seems well pleased and urges me to stay longer. I shall make an agreement Saturday if nothing happens. Labor faithfully while young in some good cause. Fit yourself to enjoy life when old.

June 9, 1863

The sun shines very brightly this morning and there is a strong wind from the south which gives some indication of rain which we are no great of as it is getting very dry. The sky is clear and it will not rain for sometime. This evening I can say that it has been a very warm day and one that has placed me in a position that I was never in before viz. to have the charge of one hundred and thirty scholars in a school room large enough to accommodate seventy-five. It has been a severe day's labor for me and also for Miss Cundy although she sits in her chair and has very little to do with the management of any of the scholars.

Young Mr. Tresider, living at the [Eagle] River, who has just returned from a year's schooling at Ypsilanti, made a visit to my school today. He examined the grammar class and found them ready on any thing they had passed. He is a tall, slender, young man who enjoys very poor health, has a remarkable memory [and] also a good command and flow of language. He intends taking a college course and if his health does not fail will doubtless make something if he has life or energy enough to put his knowledge in practice.

A man with a fine classical education, with a mind disciplined and polished in the very best style, is a worthless thing if he never puts it to some good practical purpose and fails to give mankind the benefit of his labors. He will not contribute so much to the growth of society and the advancement of science etc. as the man with a practical education whose energy urges him on in his labors for science, morality & truth. Latin grammar will not make the man although a good aid, in disciplining the mind.

June 11, 1863

I find an unpleasant change in the weather has taken place during the night viz. It is a cold foggy morning, very damp, and there is a strong wind from the north. This change was unexpected and I find that I have taken cold. I had a very pleasant spelling school last night. There were a number in and the scholars spelt well. The work towards repairing the schoolhouse progresses slowly.

The study of the various phenomenon connected with the eruption of volcanoes is very interesting. There are about a hundred active ones and two-thirds of them are situated on islands; the others are on continents but not far inland. The center of the earth is a mass of lava or fire and this is surrounded by the crust of the earth or the surface. The water on the surface penetrates the sandy portions to this lava where it becomes various gases which must have vent, and the volcanoes act as safety valves throwing off the surplus gas, in the same manner as the safety valve of an engine works. Were it not for these vents, the earth would be thrown to pieces; therefore these are arranged by the divine hand to prevent such a consequence. People look at the accounts given of the eruptions, the cities destroyed the great number of persons killed & declared God's not just but when the cause and all pertaining to it is understood they will then understand how they act & what destructive consequences would take place were there no vent for the gases constantly accumulating in the earth.

Chemistry & Geology are interesting and profitable studies, and every scholar should make himself well acquainted with the interesting truths they unfold. *Il est temps pour commencer mon ecole maintenant. Henri.*

Tresider talks of giving four lectures here. All evil is the result of the abuse of good and is in proportion to it. Sin is a result of the abuse or neglect of good. If an individual lives in conformity to truth and good rules he will be happy or will not experience any evil effect but if he violates those truths or rules he will then experience an evil effect in proportion as he abuses the good. The greater the violation the greater the evil. This is true in everything in the apparatus necssary to the comfort and business of life. We might illustrate by means of the steam engine which is powerful and may be made a very powerful agent, so much more damage it will do when abused. Place it on a track through a city and if properly directed it becomes a powerful agent in the accomplishment of much good; destroy the track & how great is the damage to life & property as many railroad accidents prove.

By abusing virtues and morality the dangerous & evil consequences follow which should warn all to live a pure life without abusing the truths and principles of any good. If this were the case; if all would aim to promote worthy causes & truths how different would be the society throughout the country. Every good institution would be promoted etc. May we soon witness such a reformation.

Captain Jennings is here who was formerly captain in this mine and is now one of the directors.[20] He is quite an old man and has had a great experience in mining. He will climb the ladders with ease now. I was up at the shaft yesterday morning & saw him as he was going down with Captain Harry [George]. He says his head is hard enough to do without a skull cap. A brick weighing seven pounds fell on his head once, [from] fifty feet. The brick broke in two but his skull was all right. A miner has a skull like iron I should think. They often fall great distances without serious accidents to the person.

June 12, 1863

The weather is very mild and pleasant with quite a strong wind, nothing of importance has occured. Tonight I intend visiting the mine in company with Edward, W[illiam] Trewarther, John Tresider, with Captain Bennetts for guide. Although we did not go down until night, I will give a short account of our trip here.

About seven in the evening we went to the "dry" or place where the miners change their clothes. In a short time we were dressed in mining style with a candle on our hats and then commenced our descent into the mine. We went down the ladders without any difficulty and soon were traveling through the drifts. The first party of men we met were a couple of hardy Cornishmen engaged in driving a drift through the solid rock. This looks like very slow business yet a miner will cause the rock to give way with ease. It is amusing to see one of them strike the drill. They never miss a blow and every one produces some effect.

We pass on through the drifts & find men engaged in drifting, stoping, repairing drifts cutting masses of copper etc. A person must visit the mine in order to form a good idea of the business. We went down as far as the ten fathom level; from this they are sinking shafts ten fathoms further. In this drift I saw a large mass of copper. After looking around sometime we started on our way to the surface where we arrived safe and very wet.

This trip has done me good for I needed the exercise. On returning we had a meal of three cans of oysters, and tapired off a bit with a comfortable chat and at three went to seek rest. All of us except John Tresider had no difficulty in standing this trip. John was quite unwell. It is now school time as I am writing Monday.

June 15, 1863

This is a beautiful clear morning with a cool lake breeze blowing giving a purity and freshness to the atmosphere that cheers the spirits of everyone who breathes it. Everything indicates summer.

Saturday I took a walk to the Central Mine seven miles distant and all the way through a dense forest. I enjoyed the walk along the little path in the shade of the heavy timber. Now and then there might be seen an old shaft where someone had explored for copper. These old drifts and shafts are often seen along the mineral range of country.

The Central location is quite a fine one and bids fair to become one of the best mines on the Lake. From Central I went down the bluff to the level land in the bush where the Cliff Company [is] sinking a shaft which they think of finding the vein that the Central Company are working. There is a small patch of ground cleared [with] two shanties built and the shaft is thirty feet deep in a loose sand. It is very difficult to sink and progesses very slowly.

I came home with Captain Halls & made an engagement to teach one year at fifty dollars per month. Sunday I went to the river[and] saw the *Iron City*; also sent by Mr. Green for a Globe to use in school. The work on the school house is now progessing. I shall commence vacation next week. The school now numbers one hundred and thirty scholars daily.

Mr. Fitch has come here as an agent for a stamping mill for copper. He is quite a smart-looking man. Since going into the mine and to the Central & River I have been very lame.

We intend celebrating the Fourth of July in this place. I am now making preparations by canvassing the district for money & provisions. We will have a good time. The thing will be in the form of a Sabbath School celebration & the children will fare very well.

June 18, 1863

It was quite cool and cloudy last evening and threatened rain very much. It passed off with hardly a sprinkle to wet the dry earth and cool the suffocating atmosphere. The air is filled with smoke and large fires are doing much damage in the bush.

All of the buildings at the amygdaloid mine except the store were burnt the other day. It was very windy and the fire caught from the the bush and all the men in the mine could not control it. The place was all in ashes in less than two hours. This is the only news we hear of in our village.

I had a small spelling school last night which will be the last one I shall have until after vacation. I shall teach tomorrow and then close for vacation. If I ever had occasion for enjoying, it will be then. I am sick of such miserable arrangement as we have had.

The scholars crowded to death in one room & two teachers at work. It has been trying business for me.

In a new country there are very few advantages when compared with life in Vermont. Here the whole attention of the leading men of the place seems to be engrossed in the interests of the mine and they care very little about the school or anything else. They are now having an addition put on the school house when they should cast the old thing aside and build a large one for three teachers. But no it will cost too much is the very plausible excuse. They will learn that this house after it is patched will not answer the purpose.

There will be three hundred scholars soon & two teachers cannot manage them. There is work enough for three teachers now. I shall have a severe year's work to do and hope that I may succeed well.

June 19, 1863

We are now having quite a cool change in the weather. It is very cloudy and cool and threatens rain some. I now think it will be very foggy before the night and it is quite uncomfortable. It is so cool. The changes are very sudden here & a person is liable to take a severe cold which I have done I fear, but will be all right soon. I have concluded to teach four days next week before having vacation. I have canvassed that portion of the district given to me and have got fourteen dollars in money and some provision for the Fourth of July.

Mr. Rawlings is putting in new machines for washing copper at the wash, which if they work will save much labor in cleaning the copper from the sand. The men in the fitting and blacksmith shops make of a shift over time every day by working evenings. The mining business is prospering finely.

Mr. Phillips, driving the pumping engine, had his little finger taken off by putting it in a hole in the feed pump to remove some dirt when the plunger came down and took it off. It was a very careless trick, & he has lost his finger by doing so. William Trewarther is working in his place.[21] Mr. Trewarther has just come from the Portage where he has been working. He will return with his wife today, who is one of the finest women I have seen on Lake Superior. She has a good education and is blessed with a good disposition.

All the best families in the place with two or three exceptions have gone away. This is not the right way to become prosperous in business for the money is spent in travelling. Miss Cundy & Mrs. Halls are going to the Central tomorrow on a visit.

June 20, 1863

A foggy, cold, disagreeable day with nothing cheering out doors or in. Everything looks gloomy. I look at my school house surrounded by stumps and fog in the distance and it is far from being very inviting on this the last day of the week when I long for rest and a change from weary confinement.

Formerly sweet Saturday night used to bring me the sight of home and friends around the fireside—all the comforts of a good home. Now I am far away and must listen to the Cornish clamor of the miner's home. There is good satisfaction in thinking bout old times, the scenes of youth, and hoping that all are in health and happines I am reminded of the song, "Do they miss me at home? Do they miss me?"

But I must hasten to school and manage things alone today which will not be much different than every day. I shall not teach this afternoon.

I took a ramble on the bluff with Josiah [Penberthy] in the afternoon. How things have grown since I last went up there. The clover is in full bloom and the bushes are covered with a dense foliage. There is very little grass. The raspberries & mulberry bushes are in full bloom and there are immense quanities of them. I notice the shade bushes hang full of eleven green berries. I saw the rosebush growing in its wild state with as beautiful flowers as grow on the common cultivated varieties. This bluff rises from one to three hundred feet high from which a person has a good view of the surrounding country.

We came down to the wash house where Mr. Rawlings is putting in some new washing machines to separate the copper from the crushed rock as it comes from the stamps. In the evening I went to hear John Tresider lecture on things in general I should judge. I will speak of it soon.

June 21, 1863

I awoke from a good sleep this morning & was glad to hear the rain falling upon the dry and parched earth. The ground and vegetation has long felt the want of copious showers of rain to give new life and freshness to the growing things. But we received only a little rain this morning—enough to purify the smoky atmosphere. It is now very foggy and quite cool. It was cold last evening and uncomfortable.

I listened to young Tresider last evening. He is a young man about twenty, very tall and of delicate health which I am confident is owing to bad habits. He is brimful of self-conceit and pride, thinks he knows everything and likes to show off. He has a fair command of language, posesses a remarkable memory, reads much and remembers it. His knowledge consists in the little he has read for there is nothing original about him. A thorough scholar who has common sense will never be continually telling about the principles of Philosophy, Chemistry, Geology, as this young Cornishman does who has studied nothing thoroughly but read a little of everything.

He has a very weak voice, quite feminine, & poor delivery & takes great stock in flattery and praises. A few words will make him think he will make a Seward & he will swell off in a speech on anything at once. If I were to give my opinion I would not hesitate in declaring the young man out of his head or a little cracked to use a common expression. Such is young Tresider, the Goliath of Lake Superior, in his own estimation.

The upstart declares he will show the Cliff how remarkable he is in the sciences and thinks he will have my school & says he knows more than any teacher they have had yet. Hence notice was given out that he would deliver a lecture on science & things in general. This he done disgusting everyone and making a perfect Ass of himself. A self conceited Greenhorn goes to school a term & comes up here bragging of his talents & ability. Says he was the smartest scholar in the school & had the greatest piece at the exhibition that was ever spoken there. Talk with him about what he studies & he studies nothing particular, read a little of everything & was the smartest young man there. In my opinion this smattering is far from being genuine scholarship & he is very far from being a sound scholar or a young man of sound mind.

He visited my school & criticised things closely but my little class of beginners in Grammar were ready for him & could show him the beauties of analysis. I am willing anyone should criticize my classes & will not say anything about teaching but this young man is not fit for anything.

There are other young men here who cannot read a common newspaper & will come into my school and tell their great talents always analyze what they read in the manner that I have learned my class. What ignoramuses. They assume to know three times as much as I do. They are worse than the common Vermont stock of young men. I often wish they could go to an academy in Vermont. They would be the laughing stock of the school.

What does a young man gain by assuming to know every thing when he knows comparatively nothing. He will expose himself to ridicule sooner or later. Well, the lecture he commenced by speaking of some of the principal truths contained in astronomy & philosphy making a number of false statements in the operation, one viz that bodies invariably expand by heat & contract by cold.

He then spoke of American antiquities & his language may be found word for word in the *History of the U. S.* by E. Gurnsey . . . & concluded by saying that the remains of old forts in Ohio & along the Mississippi resemble the forts of the Romans & Egyptians with them & they crossed the Atlantic.[22] There is no record left that such was the case while there is a history of the doings of these nations in the old world.

In my opinion there are very few circumstances to support this theory, neither is it a fact that all the fortifications along the Ohio & great Mississippi are square like the Roman & Egyptian forts. Very many of them are circular. These remains are curious and date back to a distant period. I am of the opinion & there is much to support the fact that the ancient inhabitants of this continent crossed the Bering Straits from Asia & took a course through the Canadas down the Ohio & Mississippi & finally settled in Mexico for there is a similarity between the ruins in Mexico & Asia. There are evidences in Mexico of a superior civilization in fact when Cortes landed to subdue the country he found many equal to his own followers. The old remains of Forts & other antiquities commence in N[ew] York & Penn[sylvania] and become more apparent & extensive down the Ohio & Mississippi through to Mexico on the very route for those from the Straits while in search of a warmer climate. Everything goes to show this to be the case and it does not appear like an impossibility.

The idea that a party was driven across the Atlantic by storm & tide while the ancients knew very little about navigation is a poor theory, & poorer still when we think of their drive through the Gulf of Mexico & up the Mississippi. The antiquities of this country are worthy of study.

Geology is still in its infancy and when more fully developed will be worthy of attention. About one dozen persons left the house while listening to young Tresider which must have been discouraging as there were only a few there. He proposes to deliver another lecture next Saturday evening on the aqueous agencies or the changes continually produced by water. I doubt not that it will be very interesting and will doubtless be worth the twenty five cents charged for admission.

June 23, 1863

The cheering light of the sun breaks forth this morning in all its beauty and brightness dispelling the cold, foggy, fall weather of the past few days and giving promise of a warm summer's day. How pleasant it is to have warm weather imparting vigor & life to the crops & causing the birds to sing. Nothing has occurred in our place worthy of notice.

I have received a couple letters from Vermont bringing sad news. Miss Hattie Chadwick died after a short illness with Typhoid fever which is generally a very fatal disease.[23] It seems bad to think that this young lady of fine talents and good health with the most flattering prospects of life before her, the idol of kind parents, should this be cut down in the vigor of youth & health. How unexpected to her parents who lavished all the care & attention that kind parents could on an obedient and beautiful child. A wide circle of friends will mourn the loss of one who was respected and esteemed by all who knew her.

The same letter brought me the sad news of the death of our young soldiers, Lucius Bostwick & Chauncey L. Church.[24] Both smart young who left good homes to fight in defense of the Government. Very few of our young soldiers can stand the trials of a soldier's life. They are falling before the enemy in battle & by disease.

I often wish I was there to help defend the Government and am inclined to go now. Everyone of my young acquaintance are going with very few exceptions. How sad must be the condition of things in Vermont. A State of mourning which is the case all over the country. How many more of our brave young men will fall no one can tell. How soon this terrible struggle will be brought to a close no one can tell, but soon or later the country is in a sad condition. War has blasted the fair prospects of our land & slain her noble young men.

Tuesday Evening

This has, truly, been a warm pleasant day very like summer in Vermont. Mr. Fred Hynes visited me today at my school house. He is clerking in a store at the Portage and came on a visit on one of the boats. He is a fine young man and one of my best friends here. I was sorry that I was obliged to teach as I should have enjoyed a ramble with him. He thinks now of returning to Vermont with me and I hope he may do so.

Mr. Rawlings is quite unwell as he has a severe cold. The news that we now receive from the war is not very flattering. Lee, the Rebel leader, is making a demonstration north toward Pennsylvania. The country is in a state of great excitement and rushing to arms. Hooker is moving & there is uncertainty about the moves of both. What is to be the result of these moves time will disclose but there is a great anxiety about the matter. Vicksburg is undergoing a siege. Grant has not taken the city yet. There is no very important news, that is favorable news.

Government of Children

I have been convinced fully in my opinion that the use of kindness is the true way of governing the young or that any other system is a poor one. After witnessing the cruel practice of beating, scolding, shutting up in dark closets, lying up etc. that is generally adopted here and the character of the children I fully believe that they are not near as well behaved as those who are managed by kindness & correct training. The practice of continually punishing a child causes him to be in a raging passion & he knows not why he is punished. This course has made some small boys here beyond the control of their parents & perfectly unmanageable.

June 24, 1863

A beautiful morning with a mild breeze stirring the dense foliage of the forest and making a lively music. The sun shines brightly and this day brings joy to me as I close school tonight previous to vacation. This is the last day I enter the school room as a teacher with the present arrangement. And I would go home before I would pass though another nine-month siege, similar to the one I close today if nothing transpires to interfere.

I shall start tomorrow morning for the North Western five miles distant where Captain Halls is at work. I do it for exercise and to see the places. I shall take the Captain's gun to shoot pigeons on the way as the foot path is through a thick forest of heavy timber & undergrowth.

Two miners got into a quarrel about a hammer underground & one struck the other a heavy blow on the head with the hammer breaking his hat cap and a piece of it cut his head severely. The other is now in jail. A hat cap will stand a heavy blow before it will injure the head and I suppose he struck as if he was striking drill. They are to have a law suit about the affair.

I closed school in the afternoon & shall try and enjoy my vacation. I think of commencing a select school in the hall of the Odd Fellows in one week or so, for I cannot lay idle so long a time and pay my board. There is nothing very interesting that a man can see in this Country except some of the mines & to reach them would cost all man could earn. The Phoenix Company have found a new vein a few a few rods from the shaft they are sinking in the crosscut. It is in the Greenstone which is not a copper-bearing & when it strikes the trap rock it will perhaps break many feet out in another place which is always the case with a vein running from the trap into the Greenstone.

June 26, 1863

Weary and fatigued, I have just returned from a tramp up to the Central and Copper Falls mines and Eagle Harbor. I procured Captain Halls' gun yesterday morning and set out for the Central following a foot path through the thick forest. I took the gun, thinking I might kill a few pigeons or a pheasant. I soon entered the heavy undergrowth keeping the little foot path that runs along the mineral range of land. The sun shines brightly but the tall pine, cedar and hardwood make an agreeable shade and it is quite pleasant walking. I pursue my way undisturbed except now & then a long-billed mosquito will perform the delicate operation of lancing my face in some tender part bringing such thought and feelings in my mind as would soon sink the whole race of flies if in my power. I pass on & soon a large woodpecker lights within easy & I bring him to the ground in Yankee style but I will not boast of my shooting powers. In a short time, I bring another to the ground and then pass on without seeing any game.

I soon reach the North Western a few rods below the Central where Captain Halls is sinking a shaft. Spent a short time there and then took up my journey toward the Harbor. From the top of the bluff above Copper Falls, a person has a fine view of the Lake, Eagle Harbor and the level tract of timber extending through on the Lake shore.

I looked at Balls Stamps at Copper Falls for stamping rock & washing.[25] There is a great deal of machinery about it & it is liable to get out of repair. Still it works well. When I arrived at the Harbor, the *Illinois* came in bringing no important news.[26] Saw the same clerk and steward on her as when I came up last fall, I remained overnight and came back next day. Saw plenty of pigeons but had no shot except one charge with which I killed one. Took dinner at Mr. Williams' place [at] North Western. Arrived safe at home tired enough.

The North Western

The Cliff company owns land just below the Central Mine which is situated on the Bluff on a very rich vein of copper. The Cliff company is sinking a shaft in hopes of striking this vein. The place is in the bush about fifty rods on an elevation of the swamp or valley. The shaft is very difficult to sink as it is in a kind of quicksand. And the sand is constantly boiling up so that some weeks they make no progress. The shaft is made tight & very heavy weights or timbers suspended from it cause it to sink as they go down. The dirt & water is raised by means of a small engine or locomotive. The shaft is now a little more than forty feet deep.

Captain Halls is managing the sinking of this shaft which will cost a very large sum of money & may then be worthless as a mine. The timber is cut away by a few rods & two log shanties built. It is so completely surrounded by trees that the wind does not reach the place and it is quite uncomfortable at times. The black sand flies are very troublesome and will soon cover one with blood. I should not like to live there very well for it is not a pleasant place.

There is a very heavy expense attending the opening of a mine and a company must have a great capital to commence with. I doubt not that good mines will be opened in the country twenty years hence. It is full of copper, and mining here is in its infancy. Success to Captain Halls and the North Western.

June 27, 1863

This is a very hot suffocating day with a slight breeze and the large thunder clouds rising up from the south which is an indication of rain. It is now very dry, the gardens are a failure on account of the warm weather and bugs that cut down all the plants. All kinds of vegetation are suffering for want of rain. May we soon receive it.

I spent the day in reading and resting which is a privilege I have not enjoyed for many months. In the afternoon I attended to the library and met the Committee to make arrangements for celebrating the Fourth which I will speak about after the event takes place.

In the evening John Tresider came up to deliver his lecture on the aqueous agencies that are at work on the surface of the earth. No one came to listen to it so it proved a *gigantic humbug* which he would have known to be the case if he had had common sense & thought of the matter soberly.

There was a sad accident in the mine today. A man coming up from the 120-fathom level in a shaft he was helping to sink; when he arrived at the 110-fathom level on the top of the ladder his hand missed the top round and he fell backwards to the bottom, a distance of seventy-five feet striking on his head on the solid rocks. His skull was broke in pieces & he was brought up senseless and is still living though very little hopes are had of his recovery, he has a wife & several small children whom he left in the morning in health and expecting to welcome him home at night. In three hours he is brought home in a senseless & and dying state. The miner is constantly exposed to danger; still, he would not work on the surface. It is very cool in the mine and they do accustom themselves to the work that they would never work on the surface.

June 30, 1863

This is the last day of the moth, a bright warm summer day rendered very pleasant by the cool breeze of wind. It is truly a Lake Superior summer. The air is bracing and cool which is the case near bodies of water. There is a purity that is not enjoyed by the inhabitants of countries far from the water. It is truly pleasant to climb the bluff back of our village and over the broad level expanse of timber below, along the Lake shore. Lake Superior stretching its blue waters as far as the eye can see. On the other hand, there is a birds-eye view of the village and the forest in the distance. This [is] the only pleasure a person can have without business. There is nothing interesting to see or profitable I am having vacation & have nothing to do but look around the country. I prefer working to spending time & money in a country like this. How very little pleasure there is then about nothing and living where there is nothing to be seen.

Miss Mary Dee, one of my scholars, died yesterday morning. Disease was some sudden derangement of the liver which gave her sudden death. Her little brother died last winter very suddenly.

The frame of the addition to the schoolhouse is up and I am anxious to see it finished. Miss Cundy commences school tomorrow in the Odd Fellows Hall to continue during vacation. I shall commence next Monday.

Squire Vivian is here enrolling names on the militia roll. I suppose drafting will soon commence at least I should judge so from the fear that prevails in the community in relation to the matter.

The children are to have a fine treat on the Fourth. The articles purchased will amount to some seventy-five dollars consisting of lemonade, candy, raisins & nuts.

Notes for May-June 1863

1. The steamer *The City of Cleveland* weighed 574 tons and was built in Newport, Rhode Island, in 1852. It was wrecked in Lake Superior in 1864. John Brant Mansfield, editor and compiler, *History of the Great Lakes* (Chicago: J. H. Beers, 1899), p. 808; Grace Lee Nute, *Lake Superior* (New York: Bobbs Merrill, 1944), p. 312.

2. The *Michigan State Gazetteer and Business Directory for 1867-68* (Detroit: Detroit Post Co., 1867), p. 197, lists a J. Betzing as a saloon keeper in Eagle River.

3. William Allen Johnson was born in 1823 in Littleton, Colorado. He graduated for Columbia University in 1857 and served at the Grace Episcopal Church from 1862-1864. *Hancock Journal*, December 23, 1908.

4. Silver Creek enters Lake Superior at Agate Harbor, a few miles east of Eagle Harbor.

5. The *Iron City*, a 934 ton steamer propeller, was built in 1856 and operated between Cleveland and Lake Superior. *Detroit Tribune*, May 2, 1863; Mansfield, *History of Great Lakes*, p. 841.

6. The *8th U. S. Census*, Houghton County, 1860, lists Richard Carter, age 26, a miner, born in Ireland. His wife, Annie Carter, age 24, also born in Ireland, is listed as a schoolteacher.

7. John M. Fay was a classmate of Hobart's at Williston Academy in 1859, according to the *Catalogue of the Trustees, Officers, Teachers and Students of Williston Academy* (Burlington, Vermont.: Free Press Print, 1859). He was the son of Henry, age 47, and Mary Fay, age 50, who had three children, John, age 16, Edward, age 14, and Louisa, age 8, according to the *8th U. S. Census*, Underhill County, Vermont, 1860.

8. John Yale was a classmate of Hobart's at Williston Academy. Ibid. He was the son of William, age 52, and Cordelia Yale, age 51, according to the *8th U. S. Census*, Chittenden County, Vermont, 1860.

9. Reverend Joseph Sargent was born in 1820 in New Hampshire. He was a strong abolitionist and pastor of the Universalist Church in Williston. He enlisted in the 13th Vermont and served as chaplain until his death on April 20, 1863, of typhoid fever. "History of the Town of Williston, 1763-1913." Typescript in Vermont Historical Society, Burlington, Vermont, p. 54.

10. William Tonkin was born in Devonshire, England, on May 1, 1829. In 1849 he came to the United States and worked at the Northwest Mine under Captain Joseph Paull. After working in other mines he returned to the Northwest Mine in 1859 as superintendent of the stamps. He later worked at the Central and Phoenix mines. In 1849 he married Ann Coade of Cornwall, England. They had three children—William, Joanna and Louisa. *History of the Upper Peninsula* (Chicago: Western Historical Society, 1883), p. 320. Tonkin's report to the officers of the Central Mining Company is found in *Central Mining Company Report* (New York: 1864), pp. 11-13.

11. The Gratiot River probably refers to Gratiot Lake, or Little Gratiot River, both located a dozen miles east of Clifton.

12. Charles, age 24, and Elizabeth Barkwell, age 26, had three children, according to the *8th U. S. Census*, Houghton County, 1860.

13. The propeller steamer *Northern Light* weighing 857 tons was built in Cleveland in 1858. It ran between Cleveland and Lake Superior ports.

Detroit Free Press, May 7, 1858; Nute, *Lake Superior*, pp. 95, 103; Mansfield, *History of the Great Lakes*, p. 867.

14. Samuel Bennetts was born in Cornwall, England in September, 1830. He came to the United States in 1854 to work at the Cliff Mine, which promoted him to captain in 1861. He remained at the Cliff Mine until 1872 and later worked at the Allouez and Central mines. In 1860 he had a wife, Grace, age 29, and three children—William, age 9, Elizabeth age 7, and Emily, age 5. *8th U. S. Census*, Houghton County, 1860; *History of the Upper Peninsula*, p. 343.

15. "Cousin Jack" was a slang expression that Americans used for the British.

16. The steamer *The Traveler* was built in Newport, Rhode Island in 1852 and burned at Eagle Harbor in 1865. Mansfield, *History of the Great Lakes*, p. 894; Fred Landon, *Lake Huron* (New York: Bobbs Merrill, 1944), p. 352.

17. James Willis was a School Inspector for the Clifton School in 1865. Michigan School Inspector Report for Year Ending September 1865, State Archives, Lansing, Michigan.

18. E. S. Whitcomb was from Jericho, Vermont. *8th U. S. Census*. Chittenden County, Vermont, 1860.

19. William Van Orden, age 21, is listed in the *8th U. S. Census*, Houghton County, 1860; *History of Upper Peninsula*, p. 339.

20. William Jennings was born in England in 1831. He and his wife Elizabeth had two children as of 1860—Mary, age 7, and William, age 2. *8th U. S. Census*, Houghton County, 1860.

21. William Trewarther was born in England in 1839. He was employed as an engineer at the Cliff Mine and lived with his brother Abram and family. *8th U. S. Census*, Houghton County, 1860.

22. Egbert Guernsey, *History of the United States* (New York: Cady and Burgess, 1850).

23. Christopher and Eleeta Chadwick of Cambridge, Vermont had two daughters to whom Hobart may have been referring—Helena M., age 23 and Harreitt E., age 21. *8th U. S. Census*, Lamoille County, Cambridge West, Vermont, 1860.

24. Chauncey L. Church was killed at the Battle of Salem Heights on May 4, 1863. He had enlisted at the age of 21 on August 20, 1862, in Company G, 2nd Regiment, having just completed his first year at the University of Vermont. Lucius H. Bostwick, age 22 in 1860, was the son of J. H. and Columba Bostwick, ages 54 and 43 respectively, of Jericho, Vermont. Promoted to captain on March 3, 1863, he resigned June 3 of that year on account of sickness from exposure in camp and died later that month in Washington from rheumatic fever. *8th U S. Census*, Jericho, Vermont, 1860. E. H. Lane, *Soldier's Record of Jericho, Vermont* (Burlington, Vermont: R. S. Styles, 1868)

25. Balls stamps, an improved version of Cornish pestle stamps, were introduced in the copper mines in the 1850s. The shafts were made of iron rather than wood, the number of units were increased and more powerful engines were used. Paul Gates, *Michigan Copper and Boston Dollars* (Cambridge, Massachusetts: Harvard University Press, 1951), pp. 26-27.

26. The sidewheeler *Illinois* was built in Detroit in 1857. On June 18, 1855, she was the first vessel through the new St. Mary's Falls Ship Canal. She ran aground at Eagle River in June 1864. Frederick Stonehouse, *Keweenaw Ship Wrecks* (Au Train, Michigan: Avery Color Studies, 1988), pp. 43, 63.

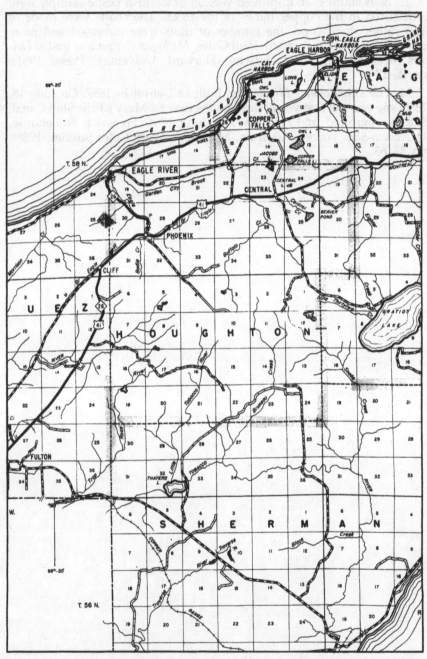

Above is a contemporary map of the Cliff area. On the following page is a group of children—circa 1900, generations later than Hobart's "scholars"—at an outing in the by then deserted village of Clifton.

July 1, 1863

I commence another month today in my journal and my first July at the Cliff. I am fearful that I shall not write very often this month; still I am in hopes of completing this book by the first of next month. If I do so I shall have to do better than I did last month. I can hardly realize that it is now July, that it is summer and that I have been far from Vermont for nearly ten long months, and that I have passed through a siege of nine months schooling with a roll of 225 scholars.

I have been well and in fine spirits although I find very little enjoyment. The style of living I should always dislike. It is so seldom that I see a potato on the table that I have almost forgot their taste. My breakfast is dry wheat bread & water with a little milk in it to drink. The butter is so filthy I can hardly get along with it on the table much less try to eat it. Sometimes I have some fish but I dislike the idea of always making a meal out of wheat bread. My mouth fairly waters for a home meal.

I could never enjoy Cornish living. Wipe the knives & forks on the towel, wash the plates in the wash dish & perhaps in the same water that some nasty little urchin had used. The bread is molded

177

on a board that looks like a stable window. O horrors! I feel like crying out at times.

An old English woman is as tight as the bark to a tree & the perfection of tyranny in her management always boasting about how smart she is & how her hired help & everyone else are good for nothing. This is a part of one side of the picture & it is a no small part either. The children of such a woman are self-conceited, tyrannical, foolish, silly things who are superior to everyone in their own minds. It is quite humiliating for one to resign himself to their abuse & always without expressing his mind. If I were in any other position but teacher, I would denounce their foolish & dirty ways.

Mail Day—Lake Superior

The sharpest lawyer in Yankee land would find it dificult to tell when we are to receive a mail here and how often; in fact we have no regular time for expecting a mail or when it does come we have very little hopes of receiving anything. I feel as if I was living in another country & believe I should receive my papers oftener & nearer the time that I should receive them. A boat will bring a small mail sometimes and all kinds of war rumors. I prefer living where there is a regular mail and if it comes daily all the better. So much for mail day on Lake Superior. I will now "tapir a bit" and wait for dinner.

Singers—Cliff Mine

I was authorized by "Committee" to invite the Episcopal choir to join with the Methodist choir and sing some national airs for the "Fourth." I've done so. Edward Penberthy assumes to be leader of this choir or at least has everything to say on account of his self-conceit. Mr. Rawlings the best one in the choir, a man of sense, is disgusted with the swell and affectation of this silly youth and I do not blame him for not wishing to sing on the Fourth with one who tries to show off, disgusting the most illiterate. He wanted to sing alone. Why, so as to beat all others and spread himself as only an ignorant, self-conceited person can. Living in a perfect nest of such characters I am disgusted with such nonsense. If it was in Vermont all the choirs would meet & sing but there is so much jealousy here that they cannot think of doing so patriotic a thing as to sing a national air together on a day like the Fourth of July. It is a time when everyone should aid in commemorating the great event the birthday of Independence and liberty. Patriotic sentiments should animate every citizen.

July 2, 1863

As I take my pen to record a few words today the rain is making fine music as it falls from the sky on the dry earth. By looking over the pages of this book, I find I have spoken seldom of rain and the reason is we have had none of any account but now the refreshing drops are falling, giving new life to the growing things. How refreshing is a shower of rain in a dry time. The potatoes I put in the ground last spring will grow finely. They are large enough to hoe. Crops are very poor here.

I have been reading today and writing some. I am very lonesome with nothing to divert my attention and no business to engage in. Miss Cundy commenced her school at the hall yesterday. She has only six or eight scholars. I shall commence mine Monday.

Naomi, the daughter of Enoch, was 580 years old when she was married. "Courage Ladies."

There never was a goose so gray,
But some day, soon or late,
An honest gander came that way,
And took her for his mate.

Recollect the child's mind is nothing better than a sheet of letter paper. So mind its address in afterlife will depend entirely upon the way in which you direct it.

There is only one "Mail contract" says a young lady that she would care about embracing, or embarking in & that is a promise of marriage.

The stamp ally broke the other night square off. It is nearly one foot in diameter. Mr. Rawlings is engaged in repairing the thing. He bosses all the mechanical engineering and blacksmith work. He has a fine birth and is an excellent man.

July 3, 1863

It is a rainy, damp day and not very agreeable, drizzling, foggy, cloudy, muddy kind of day & if anyone should ask when we should enjoy sunshine or a right, good, earnest, rain we should reply as an eccentric old chap did his tailor who seemed over anxious about that little bill of his that he could not pay it then and the

Lord in his infinite mercy only knew when he could and it's about so with this damp day. But we shall while it lasts warm our indignation at its continuance, and thus verify the old adage about its being a very cold breeze that blows nobody any good. But we will not disturb the weather and will wait patiently for a change hoping that things will be favorable for tomorrow. I went around and finished collecting money for the celebration to morrow. The singing will be a failure I fear on account of jealousy, pride etc.

Preparations

Under this head I will speak of one thing which shows that an ignorant man is totally unfit to have anything to do with the management of any public doings. The Committee of which I am one have bought the candies, raisins, nuts & have provision enough for a good time. It is therefore right that good speakers be secured for the occasion. Mr. Baughman is the principal speaker & it would be fair to invite Mr. Johnson, the Episcopal minister. At such a suggestion Mr. [Thomas] Williams was exceedingly put out & would resist the thing to the bitter end. What an idea. It would be a mark of respect and certainly worthy of a Christian to invite him on a public occasion like the Fourth. Nothing but a Methodist can celebrate the day here. For shame. An ignorant man is unfit to be the member of a church for it is perfect popery in his presence. Such feelings are far from being the feelings that should actuate a true Christian. Every one should be allowed to celebrate the Fourth.

The Fourth

It has been my fortune to pass a Fourth in the village of Cliff Mine, Lake Superior.[1] On an occasion of this kind in a new country a celebration is attended by many sad and disgusting scenes especially where "Paddy's eye water" is plenty and beer by the half barrel or as a Cornishman would prefer by the quert or bloody drop.

The preparations for a time in this place were made by the following Committee of arrangement, Henry Hobart, Abram Trewarther, Thomas S. Williams & William Osborne, who canvassed the town & secured $78.70 in money & provisions enough to give all present a plenty.

The Methodist Sunday School started the thing and it was on their behalf. First there was marching after martial music the committee acting as marshals for the scholars who made a long procession with banners flying. They then stopped by the side of the church where were seats & a platform built. After Prayer & singing I read the

Declaration of Independence & the Rev. Mr. Baughman followed with a fine speech. The committee were then very busy passing lemonade, candy, nuts, provisions to the satisfaction of all.

Everything in the vicinity was quiet & orderly, but there were serious fights in one of our streets at the River & other places by drunken men. I witnessed one where two Irishmen were trying to come together & several women were separating them, at last they went in pulling hair, yelling, knocking, swearing, kicking etc. Three or four others rushed in and the fight was very amusing for they were all tight & old women might be seen carrying their husbands away after they were rendered *hors de combat* [disabled]. Two or three of them were covered with blood but no one was seriously injured. This is the way drunken men fight. So it was at every grog shop in the country. How much misery and trouble is caused by intoxicating drink.

This is the eighty-seventh anniversary of American Independence and the Fourth of July has been held in special honor by Americas ever since the passage of the Declaration. The men who nobly asserted their rights then were actuated by feelings of the true patriot: the love of home, liberty and country. They fought nobly in defense of these principles and resisted the tyranny and oppression of their mother country. Their efforts were crowned with success and we now enjoy or have since enjoyed the free institutions for which they offered their lives on the alter of their country. A look at our career since gives evidence of astonishing progress.

Look at the vast population scattered through our land from Maine to the Gulf of Mexico and along the Pacific Coast. Look at the general intelligence that prevails. The institution of learning & religion. See how our land is covered with large cities, railroads & canals, running here and there. Now She has been taken from a dense wilderness to become the abode of the most flourishing nation and the best government ever known. There are some of the blessings we have derived from our Independence.

But how different are the feelings that animate the loyal men of our land as they meet today from their feeling on former occasions. A terrible civil war, unparalleled in history, is raging and desolating the fairest portions of our Land. It is a result of slavery—of the same aristocratic feeling that was planning our submission & carrying it out at the time of the revolution. Its origination

[was] from the dregs of aristocracy, the seed from England that were sown in the parts of our land. Slavery extended its influence under the protection of Government until it received a check by the election of an administrator whose views were for liberty; then it came out in open war with the Government. This step was not taken without preparation. The resources of the Government were in the hands of traitors. The Government was crippled. How nobly the loyal men of our land have come forward in defense of the Government. Like the heroes of '76' who closed their war by taking one Lord Cornwallis & his army at Yorktown and the Yankees dealt with him so finely that they shelled the corn all off of him and he was called Lord Cobwallis.

May we bay the traitors of our land and soon put an end to this contest. We have spent millions of dollars thousands of our noble men have fallen in defense of our country. There is a class of poor, snarling, sore-eyed mortals in our midst under the protection of our flag who feel terribly for traitors. Poor, forsaken fools who will say words of sympathy with traitors. They should receive the same punishment as the Green Mountain Boys gave the traitors viz. Whip the traitor's principles out of them with the blue bleach and then give them a ducking in some cool body of water.

Some of the territory that is now in rebellion cost the Government millions of dollars. They secede after the Government has been to this trouble but Yankees say you must come back or we will make you. We are now nobly fighting for our Government and will overthrow this great rebellion sooner or later. Treason must be put down if it cost treasure and the blood of our noblest citizens.

The youth of our land should be educated and their minds imbued with the spirit of liberty & truth for if we are successful in this struggle if treason is put down. Our institutions, our Government must look for support and portection from the rising generation, from those who are soon to step upon the stage of action. Then it is the duty of all to learn them to love and respect the principles of liberty & truth. To have their characters grounded on a sure foundation for then they will become patriotic men & women, lovers of the institutions of liberty.

July 7, 1863

It is a very hot day and no air stirring. It is almost insufferable. Last night it was almost impossible to sleep or take any comfort. I went to bed at midnight not feeling well. I am quite unwell. I have not taken much to eat for a number of days & am in hopes of being better in a few days. I think my labors in the school room or in an place of confinement will close in our year. At any rate I will not teach summers as it is injuring my health. I do not feel well while undergoing such labor in a warm room. And I am confident there is very little money to be made after paying expenses. If I had a school where there was only one teacher I could make more for the assistant lessens my pay a great deal. I shall take very little money back with me on my return. I am glad I came out & would be glad if I only paid my expenses. I am teaching in the Odd Fellows hall during vacation and have just learned that what I will have to pay for the hall will cancel all I can make there. But I shall not be idle and will be doing good. There is no chance to spend time in seeing anything for a person that has been here awhile cannot find any thing interesting.

I learn that the Paddies who were tapering off in a general fight on the afternoon of the Fourth are fined about twenty dollars. apiece. This is a good thing but it would be much better of the grog shops in the vicinity were burnt to the ground and a war waged with the cause of this evil which is so detrimental to the business of the country and causing so much disturbance wherever it is used. I do not approve of the use of gin or beer in any form, although miners claim it is necessary.

July 9, 1863

We have experienced a curious change of weather since I last wrote and it is considered very peculiar by everyone who noticed it. I never witnessed a similar thing in my life. It has been very windy and foggy for some time, very warm weather and boats have found serious difficulty in approaching the ports which could only be done by firing signals etc. The air has also become smoky from some cause; even today it is impossible to see far on account of the smoke. Yesterday the smoke seemed to mix with the fog settling down so as to make it almost night around our place. Some said it was similar to the London fogs which are so dense when mixed with the cool smoke of the city as to compel the people to light the street lamps.

Superstitious persons here thought the world was coming to an end & the fact that grasshoppers which were very plenty seem to have been killed by some agency even where logs were covered with them they had expired. This doubtless has great weight in causing them to look upon the end of the world as near at hand. One thought it was a special interposition of providence be that as it may I have nothing to offer only a strange thing.

I have just received a fine letter from sister Florence. Everything comfortable at home.

There is a new vein of copper discovered by the Phoenix Company between here & the River. It is one of the finest things that has been opened on the Lake. The stock was selling at seven dollars per share and if a man had secured a number of shares he would have made a fortune. Most everyone has sent money & the stock will be very high soon. How easy to make a fortune if attended to in season. Old Mr. Farwell owns four thousand shares & was a poor man.[2] He will now become immensely rich. Luck to the mining interest on Lake Superior.

July 10, 1863

The chief feature in the weather at present are the banks of fog and smoke that prevail constantly and the dryness of the weather also that is the want of copious showers of rain. These are the striking peculiarities of the season. I suppose there is always fog on account of the near proximity of the Lake. But the want of rain is a strange thing. The sky was overcast last night with dark heavy clouds and the thunder and lightning were very sharp but no rain. It is cloudy today and the noise of distant thunder is constantly heard; still I fear it will not rain. There was a great excitement here yesterday on account of the new vein at the Phoenix. Men have sent all their money to Boston to purchase stock in the mine. If I had known in season I should have invested my money. But when captains & agents have the first chance there is very little chance to find any of the stock for sale.

Four darkies came into town last evening and are going to give a miserable, silly show tonight, and miners will doubtless give their quarters to witness their foolish actions. I should prefer patronizing a good sound lecture.

Last evening Mr. Rawlings gave Miss Cundy & myself a lesson in singing; we are making very good progress and I am in hopes to learn something about the principles if I cannot make much music. We experience remarkable weather today—very smoky and cloudy [and] also a dense fog. The sun is almost as red as blood. The thermometer goes down as low as fifty-four degrees and although the clouds seem light it thunders constantly and grows dark at times. Everyone is remarking about the strange appearence of these days. The boats cannot come in on account of the density of the fog and there is constant whistling from them.

I have just sent a letter to John Fay and one to L. Putnam. Yesterday I mailed one for G[eorge] Eastman and one friend Jesse B[ushnell], also one to the Post Master at the Portage in relation to a letter in that office for me. I shall not keep school tomorrow.

Mr. Rawlings commenced drawing a map of Keweenaw Point for me to take home with me. I am glad I can get one for I can see where I spent a portion of my life in the Lake Superior country. I find that a number of these self-conceited miners thought I ought to hire the hall & instruct their children for nothing while vacation continues. I must pay my board, hire the hall and give a months labor to the district after I have spent evening and worked hard for them. They have very little sympathy for a teacher as they know nothing themselves. I am too much of a Yankee for any such thing and will not teach without good pay. A teacher has difficulty enough without giving his labor free and then pay his expenses.

I noticed another thing here that is shameful to behold viz. The self-conceit, pride and affectation of the young men of this place who are as ignorant as jackasses & full blood Cornish of course. I can never accustom myself to their ways. How disgusting to have them come round and in a pompous style and without a request explain something that they know nothing about and say they showed when it was a thing that I knew & was able to explain long ago. A person must keep silence in my position but it is hard to do it sometimes. There is a nigger show at the hall this evening & William Penberthy who is black as one and acts like one is delighted. His old guitar is all he things about & is right cut & has a natural taste for some silly nigger nonsense.

Evening

Tomorrow morning I shall go up and hoe potatoes if the weather will admit. I think the exercise will do me good. My friend William Trewarther has been discharged for refusing to work evenings when there was a hurry for the work. He was in the fitting shop [and] has driven the engine for some time in this place. He was intending to go away and thinks about going to California. I wish I could go with him for I could do well there. I should see that beautiful state and enjoy the healthy climate. I expect a letter soon from a friend who has gone to Pikes Peak from here. Wages are very high there. There is a fine charge in a rich mining country for a young man. Everything commands an exorbitant price.

I have been reading an account of the war in Kansas by "Brewerton" who was correspondent of one of the New York papers and from the style of that I should judge him to be a pro-slavery man. At any rate I dislike his sentiments although he gets off many good jokes and some good ideas. He was one of Kit Carson's companions in his hunting excursions, and seems to be an old boy at hunting. The book will pass as well as many others that people read. They are worthless so far as conveying any information worthy of remembering or treasuring up. Of late I have found very little time to read as I have been answering letters and writing. I intend to read the *Second War with England* by J. T. Headley which will be worth remembering as it contains valuable historic accounts of the transactions during that time.[3] The truth is there are many books that I should read and must as soon as I can find the time or a leisure spell from labor.

July 11, 1863

The sky is as clear as crystal and the sun shines brightly. It is a fine day although the wind blows quite strong. The rain has proved a humbug like many other things & by the way I often think of that solemncolly word as I write in this book. I think the reader will cry humbug, but I must speak of the weather which is no humbug I am sure. The thermometer was low as forty degrees this morning & it was quite chilly.

I took my breakfast, donned a ragged suit & with hoe on my back started for the potato patch. Met Mr. Wilson, the farm boss, haying with a gang of men.[4] Took the scythe and showed them how a Yankee could handle the tool. He wanted to hire me anyway. I spend the day hoeing & finished the business. I paid up my board yesterday to the first of August.

The work on the school house is progressing finely and in about two weeks I shall be at work again. The news that Lee's army is cut to pieces and Vicksburg has fallen reaches up today and the Stars & Stripes are flying from the flagstaff in honor of the victory. I hope it may be true yet it seems most too good to prove all true. It is difficult to tell what is true there are so many false rumors but I am inclined to credit the defeat of Lee as he was out of his fortification where our boys could have a fair chance with his ragged traitors It is also true that Vicksburg was so completely hemmed in that they must yield for want of food or the means to fight. It was a well known fact that they were on short allowance and had no guncaps to use. I am inclined to credit these statements although they may not prove true. What a joy it would bring if it were so. Success to our troops and cause.

July 12, 1863

I intend to give from this date, the degree of temperature indicated by the thermometer on the last page of this book taken three times each; viz at six in the morning & evening and at noon also the mean temperature for the day. I should have done so before if I had had a thermometer.

This is a fine day, a day of rest; the sun shines beautifully and although it is very dry still everything looks fine. There is no breeze today and how beautiful and smooth the surface of the great Lake looks. It would be pleasant to be on board of one of the boats during a calm sunny day like this. I took my usual breakfast of white bread this morning with an unusual yet agreeable change of a piece of apple pie, which mother knows I never object to.

I went up to the Methodist Sabbath School this forenoon. The officers were elected this morning. I was chosen as librarian, Captain Souden is to be Superintendent. The school is in a good condition and we will soon be in the new church. It is to be dedicated the last Sunday in this month. The Society of Odd Fellows held a meeting for the installation of officers. It was not public, however, to the disappointment of many.

There was considerable stir last evening in relation to the cheering news from the army. The boys were out playing the fife and drum and all were jubilant. Cornishmen care nothing about it only hoping it will prevent a draft. They would do most anything rather than go fight for the country. Those who enlisted from here after getting their advance pay deserted in Detroit fleeing to Canada. Very little sympathy is manifested here for the Government that is among a certain class of Cornishmen. It is true there are patriotic Englishmen even in this place.

I am convinced by a fair course of logical reasoning that there is a power in me superior to matter, a "something" that has capacities of a nature far superior to any of the properties of matter, that cannot be comprehended. This wonderful power in me is called mind. I look at my hand, at its various members called fingers. It has a peculiar shape. I notice farther that there is a certain muscular power about it. I can open it & close it, use it in various ways. It is capable of grasping & holding in obedience to my mind. There must have been a special object a fixed purpose for its use. It is not shaped like the foot and therefore could not be designed to walk with. It has a particular office like all the members of my body to fulfill. Then it follows that I was made for some purpose.

I look around & see the sun, moon & stars. This earth all working in obedience to some law. Who was the author and for what purpose are these laws at work. I am convinced that no man every was able to make the sun. I see it shine; there must be a purpose in its shining. I therefore see design. There must have been a designor and by sound reasoning I am convinced that the designor was superior to man. I see a limit to matter. Stretch forth my hand. It cannot comprehend matter out of its reach, its power is limited I can comprehend matter through its agency only as it comes in actual contact with it but I know that the mind is not thus limited in its action. I can send it to the heavens, to England, anywhere. Who can limit the power of thought. How great then is the capacity and power of mind. I therefore conclude its author is great. "The infinite God."

My reason teaches me. I am forced by the power of sound reasoning and argument to believe I was created for a good purpose. That all this wonderful machinery of worlds was created for some good purpose and acts in harmony to certain laws. I reason that further and conclude that a violation of these laws causes evil or the offender must be subject to its penalties. It must cause sin and evil if these things act in obedience to law for a good purpose. I see a wise and good design in everything and therefore conclude by fair reasoning that evil results from the abuse of good from the violation of some law. I can trace all evil & crime to this point viz. It results from the abuse of good. But further I know that I do not carry out fully the wise purpose of my creation. There is a feeling within me that convinces me I am a violator of the divine law that I am a sinner. I am forced to this conclusion by sound argument. I cannot avoid it. I look farther & try to reason a man's or way of escape. How can I avoid the penalty I find my efforts fail I cannot reason out any course or way.

How beautifully the Bible came in here showing me the way. Where my reason fails divine revelation points out the way. This is a beautiful thought, a wise arrangement. The Bible comes in where my reasoning powers fail or are brought in difficulty. Therefore follow its teachings. Treasure up its precepts. There is a class of persons who deny the truth of the Bible. There never was a man that could make such a book. Moses never could never have made his people believe that they passed through the Red Sea and similar miracles unless they actually done so. I might as well try to make Americans believe that they were celebrating the discovery of America every Fourth of July. The thing is impossible. No man could devise a system of truths like the Bible & impose them on any people. The Bible is true. There is not one particle of good in Mohammedanism but what was taken from the Bible. And Mormonism is one of the most damnable & cursed systems that ever a people supported. Neither of them can be compared with Christianity; my reason rejects such an idea.

July 13, 1863

It is a cloudy mild morning and there is a slight prospect of rain. The wind is increasing and it grows cooler. It is quite different from summer and quite a change from the weather that we have enjoyed for some time past. There is no fog now. The clouds are heavier and thicker this evening and it is cool.

I closed school today as an artist has rented the Hall where I am teaching. Miss Cundy will close tomorrow. Mr. William Trewarther has just returned from the Portage where he is going to work. He likes the place and there are a large number of men wanted there. Business is very thriving. A number of men will go from here as they can obtain better pay there than they can here. Mr. Rawlings gave me two or three specimens of copper—he has nearly finished my map

Mr. McKenzie, editor at the Portage— a fine young man— was here today.[5] I did not obtain an introduction to him as I was in school. The Phoenix stock is rising. It has doubled since the discovery of this vein.

School Houses

Every teacher of experience must be aware that the school houses of the country generally are not adapted to the purpose of a school. There are three very important things to be considered in their construction that are looked upon as of very little importance in their construction viz, proper height of room & ventilation, warmth & a convenient arrangement of seats and those of a good kind. In the construction of public buildings height & ventilation is very important to be noticed & in school rooms it is neglected. Scholars are always uneasy where there is a lack of ventilation & it is very unhealthy in a low room. The seats should be made for comfort & not for torture as is sometimes the case. Everything should be so constructed as to add to the comfort of the school and also convenience.

July 14, 1863

I suppose I must speak about the weather any way so I will affirm that it is a damp foggy day, cool disagreeable, sneezing kind of weather. I went up on the bluff this morning; work is progressing finely. A new engine for hoisting is to be put up there soon. I notice the berries are getting ripe. There is a great plenty of raspberries, very few strawberries.

I have no work to perform now but writing and reading. I shall work at the school record. I find this evening that I have done very little except reading some. Having nothing driving I have felt like running around. I went and gave directions for placing the seats in the school room. The work is progressing very slowly for want of good help. I am going to fix the sidewalk soon & think I shall work in haying also, for I cannot spend my time in doing nothing.

This afternoon the fog cleared away and the wind was north. The sun shone out quite brightly yet it is quite cool. It seems like the Fall of the year. Nothing important has taken place to day. There is a sameness in the weather and transaction each day & I find very little change in my writing.

The Sunday School Library

I have received the appointment of librarian and secretary of the school. The library is in a sad condition; the books are torn and many lost. I shall try and make out a new list and put things in working order soon. It is a disgrace to have such an arrangement. A library if not attended to will soon be destroyed and especially is this the case when children take the books. And children here are very severe with the books; they cannot or do not try to keep them neat and clean.

July 16, 1863

Although yesterday was a clear fine day and a good prospect of a clear day today, this forenoon it was quite cloudy but has cleared off again and is quite warm. I spent yesterday in laying the side walk to the schoolhouse. Today I have likenesses of some of my scholars taken to take below with me.

There is to be a war exhibition at the hall this evening.[6] I went and saw it. The pictures were very good representations of the war although on a small scale for a good thing. The Lady is a fine singer and sung many touching songs. One was called "My Mother" and was very good. They are to show tomorrow evening.

Mr. Rawlings has gone down to the North Western to inspect the work where Captain Halls is sinking the shaft. He also went to the Harbor for a box of his tools that came down on the boat from Ontonagon.

I have felt quite lonesome today as I have no business that is very driving. I cannot avoid noticing the difference between many young men. It is a commendable thing to see young men below take pleasure in a good sound lecture or discourse and anything like nonsense or nigger shows are not patronized. This will certainly determine the character of the people in any place. A silly show will take here best and young men will look upon it as a wonderful thing. Very little is thought of a good lecture or discourse. The aim of the principal class

191

of young men seems to be to witness or aid in doing some silly thing. The patronage that the majority of principled ones give to either class will soon determine the aim of their minds, the object of their endeavors & course of conduct.

July 17, 1863

It is a cloudy warm morning & I think the sun will shine very bright before noon and it will be warm. There is a brisk breeze this forenoon, which gives signs of blowing quite strong before night. Captain Paull's girls are coming up this forenoon & I will get their pictures taken.

In the afternoon I went up to and commenced work on the farm for Mr. Wilson for a while. There is some laughing around the village about the idea of a schoolmaster taking a little excerise with the pitchfork but those who laugh are the biggest fools. What is a young man worth who has that false pride about him that will influence him to regard labor as beneath the dignity of the gentleman. I wish I had a good Yankee. I would show the lazy men how Vermonters put in hay. If Ruluff was alive & here I would like to pitch hay one week. The idea of getting in only two loads of hay in six hours would sicken a Yankee. There is no life in the help. Mr. Wilson has lazy, indolent, ignorant fools in fact. I shall work with them.

I shall try & help paint the school house as I am in a hurry to see it done. The work on it is not progressing very fast and I dislike to spend time without pay. I went in the evening and saw the closing pictures of the war panorama. It is quite a good one taking it through although not on a very extensive scale. I doubt not that we may yet see very fine paintings of this war on a grand & extensive scale. I have six pictures taken in all. Three persons in each. I shall be able to see my scholars when I am in Vermont if I return home safe. The artist is quite skillful and takes them quite well.

July 19, 1863

With what pleasure should we hail this day as the weeks roll by. It should awaken in the mind elevated and noble sensations and should not be hailed by anyone as a time specially set for spreeing, for drinking and groveling in low, debasing, & sensual thoughts, practicing evils thus converting the man into the brute. It should be regarded as a day of rest for sober & serious thought for attending religious worship for elevating the mind above earthly things.

How beautiful & pleasant the thought when the true idea enters the mind & is understood. There is a satisfaction in hailing the sabbath when the true purpose for which it is specially set apart takes possession of the mind. How it is violated here among the ignorant people who make it a day for carousing etc. I went to Sunday School today; there were only a few present as it is quite wet. The next Sunday the new church will be dedicated.

Every person has a longing desire to be happy. It is one of the most prominent aims of the mind to seek after enjoyment. It constitutes an essential element of man's nature. This desire is universal and every class of persons aim to secure this object although in a very different direction. There is a wide difference among the different principles that move men to action. Some are actuated by selfish and improper motives, motives that influence them in a course of life unproductive of genuine and pure happiness. In order to secure pure substantial enjoyment a correct moral course must be adopted in conformity with truth & christianity. This will give the possessor enjoyment, pleasure & satisfaction that is lasting and worthy to receive.

July 20, 1863

A variety of weather today. In the morning it is very cloudy and there is a cold damp fog and much wind. In the afternoon, it clears away and the sun shines brightly. It is quite a fine one for hay but I will not go out this afternoon. I think Squire Wilson will not draw but put his men mowing.

Mr. Rawlings has finished my map and I gave him fifteen dollars in money for it although his usual price is twenty-five dollars for the same. It is a splendid ornament and I am very glad to get one of this place for I can see where I labored as a teacher. I can show friends the situation of the mines and many things of interest in relation to this rich copper country.

Mr. Lamb, who had the job of repairing the schoolhouse, has turned out a mean rascal. I often conversed with him and saw nothing very much out of the way in his actions. He was pleasant spoken and showed good intelligence, had been a schoolmaster according to his own assertion and was a native of Long Island. This smooth-tongued rascal for such, I must now call him, came here and took this job for a good price and went to work. I often told him that I was anxious for him to complete it as I was idle. He drew about three hundred dollars in money and has gone below without paying for anything. A meaner thing he could not have done to me at least. I am paying my board & cannot teach. When the house will be ready I cannot tell, for there is not a spare carpenter here. I sincerely hope he may lose every cent of the money before he reaches Detroit for I feel bad to think I am thus on expense and no way to pay it wholly on his meanness in thus running away and leaving the work incomplete.

July 21, 1863

It is a fine hay day and quite warm & I work for the Squire haying. I raked after the cart as there was not a man who could keep up. We drawed in twelve loads of hay and went over an unusually large rough bushy wet swampy hilly piece of ground. It is a tiresome place to work as there is so much running. I am tired & as I am going to work tomorrow I will go to bed and take comfortable old snooze in my old bed. I will fill out this page some other time.

Mr. Rawlings is mostly engaged on the bluff seeing the building of the foundation for putting up another engine for hoisting masses of copper. This will save much labor under ground as the masses come mostly beyond or near No. 4 shaft on the bluff & they must be carried through the drifts to No. 2 shaft now, before they are raised to the surface.

July 23, 1863

I awoke this morning from a good rest & partaking of some bread & milk started for a day's work on the farm. I am sure the day will not prove fine as it is very cloudy. We draw hay until eleven when it is very foggy and we stop work. I clean up and take a walk upon the bluff picking a few blueberries to eat. The sun shines out bright this afternoon. We shall draw hay tomorrow if it is fine. There are six teams drawing every day we went over nearly eighty acres in a few days or less than one week. I shall work very little as it would make me lame & unfit to engage in teaching.

The masons are building a chimney in this house. The Ladies are carpeting the church, and it will soon be ready to enter. There is no news. John has a small squirrel at home that came into the office where he was at work. It is very handsome but Edward pulled off his tail this afternoon in trying to catch him.

July 26, 1863

How I am neglecting to write in this book which is for this reason. I am working mostly every day and therefore I have very little time to attend to this business. I was in hopes to write a few short sketches in the last pages of this volume of my Lake Superior life, but must now fail so to do. I am aware that there is very little of interest recorded here as it has been done in great haste without much thought yet notwithstanding these imperfections I shall prize the book as giving some idea of my western home and experiences.

On walking from a quiet rest this morning the cheering sound of rain fell upon my ear. How seldom has the refreshing showers fallen here this summer. I supposed I should hear the music of falling rain very often, but this is a dry season. This shower has moistened the ground very much although there was not a heavy fall. It is cloudy & mild with quite a breeze stirring. We have not experienced much hot weather that is it is quite cool most of the time.

It is Sunday today—a time for rest and sober thought. I hail this day from week to week with the greatest of pleasure.

Our new church is to be dedicated to day. I spent yesterday and last evening in laying down the carpet. It is a fine building and we have a man of large talent & long experience to preach an interesting discourse whenever he enter the pulpit. He is a Dutchman whose hair is now white from the effects of many years labor and possesses a vigorous body & mind rendered so by the most temperate life and proper training. He has a strong voice and is a fine speaker. He is one of the smartest men in the state & has a thorough knowledge of ancient & modern history.[7]

Notes for July-August 1863

1. The Fourth of July was celebrated in all of the mining villages and towns in the Upper Peninsula. At the Rockland Mine, the celebration started with a parade led by Robert's Rifle Guard, followed by the Friendly Sons of the St. Patrick Society and some 200 children carrying banners and flags. Following the reading of the Declaration of Independence, the Reverend M. A. Fox gave a oration. In Houghton, the celebration featured a parade, speeches and fireworks in the evening. School children were treated with cakes, nuts and candies at the Methodist Episcopal Church. Nearby at Paddy's Creek, a group of Chippewa Indians celebrated the "Feast of Dog Boyeau." *Lake Superior Miner*, July 11, 1864.

2. Oliver Farwell, a respected mining engineer, was placed in charge of the Cliff Mine in 1871 and remained in that capacity until his death on June 22, 1881. *History of the Upper Peninsula* (Chicago: Western Historical Society, 1883), p. 32. Henry M. Pinkham, *Lake Superior Copper Properties* (Boston: Printed for the author), p. 8.

3. Joel Tyler Headley, *The Second War with England* (New York: Scribners, 1853).

4. The *9th U. S. Census* for Houghton County, 1870, lists two Wilsons as farmers at Clifton: Joseph Wilson, age 39, born in Ireland and married to Margaret, age 34, and William Wilson, born in England, age 34, and married to Sarah, age 23.

5. Henry McKenzie purchased the *Portage Lake Mining Gazette* in 1860 and operated it until 1870, when it was sold to J. R. Devereaux who had founded the paper in 1859. *History of the Upper Peninsula*, p. 221.

6. The Douglass House Hotel Register for July 18, 1863, had the guest signature "Warren Bardwell and Lady with Banvard's   Polyoroma of the War." This is undoubtedly the same exhibit that appeared at Cliff. The register is at the Bentley Historical Library, University of Michigan, Ann Arbor, Michigan.

7. The Reverend J. T. Hankinson served as a minister to the Methodist Church in Cliff in 1863. R. C. Stetter, *Central Methodist Episcopal Church: A Short History* (No publisher : no date), p. 75.

Hobart taught some miners in his short-lived night school and was teacher to their children as well. He traveled down into the Cliff Mine (two drawings on the following page) and described its workings.

SCALE IN FEET

September 19, 1863

It will be seen by the above date that I have not written for a long time in this book. I am sorry that circumstances have taken place forcing me to submit to such a course which has been a sad detriment to my improvement in penmanship etc. But I realize the fact that everyone should adapt himself to the various circumstances in which he may find himself placed, and strive to make himself useful or at least shun idleness.

I spent a few days in the hay field and as a carpenter in repairing the store. The rascal (for such he proved) who was repairing the school house ran away and there was no one to finish repairing it as every carpenter is employed about the mine. Captain Souden (director) came to me & told me to go at it with two men to help. I bought a pair of overalls and assumed the dignity of a carpenter & completed the work. Now there was no painter to be had & I stepped in Yankee style calling myself very good in that line. I saw an old Friend who gave me a word of advice in relation to mixing the article & I soon found myself styled the Yankee painter. I painted it inside & out and to tell the truth done a fine job as all admit. I was lucky enough to make a good color and trimmed the building off in fine style. Painted the large bookcase holding the public library which is in the school room under my charge. I made a mixture that causes it to look like black walnut (to perfection). I now found everything ready for school and determined to commence the next Monday.

The building is now seventy-five feet in length divided into two rooms very high. I thus was able to pay my board bill while I could not teach. If I had done nothing I might have been compelled to wait three or four months doing nothing but running in debt.

But instead of commencing school I was taken sick with a bilious attack resulting in Yellow Jaundice severely. I have now been sick three weeks employing the Doctor. I am now on the gain, I hope. When I was first taken, being aware that my stomach was out of order, which I do not wonder at when I think about the Cornish style of living, I took a severe emetic, and have been taking physic & etc. My skin & eyes are the color of Gold although my pockets are not lined with it or will not be when I recover. It is a disagreeable sickness & there have been many cases here. I do not wonder that people have bilious attacks in a country where they live as they do here.

Mrs. Rawlings has been very kind although I cannot help noticing her ignorance in the cooking line. She claims to be very neat, clean, and fine nurse & cook. I could eat nothing and what did I get but a dish of soup or broth that the beef cabbage onions dumplings are boiled in one-half grease, bread & onions in it [and] perhaps the onions were sliced in raw. The dish is taken up dirty & wiped with the towel that they all use. Oh, what a dish of nice soup.

There is nothing but the towel to wipe hands with to use for the dishes. The bread is taken out on the floor when taken out of the dishes in which it is baked. We have had only a few meals of potatoes this summer, never a pie or piece of cake and no kind of sauce. I have often set down to a meal of bread and water, but never a piece of corn bread. Oh, when shall I see a meal at home. Since I have been sick, pies have been making me mad to think I could not eat any. I now eat oat or corn meal gruel. The old lady says a pie or any of those things are not good & she will not make them.

The Yankee style of living can be had by paying twenty or twenty-five dollars per month. The doctors and clerks do it & make nothing. I am aware that I pay high enough. Cost what it will I shall have a supply of apples to bake this winter and enjoy myself some. I have a good room & have bought a stove for it & shall bake apples, read, write & enjoy life well.

I have fine times with Mr. Rawlings but I think the Mrs. is rather deeply imbued with the English ways. It is hard to keep silent and listen to her talk but I can do it. She does not know anything about things. Totally ignorant of everything except what she has seen. How many are similarly situated I hope I shall be pardoned for expressing myself partially about these things. I could write pages about their foolish & disgusting ways.

There have been various changes since I last wrote that would have called forth a few remarks from me if I could write, at the time. Edward [Penberthy] has left the store & gone to Copper Harbor. His course of action I will not speak about. I was so thoroughly disgusted. Proud, foolish, saucy, ignorant. Dressed like a dandy strutting like a simpleton disgusting everyone. Mr. F. Ten Broeck is now clerk in the store. Shall speak of him after further acquaintance. The clerks now receive fifty dollars per month & doubtless spend it all.

My assistant, Miss Cundy, has gone to Ypsilanti to school and there is no one here to fill the place. Captain Souden has sent to Wisconsin for one, a daughter of Mr. Philbrick, boss carpenter of the mine. Miss Mary Tresider, brother to the invincible John, was married to Captain Vivian Q., called the governor on account of his haughty appearance.

There has been quite a number of accidents in the mine. One man killed by tons of rock falling on him. One or two had legs broken, fingers & toes smashed. Many men have gone away to other mines and there is great want of help everywhere but things are so dear that men find it difficult to lay up any money. Clothing is very high.

September 20, 1863

It is a wet foggy morning. The ground is soaked and covered with water from the past few rainy days. It snows some, freezes nights, and looks like fall weather generally. The leaves show the golden color giving assurance that they must soon fall to the ground. There is beauty in the immense forests extending over these hills and valleys clothed in their rich foliage of various hues. There are scenes here that cannot be far surpassed of color & beauty. I imagine myself seated in a birch canoe out on the placid surface of Gratiot Lake, ten miles distant in the woods, the beautiful trout are busy at the hook, the sloping hills extend back in the distance unmarred by the ax in all the richness of their ancient beauty. Everything is pleasant to the eye & sweet sounds meet the ear. Yonder . . . beautiful trout of twenty pounds darts to the surface of the water after the hook; ducks & water fowls are seen everywhere. What a scene for the painter. Thus it is all through this region.

For the past few days there have been very sudden changes in the weather viz within a dozen hours the thermometer would stand at ninety degrees then at thirty-five degrees. Very sudden changes.

The usual storms on the Lake have taken place & one or two sad accidents is the result. In one of these severe blows the *Sunbeam* with thirty passengers on board was sunk about forty miles from here.[1] The waves dashed her to pieces, the steersman lashed himself to a door & was driven ashore in thirty-six hours & saved by a pleasure party down the Lake in a small boat. He was just alive & the waves had beaten the flesh from his limbs and body.

The others got into a small boat which sunk at once. Rev. Mr. Bird was among the lost.[2]

Mr. Baughman, our respected preacher, is now attending a Conference. There is so talk of removing him from here to the Portage. All here are opposed to the change and hope he will return. Captain Halls has taken his family to the North Western. He is now sinking the shaft in the rock having got through the sand. He expects to find the vein soon. The store is now nearly done and new Goods are coming from below. All are active in preparing for winter.

I received a letter from cousin George Eastman teaching at Winooski Falls, Vermont. I hear teachers are very scarce in that place. There has been a draft & the drafted men paid their three hundred dollars. Captain John Woodward was killed at Gettysburg.[3] His father is at home & represents the town this fall. I think I will write home today. More Soon.

Afternoon

I find myself recovering from my sickness quite fast. I shall continue taking medicine a few days longer and expect to commence school Thursday cleared giving promise of some fine weather.

We hear the good news that General Gilmore now holds Morris Island having taken Battery Gregg & Fort Wagner. Cumberland Gap surrendered to Burnside September 9. The Union cause is steadily advancing. Success to our armies.

I shall close this book soon and commence a new one, October 1, in which I wish to give a particular account of everything and especially the weather & different changes indicated by the Thermometer. Also speak of the manner of living & everything that comes under my notice. How faithful I shall be in writing I cannot say. I hope I may write some each day.

I wish I had my gold pen which I lent to one of the clerks & cannot now be found. I intend using one pen and no other and if I write each day. I expect to improve some I will do no more today in this line.

September 23, 1863

Although it was cloudy and cool this morning there was no good sign of a severe day or prospect of a change for fine weather.

Everything indicated a cool day without change. It has proved to the contrary. The breeze up and a line of sleet and rain has been falling. It is much cooler and very unpleasant. It is one of those days in which a person in a snug room with a good fire burning, a dish of apples on the table, the latest paper & good stories at hand, feels at home and delights to think the howling storm cannot injure him. How good to have a home and plenty to make it comfortable. I had a fine berth today.

I commenced my school without an assistant. This is business that I have made myself thoroughly acquainted with and must say that I feel at home and enjoy myself well in spite of the many drawbacks. I can see very plainly that I shall have a good school if I secure a good assistant. It was not large today I am to be allowed fifty-two dollars for the twenty-six days I worked on the school house which will cancel my board for the three months I have been idle.

I finished my report of the last term of school yesterday. I had two hundred and twenty-eight different pupils & the school averaged eighty for nine months of twenty-six days each. I could pick months that went far above one hundred.

I learn this evening that the *Illinois* was sunk below the Sault river. No particulars. It is strange that they do not run boats of a stronger pattern on these Lakes. We hear of boats going down every year. It is strange that the people trust themselves on such crafts. I think sea boats would be the best.

September 25, 1863

It was a cool day yesterday and everything passed pleasantly with me. It was very cold last night. The mercury stood at twenty-two degrees this morning. Ice was an inch thick on water and the ground was white. The sun shines very brightly. I received a nice letter from Florence with her likeness yesterday. How glad I was to receive it. I send mine this morning and a letter.

September 28, 1863

How sudden and great are the changes we have in the weather. It is a very hot day almost one hundred above zero. The sun shines brightly and the wind breezes up now and then giving signs of a storm. I find it quite cool in the school room.

I had several new scholars to day. Annie & Sarah Paull have come to learn. Two pretty girls, always good scholars, in whom I feel much interest. I put my roommate "Josiah" to assist me in school. Close every afternoon at five

This evening the annual school meeting was held. Captain Harry George, Moderator; Captain Souden, Director; Abraham Trewarther, assessor; Sam James & myself present. Voted to raise money to pay debts, build sidewalks, buy Globe etc. Passed a vote of thanks for myself for my efforts in finishing up the school house. Adjourned feeling well.

As I have nearly closed this volume I will give a sketch of a visit to the river in my next book. Shall only speak a few words in relation to the events of each day until the first when I open the next volume of my Journal. The store is now closed as the clerks are busy opening the new Goods. I must go and see if my apples are baked. I have partaken of the apples and feel fine. I enjoy a few baked now and then as well as any person. Give me apples & pies.

Journal II

In this article I wish to give a general view of the customs and habits of the miners, the aspect of the county, villages, mines, and more particular some account of my own experience as a teacher at the village of Clifton. I shall pen this without any previous preparation writing in plain terms as the thoughts occur to me and may thus make many mistakes or fail to arrange everything in as precise and correct a manner as I might by writing and giving every part a thorough correction.

The Northern Peninsular of Michigan is rich with Copper and Iron. The Copper region extends along the southern portion being in Keweenaw county and around Portage Lake. The iron region lies south of this. Keweenaw Point is covered with a thick growth of timber consisting of hard wood and evergreen. Civilization has made a few encroachments upon this wilderness in search of the rich copper beds. The attention of the public has been called to the immense mines of copper here within the past twenty-five years, and so great has been the rush to this region of wealth that flourishing mines are in operation all through the county along the mineral range, raising hundreds of tons every year. Great has been & will be the speculation in mining stock by money men. The public are becoming aware of the immense wealth that lies buried in the rocks of this point.

The country is uneven—a high bluff running along about four miles from the Lake Shore. The veins of copper extend through this bluff in a direct line toward the shore. They run this bluff at a sharp angle going deeper and deeper. The copper is found in the Trap rock. The Greenstone lying above & constituting the Bluff. There is a very marked division where the Greenstone meets the Trap rock appearing as if the Greenstone was laid on the Trap there being no solid junction between. When the Trap is removed in taking out copper the junction of the two is smooth and is called the Slide projecting down at an angle of forty-five degrees perhaps. The heavy copper lies in the Trap or copper bearing rock under the slide. The Greenstone is not a copper bearing rock; therefore mines on the north side of the bluff or in the Greenstone are poor generally.

The ash beds are north of the Bluff being belts of rock about twelve feet wide filled with fine copper. Veins are from one inch to three feet wide and are readily known by the white spar with which they are filled. It looks like a partition running down through the rock. The copper lies in these. When they pass through the Greenstone and come to the Trap they are thrown one side fifty or one hundred feet and may be found by drifting east or west distance. Why this is I cannot explain.

The mines are opened by sinking a shaft on the vein, the rock being raised by means of a rope around an axle turned by hand. The horse whim is used & if there are indications of a good mine an engine is used. After sinking a number of feet the miners commence drifting, that is blasting a road about four feet wide and six high along by the side of the vein. This drift is timbered up & a track laid for a wagon or car to bring rock to the shaft to be raised to the surface. The rock directly over this is blasted down & removed. The vein by the side of this is now thrown out by powder and dropped through holes called mills into the cars below to be taken to the shaft.

While some are thus engaged others are sinking the shaft twelve fathoms more when another drift is made when the rock overhead is blasted down—called Stopeing & copper removed. Thus they continue sinking. A winze is a small shaft sunk from one drift to another when they are long for passage. If the mine is prosperous there will be four or five main shafts from the surface for raising the rock. There is one large engine pumping water out of the mine, day & night. All the work above and underground is carried on night and day. A portion of the men working night one week & day the next; the other portion working the remaining time.

A large drum is attached to the engine & a wire rope from one to two inches thick attached to this with an iron bucket to lower into the shaft that will hold seven tons. The rock is raised in a square bucket six feet long & three square with guides on the back running in a groove. It comes up very steady & swift while in the other way to let swings through the shaft, especially when hoisting one hundred and twenty fathoms from the surface sometimes the chain breaks & the bucket falls through the shaft making the fire fly. The masses are raised in the main shaft with a rope four inches thick. It is terrible for ten tons of rock to fall through a shaft one hundred and twenty fathoms when the chain breaks.

The men wear pants & a sack coat with thick flannel under clothes. The pants & coat are made of bagging & are the color of copper after being worn once. Thick flannels must be worn as every man comes up very wet from the dripping water. Suspenders are never worn but a belt above the hips so as to give the arms play in running the ladders. The hat is made of wool and resin etc. as hard as a rock fitting the head & the rim is about three inches wide. A lump of clay holds the candle in front & three or four candles hang on a button of the coat.

Thus equipped the miner places his drills & hammer in the bucket to be sent down & with a good "crib" in his pocket which generally consist of a "Cornish pasty"—plenty of fuse in pocket, he is ready to descend. The ladder is about twenty feet long standing straight reaching to a platform & then comes another, so on to the bottom. The hole through each platform will just admit the body of a man. How fast the miner ascends & descends on these ladders singing all the time. It sounds fine through the drifts.

I cannot give now an account of matters underground. It is amusing to see twenty men swing the hammer & striking the chisels in cutting a large mass of copper. I have been down twice and find it very pleasant. Make a good looking miner. The large masses are cleaned from the rock by picks & wedges in the mineral yard. The vein stone filled with fine copper is broken with the hammer into pieces about the size of a man's fist or larger. Some of it is burnt in a large heap on a pile of wood— softening the rock & then broken, it is then taken to the stamp mill where it is crushed & the copper taken in the wash house.

Large iron lifters with heavy iron heads are raised by machinery & fall on the rock crushing it. Plenty of water is used in the iron buckets where the heads fall. They are cleaned twice a day— all the fine copper and fine rocks washes out through a sieve in front as the lifter falls. The cleanings taken out when they are cleaned consists of pieces of all sizes from one cent to the size of one's fist. The silver is picked out of this. This is barreled as well as the fine copper from the wash & sent below.

Mr. Rawlings has invented & put in operation a machine for separating the copper from the sand. It works fine—the copper coming out clean from it. The Cliff mine has raised about two hundred tons some months, a great portion of it being mass copper.

The stove and warehouse supplies the people with what they want & the cost is taken from their wages at the office. The supplies all come from below; in consequence, the winters are very unpleasant as there is nothing that can reach the place. It is quite a lively place to live in if a person is quite contented but it is not an agreeable place for a young man, as he will be shut from almost all society and comfort.

The English are coarse, uneducated, people, very rough in their manners and lack most of those qualities that make the man. It is true there are very honorable exceptions. The Germans are better informed. The Irish are of the rougher sort. They are all free partakers of strong drink and all evils of imtemperance in its worse stages are seen here.

I might relate many circumstances to illustrate the character of the people & give some account of the prospects of the country which are very flattering but having neglected to do so while living there I will merely close this unfinished article by saying that I was well pleased living there, have many firm friends and hope that I can visit the mining country of Lake Superior sometime.

Henry Hobart

October 2, 1863

Yesterday was a mild damp one and not over pleasant. In the afternoon it rained some. I spent the day at my sanctum viz the

Schoolroom laboring as hard as ever. I have no assistant. Emily Edwards, one of my pupils, helps me as Josiah is in the store which is opened with new goods. He is to work there for one or two weeks until the rush is over. I enjoy my School much better than last term.

It has been a cloudy foggy day [with] a mist falling this afternoon. I close teaching for the week. I shall dig potatoes tomorrow if nothing unusual occurs. I bought two pair of drawers, two undershirts & one outside flannel for eleven dollars this evening. I received a line from home yesterday. I am sorry that they have to work so hard in my absence and hope nothing bad will befall the dear ones at home. How seldom I receive any welcome news. I have had very few letters of late.

Mr. Vivian from England is here on a visit.[4] He is a tall well educated old Gent and a pure specimen of the Aristocracy. Although very Social and pleasant in conversion, I am constantly reminded of a "Lord or noble" when in his presence. Of course, he praises everything of the English Stamp, of the church of England etc. while his ideas of Yankees and their happy land are foolish and incorrect. He was disgusted with the River village and thought this place quite comfortable. I admire him for that for there is not a more God-forsaken hole in any part of the state. I will give some account of this filthy place in the chapter in the first part of this book.

October 5, 1863

Yesterday was a cold damp snowy day very muddy under foot. More dismal weather cannot be enjoyed this season of the year than we experienced the first of this month. It is well calculated to stir up a feeling of dislike for the country and a longing to see once more the Green hills of one's native land. The leaves have mostly fallen. The sky is cloudy obscuring the cheering light of the sun during the day. It is foggy most of the time and sleet & snow falling most of the time. The mud is mostly of a mucky sand & in many places quicksand. There is no clay— all that the miners use to hold their candles is brought up from the "Sault.

I went to quarterly meeting yesterday. The election of officers for the Sunday School was held. Captain Souden, Superintendent. I was put in Secretary and Librarian. In the evening Mr. Isaac

Bergan, a brother of Thomas Bergan, the drill sharpener, preached a sermon. He is a young man without an education as most of his expressions were very incorrect common errors were of constant occurrence. He has come to drive the Engine at the North Cliff which has just commenced work. James Willis is Captain of the mine.[5]

Mrs. Penberthy, John's wife, is assisting me at the School house. Everything moves very quietly and pleasantly. Mrs. Souden has given me an order for fifty-two dollars for painting the School house and one of twenty for attending to the Library one year. I must now record the drawing of Books from the Library this evening.

Do wise men ever fall in love. If they do not, virtuous women must be very unfortunate.

October 6, 1863

A cool cloudy morning with very little air stirring. Everything shows the evidence of approaching winter. The trees are bare or covered with yellow leaves. The ground is cold and wet. The "hogs" of our little city go round shivering and squealing. The people repair to the store and purchase flannels to protect from the long dreary winter. The boats will soon stop running and we shall be shut up from the States below. I care not for the dreary winter for I shall be clad in warm flannels and with a supply of apples, I can enjoy life in fine or Cornish style.

Evening and I am waiting for my supper—feel rather sour of course. My mouth waters for a pie or Yankee loaf of corn bread. Thanks to the "Misses" for I have had some pie of late, but I will turn my thoughts from eating as much as possible and say that I have had the best school today since I came here. My small pupils were under Mrs. Penberthy's care and how different and pleasant it seemed. I can see that I shall have a fine school and shall labor very hard to make it a model school.

I saw Miss Bennetts today. She is coming to my school soon. Her parents are from Richmond, Vermont and were intimate friends of Mr. Robinson.[6] All are anxiously looking for the next boat which is the *Iron City* due last Sunday. My anxiety for a supper is so great that I will close for fear I shall be writing about Yankee pies and suppers—which look like Gold in my eyes when I think of my present style of passing the hours.

October 7, 1863

How beautiful the sun breaks through the gloomy weather of the past few days imparting warmth to the air and pleasant sunshine on the cold damp ground. It is a lovely morning but clouds begin to appear from the north which will when obscuring the sun give a chill to the air that is very unpleasant. I send a letter home today. The *Planet* is up from Detroit.[7] The *Iron City* will come soon. Went down to Captain Paull's this evening and spent an hour very pleasantly. The Captain came home in the evening. He has been below and brought a stock of Goods. They are fine people and have a family of five children. Four of them attend my school.

> *Far from home the truant boy*
> *Skates over the frozen mead*
> *Till careless grown amidst the joy*
> *He falls and cracks his head.*

October 8, 1863

It has been a cool day and cloudy. Nothing has taken place of any importance. The *Iron City* is up bringing Mr. Updegraff, clerk of the mine. School passed very pleasantly. I think of showing my classes in Arithmetic the true principles or rules of analysis and have placed them in the mental Arithmetic.

I saw Captain Josiah [Halls] this evening. The stock of his mine is selling for fourteen dollars per share. He said Horatio will come and spend a few weeks with me. He was one of my favorite scholars and often fought a hard battle in spelling. Mr. Phillips' family came up from below today. *Bon soir*

A Scene on the Road

Last Sunday week I started with John Penberthy and wife for the river to visit Mr. Retallick and more especially to enjoy a walk on a pleasant day down the old road to the River through the woods. We went on Sunday as it was the only day in which we were not occupied. Feeling tired after a hard week's work this would be a pleasant walk. It was warm and the woods on either hand presented a golden appearance in consequence of the falling leaves. On the whole there was much to enjoy and we were in a very agreeable state to look and examine the beauties lavished on either hand among the thick growth of underbrush & tall trees. Occasionally the crack of the rifle is heard, the baying of hounds, showing that the poor hare was in danger. Nothing unusual took place and we reached the River and spent the day pleasantly. Seeing the Boat pass without coming in which is very annoying when one is anxious to hear news.

About six we started in Tommy George's team for the Cliff.[8] It was a moonlight evening and we were enjoying ourselves in pleasant talk, when our attention was attracted by a crowd of men the other side of the Phoenix. They were near the road. We held up and went to see the Elephant. A woman in a fit to all appearance. Her husband trying to make her rise & walk. Mrs. Mitchell has been regarded as a person of bad name. Her husband has caught a man with her often & there has been much trouble. The man kept coming when the husband was at work. The night in question he was walking out with the wife to the River and the husband caught him. The man made good his escape by taking leg bail. The husband desired the wife to return & had to use force to do it. She resisted and appeared to go into a fit but it was only a sham and her ravings were of no use. She was thrown into our wagon and taken home. The next morning the husband applied the horse whip which soon cured the fit. It is strange what feelings exist between husband and wife in many places here. Many are persons devoid of sham & without principle. May I never see such a miserable scenes any more for I should feel like using tar and feathers as a remedy. Shame on such families.

Beer, Gambling and A Fight

I find from observation that these three things go hand in hand with very many. In order to gamble Beer must be had by the quart, which will bring on a dispute about the game ending in a Bloody fight or one in which vigorous attempts will be made to draw blood. If a party of Beer-drinkers meet at a grocery or saloon after having a few "querts" of beer, old man, the next is a game of cards for money but most generally for a drop of the "Eye water." Well, "Beer Bellies" will have a dispute and a row generally ensues. Someone gets a black eye or bloody nose, & all get tight and well soaked.

A fight occurred at the boarding house in this place under just such circumstances as the above and one of the parties was well beaten by four others. There was a commotion there during the entire day. The

Boss was drunk and almost all others. He got two barrels of Beer in the morning. That was the cause. Watson has full power to prevent its sale on the location & it is to his shame that there is not man enough about him to perform a right duty.

October 10, 1863

I am now standing at my desk in the old school room. I have a small number of scholars as many are at work preparing for winter. It is a cold cloudy morning yet not unpleasant. Emily has brought me a fine bunch of grapes and the little girls a number of apples. They all like me and speak well of their teacher. This is pleasant & right. I hold that there should be good feeling and perfect love between pupil and teacher. The scholar should love and respect his instructor. It is false that they will learn best through fear or that success is found where the teacher exercises a tyrannical power and every pupil is afraid of him.

It is worthy of notice that this has been a pleasant day. The clouds have cleared away and the sun shines pleasantly. We may now enjoy what is called an Indian summer. I hope it may be so as it seems too soon to have winter.

Scene at my boarding place

It is a fact that the English people are well versed in tyrannizing over all who come under their authority. There is an aristocratic feeling that I detest. They look upon a servant as a dog & treat them as such. Mrs. Rawlings is a fine specimen of a totally ignorant English woman and a poor disciplinarian. She has had four girls this summer who have left rather than listen to her jawings. Louisa Jeffrey, one of my scholars, has been there some time perhaps.[9] She is slow, still she is young. It is shameful to listen to the scoldings & fault findings of Mrs. Rawlings about this girl. Today she gave her particular fits & she has gone home. Says Mrs. Rawlings: "If you was my girl I would beat the flesh from your bones. I would haunt the life out of you." A perfect storm of abuse was let off.

I speak of it as it stirs me to hear her tell about using girls well, bringing her children up well. They are not half brought up. A ridiculous set of young men knowing about how to treat persons well-puffed full of self-conceit and possessing a domineering disposition.

212

Treating girls well—far from it. I think of the management at home. How mother brought up her children. Think of tying a little girl six years old or striking her over the head & saying you would tear her to pieces. Is this a specimen of true management? But I will not speak any more about it. I despise the tyrannical disposition I see in this family from the oldest to the youngest. I have witnessed this feeling so peculiar to the true English Gent that I am heartily sick of it. Aristocracy, may I never live where its influence is felt.

Cleanliness

It is very well to talk about being neat and clean and much better to show by everything with which one has to do the marks of cleanliness. It is a good test of this noble quality to notice the appearance of an individual. If you see the marks of filth about the person it is very good evidence that the person is devoid of cleanliness. The appearance of very many of the children here is quite filthy. I think it is generally the case. Their smutty faces are sure indications of the appearance of the mothers at home. But above all the lousy heads that I see daily is better evidence. Black hair white with the eggs of the sweet animal. There are lice enough in the head of most any child to make a cornish pasty.

October 13, 1863

Since I last wrote in this Book the weather has been fine. The sun shines out very pleasantly every day and this weather is the "Indian Summer" that is enjoyed here before the winter comes with its chilling blasts of wind & snow. So soon as the boats stop running we shall not receive any mail for six weeks. It will be a lonesome time but we do not receive much mail now.

I commence evening school last night with twelve scholars.[10] Some of them have come to learn to read. These are mostly Germans. My labors have fairly begun for the winter. My school was very large today and by severe exertions I was only able to close school at five. I commenced again at six and kept until nine.

On going home found that a mail had come in during the afternoon on the *City of Cleveland*.[11] Nothing for me yet. I had some sport reading the papers. There is no important news from the war. Rosecrans was not beaten severely. He is now ready for another brush.

Public libraries

In a country like this where a majority of the people are unable to purchase books for want of means such an institution as a public library with a good selection of books is a good thing; but there are very few who can read or take any interest in it. If it is well supplied with stories it will have an extensive circulation; on the contrary, it will not. I am in favor of libraries in places like this and they should be good ones too. No trash but sound reading and plenty of it.

October 14, 1863

How pleasant and refreshing the air is. There is a slight breeze that gives a freshness to the atmosphere as it comes from the Lake. The sun shines brightly. School passes pleasantly.

October 20, 1863

I cannot find time to write anything here worthy of notice. My evening school takes all my spare time. The weather has been cool. Sunday it rained severe most of the day & also Saturday night. The brooks are very high. The wind blows quite hard this morning.

I will give here a sketch of a visit to Captain Halls of the North Western saying first that Mrs. Vaughan died last night.[12] She was in apparent good health.

Everyone here who ate some of the veal sold by Mr. Wilson has a turn of the back door trot or "Dictionary." What was the cause?

We have just received the papers informing us of the draft [with] 108 to come out of this county or almost every able-bodied man. I shall give some account of this scene when it takes place.

I received a good letter from home last night. Everything in a good condition. I am glad & doubt not they had a hard time during the Summer. Everyone who was drafted at our place paid the three hundred dollars & stayed at home. Some of them have become Copperheads in consequence of being obliged to pay three hundred dollars. They must have firm principles to be disturbed by so small a thing. Shame on the weak principled fools.

A tramp

Saturday about ten AM I started for the North Western to visit Captain Halls. It was quite pleasant but the roads were muddy and having only a pair of shoes I did not expect to find it very agreeable for the feet. I pursued my way calling at Captain Paull's and also at the new mine at the Phoenix and the Bay State mine. I then turned off into a path through the thick bush. The rest of my way, six miles lay through the woods along the foot of the Bluff on where a road is to be made called the mineral range road. The bush is composed of thick under brush and heavy timber. Now and then a few men could be seen digging in the side of the Bluff in search of copper. But the way was mostly lonely.

I arrived safe at the Captain's and found them in good health. I went down to the shaft they are sinking to strike the vein of the Central Mine. It has received the name of the "Bull Frog Mine." I spent the afternoon with Horatio looking around the Central.

In the evening I went with the Captain to a school meeting and like all school meetings in this country the officers of the school are the only ones present. This is a shameful practice and shows that there is very little interest manifested by parents to give their children a good education. They are generally willing to pay their tax but take very little interest in the school. They are about to build a large school house at the Central and North Western. A good place soon. I arose Sunday morning feeling well. It was quite stormy and there was a strong wind.

Captain Halls took the gun & shot at a rooster but missed him. I fired and knocked off a few feathers. The next time I took him in the head and neck. We did not shoot at the body and he being wild it was difficult to hit his head.

Had a fine dinner and a good talk. Gave my old Scholar Horatio a few lessons about making up ground, and at two I bade them farewell and started for the Cliff. The Captain & Horatio went about a mile with me.

I entered the bush and all went well until I met two Cornishmen carrying a Hedge Hog on a pole. They had a small dog that had caught one and filled his mouth and head full of the quills. One of them took the strap from his pants and put it around the Hog and swung him on a pole alive. He was very fat and I doubt not that they will use him for pasties. The little dog was very sober looking quite meek with the quills in his skin. I guess he felt so.

I reached the main road & it rained some, the wind blowing hard. Got home safe & ate half of a large pie I found in the pantry. It was a good treat & when Mrs. Rawlings returned from church she wanted to know why I did not eat some bread etc. but I told her I was well satisfied with the pie which surprised her some. I rested well that night and got up feeling refreshed after my tramp. I think a trip of this kind will be beneficial to me. I think I am gaining in flesh for I now weigh 163 pounds. Hope I may gain until I reach 200 when I will be quite a man physically. More as I find time.

October 22, 1863

It is a cool morning and the ground is white with a little snow. It is froze so there is very little mud. There is some wind. Yesterday it was stormy and cold.

Captain Joseph Vivian is here for the last time before going below. He cannot eat or take anything at his brother's at the River who has a large family and everything is unclean so it makes him sick to look at it. He hates the place above anything that he ever saw. I am of the same opinion. It is a drunken dirty place. I know of no place so deserving the vengeance of a drunken dirty place. I know of no place so deserving the vengeance of heaven as the River.

I will pen a few lines before my night scholars come as I am here waiting to begin my evening work. School has not been as pleasant today as usual for I had to punish a scholar harder than I ever did before. I done it in Yankee style over the "tail of 'im" as a Cornishman would say. Mr. Rawlings is quite unwell with a sore throat. It is the result of having wet feet & exposure.

Two of my Scholars were at play this evening at home with an ax & one cut a finger off from the other. They were small boys belonging to Mr. Phillips. Parents should avoid or be careful about letting small children use sharp tools. A little care will save their little boys from many severe injuries. I learn that a small boy lost his finger in the same way at the River a short time since carelessness is the cause of many accidents.

October 23, 1863

It is snowing some and is quite cool. The ground is frozen some and I hope it will be any warmer for I prefer cool weather to the mud. This is a place where there is a constant monotony in every thing making a sameness in my writing.

I know of no place except the River so bad for an idler as this. Mr. Vivian took his farewell this morning and will go below on the first boat. My boys are out sleigh-riding this morning on the plank sidewalk.

The papers say that seventy persons are to be drafted from our village next Monday. A Schooner was wrecked on the sand just below the Dock at the River. The Captain thinks it a great mercy that he was saved from a watery grave to be drunk in the Streets every since. Quite a gentlemen I should judge.

Evening

I received a good old letter from my kind Friend Jesse of Williston who declares that he is as busy as usual and is not attracted from home by the charms of the fair sex. O, Jesse, you are always laboring for the good of someone, but I dare say you are a constant visitor to the homes of the ladies in your vicinity.

Nothing very important for me to scribble about tonight. Mr. Baughman is here on a visit and the minister for this place has come also. I intend inviting them to visit the school.

I hear that Miss Pope is to assist me in my school. If so, I hope she will do much better than she looks as if she could, but I will give a good criticism when I see more about her manner of governing and teaching.

October 24, 1863

The sky is overcast with dark clouds. A cold chilly wind from the north reminds one of the approaching dreary winter. There is one inch of snow on the ground and the Thermometer was down to twenty-four degrees. I was up this morning at six that is up in bed. I took a walk up to the mine before breakfast. I sent a line to the dock agent, Mr. Winslow, for some apples. I will write more while opening the library this afternoon. My labors as teacher are now over for the day. I shall remain until five & then I have my time. I have a barrel of apples at the warehouse. Expect some comfort eating them this winter. Mrs. Rawlings says she will not cook any more fixings; it is so expensive. She has made a few sour pies.

Form of Marriage

I, Arthur, on Monday,
Take thee, Annie, till Tuesday
To have and to hold till Wednesday,
For better for worse till Thursday,
I'll kiss thee on Friday,
If we don't agree on Saturday,
We'll part again on Sunday.

The experience of many a life—"What a fool I've been." The experience of many a wife—"What a fool I've got."

A young lady say that if a cart-wheel has nine fellows attached to it—it's a pity that a girl like her can't have one.

What medicine are we reminded of by a man beating his wife? Elixir. (He licks her.)

October 26, 1863

There is a steady sameness about the weather for a few days being in the neighborhood of freezing—very pleasant for one who is dressed warm. This afternoon the sun came out warm enough to moisten the surface of the ground.

Today is the time set for the draft. I learn that the "Marshall" is up and is going to make some arrangement to secure volunteers.[13] I think it will be very difficult.

I went and heard Mr. Baughman preach his farewell sermon last night. Everyone is sorry the good old Gentlemen is going away. We doutless have a good preacher viz Mr. Wright.[14] He resembles Chapin of New York —has been a chaplain in the army. His home is in Ohio. I hope he will be a powerful preacher and then there will be some satisfaction in listening to him.

I have so got the control of my Scholars by mild means that everyone is free from whispering without leave. I present them a handsome ticket every four weeks for being perfect. It works fine and is the best course for governing a school.

I received a letter from Miss Maria Hyde applying for a situation as teacher.[15] She was one of my Scholars when I taught in the District situated on the beautiful Grand Isle of Lake Champlain. It is now too late to secure the services of any good teacher from below as the boats will not run long. I am sorry for I shall have the poorest kind of help for the winter I am thinking. Mr. Watson, the agent, has returned from below. Everything is on the move preparing for the winter. I must commence my evening work.

October 27, 1863

Thermometer indicating the pleasant temperature of nineteen degrees. It reminds one that his bones will soon shake with the cold. This evening it is mild and pleasant. The warming influence of the sun's rays has caused the surface of the ground to moisten and a little mud appears in the roads. The ice on small ponds is hard enough to hold a man's weight. I have nothing special to write except that I hear that General [George Gordon] Meade has retreated to his fortifications around Washington. General Lee is maneuvering his troops and threatens General Meade. It is difficult to tell what will be the result of this state of things.

Confinement

How perfect an idea a person will gain of anything by experience, by allowing himself to undergo every change and passing through every course necessary to fully explain or understand its meaning. I fancy that I have a good if not perfect idea of not only the word but its meaning viz Confinement. I have a good idea of hard work being brought up as a hard worker but there is some comfort, some relaxation for an individual. In the schoolroom I find no relaxation, no rest. It is constant exertion of the severest kind under the most perplexing circumstances in order to close by five commencing at nine. Again at six & close at nine at night. The only time I find is in the morning & I am forced to employ that in writing and doing such work as falls to the lot of the teacher. I feel completely tired out this evening.

October 28, 1863

A mild day after a cold night. It is very cloudy and was quite dark when I closed school for the day— worked very hard & must go at it this evening. Nothing unusual has taken place today in our city. Without writing further I must now hear the miners read etc.

A row in which I came very near entering into a fight in self-defense.

I returned home tired after school and pulling off my shoes sat down by the stove to warm up well before retiring to rest little dreaming that I should be the object of the most violent hatred and receive the vilest abuse. Timmy and Ellen, the hired girl, & myself were engaged in quiet talk. Very soon Mr. & Mrs. Carter came in having just come from his sister's whose child just died. Carter was half-intoxicated and had abused his wife on the way home. He commenced abusing her and soon struck & caught hold of her, tearing her dress & pulling out her hair. She called on me to save her. I knew his jealous nature and did not move but had Timmy interfere & Mrs. Carter ran out the back door to one of the neighbors. In a violent & insulting manner he accused me of playing with his wife on the sly. He would stick daggers to my heart & he would fight one of us at a time etc. For one half an hour I set calmly under the worst abuse I ever heard & never said a word. I think I acted wisely in not replying or offering to fight when he was swinging his fists about me. I did not wish to have it reported that we had had a fight about his wife. I do not know how I kept my seat for I was full of wrath at the abuse.

October 29, 1863

Not cold but cloudy. Rain and snow falling this afternoon and it is very wet under foot. I think it will freeze tonight. There is about three inches of snow. I learn that Mrs. Carter is drunk at one of the neighbors. I am vexed to think that Mrs. Rawlings gives them a home & will soon procure board in another house if they are not sent away. There is a drunken row every night and someone is accused of meddling with his shameful wife. I expect that there will be some story going around the location. I am confident of one thing. I will not listen to such abuse again from a drunken Irishman. How foolish to take the part of a woman of so low a character as Mrs. Carter and I blame Mrs. Rawlings for it. If it were my house they should never have entered it.

In my experience as a teacher I have found very few Scholars who could give a proper explanation of the various principles that are brought out in the various steps in Arithmetic or in fact any study. It is certainly true that most Scholars go over the pages of the Book and yet know very little of the truths that lie at the base of every calculation principle. If this is the case quite generally it is good evidence to prove that Teachers fail to instruct right. They must take a wrong course and as a general thing they are like the old Connecticut clocks that run just so fast and long when they stop. A new interest should be created & this subject should be agitated until the evil is put down.

October 30, 1863

A Cloudy morning. Snow about three inches deep some during the night. I had my foot measured for a pair of shoes for the school house. I sent to the River for a pair of German socks to wear out. Then I shall be well prepared for the rough weather that will soon come. Mrs. Penberthy closes her labors with me today. I suppose she has done well and the little ones under her care have made good progress. She has taken pains and trained them very well. I hope her successor will do as well.

Stock speculation

Buying and Selling to make money has been quite a business in this Region of country. There has been a vast amount of speculation as copper commands a high price. Everything that looks like a "Vein" has been worked for copper & thousands of dollars made out of worthless mine by mere speculation. I saw a man who invested in one of these small mines & lost his money & he said if a white spot was found on a rock they would call it a vein & work it at once. It is true many small mines are being worked that will fail as soon as the price of copper falls. A mass is often found & the Stock is ten or fifteen dollars higher at once. Much Money is thus made. Central mine stock is now worth fifty dollars more than it was two years ago. Phoenix Stock is twenty dollars higher than it was six months ago. Bay State & North Western the same. By investing when it is low & selling when it is high the money is made. Mr. Watson is now rich by doing so; also Captain Souden & many others here. Play the Sharp and get rich in a short time without work.

Notes for September–October 1863

1. The sidewheeler *Sunbeam* foundered off Eagle Harbor on August 28, 1863, with a loss of some thirty lives. It was built in Manitowoc, Wisconsin in 1861. Frederick Stonehouse, *Keweenaw Ship Wrecks* (Au Train, Michigan: Avery Color Studios, 1988), pp. 57-60; John Brant Mansfield, editor and compiler, *History of the Great Lakes* (Chicago: J. H. Beers, 1899), p. 891.

2. The Reverend Robert Bird was minister to the Methodist Church in Eagle Harbor, Clifton, and the Portage Lake Missions from 1859 to his death in 1863. R. Charles Stetter, *The Central Methodist Episcopal Church: A Short History* (1971), p. 25.

3. John Woodward, age 21, was listed in the *8th U.S. Census*, Chittenden County, Vermont, 1860, as a college student.

4. The visit of Captain Joseph Vivian was covered in the *Lake Superior Miner*, September 26, 1863.

5. James Willis also served as School Inspector for the Clifton School in 1864-1865. *School Inspector Report*, Clifton, Michigan, year ending September 1865. Michigan State Archives.

6. Ascher Robinson was a classmate of Hobart's at Williston Academy in 1859. *Williston Academy Catalogue*, 1859. *The 8th U. S. Census*, Houghton County, 1860, lists an Ascher Robinson, a school teacher, born in Vermont, age twenty-one. He resided with Hervey C. Parke, the clerk of the Company Store, who later founded the Parke Davis Pharmaceutical Firm in Detroit. Walter Buell, "Hervey C. Parke," *Magazine of Western History* (September, 1886). Ascher Robinson is also listed in the *8th U.S. Census*, Vermont, Chittenden County, as a commercial school teacher, age twenty-nine. It is possible that Ascher Robinson and Ascher Robinson, both born in Vermont, are the same person. If so, there is a mistake in the age.

7. The sidewheel steamer, *Planet*, 1164 tons, was built in Newport, Rhode Island in 1853. Mansfield, *History of the Great Lakes*, vol. 1, p. 874; Nute, *Lake Superior*, p. 312.

8. Tommy George was the nine-year-old son of Henry and Jane George. *8th U.S. Census*, Houghton County, 1860.

9. Louisa Jeffrey was the daughter of James and Ann Jeffrey. In 1860, her parents were ages 48 and 44 respectively, and had three children—Elizabeth, age 14, Louisa, age 12, and John, age 8. James was listed as a tavern keeper in Eagle River. *8th U.S. Census*, Houghton County, 1860.

10. For an evaluation of Hobart's night school see: Marquis E. Shattuck, "Adult Education Childhood," *Michigan Educational Journal* 35 (January 1958), pp. 188, 198-202.

11. The 788-ton sidewheel steamer, *The City of Cleveland*, was built in Buffalo in 1857 and operated on the Lake Superior Line. It was stranded at Eagle Harbor in May 1863, but the damages were minor and it was soon returned to service on the Lakes. In 1867 it was made into a barge

and was operated on Lake Erie. Mansfield, *History of Great Lakes*, p. 806; *Detroit Free Press*, April 16, 1861; Grace Lee Nute, *Lake Superior* (New York: Bobbs-Merrill), pg. 312; Stonehouse, *Keweenaw Ship Wrecks*, p. 55.

12. Mary P. Vaughan, the wife of Joel Vaughan, died at the age of 38. The funeral was held the Grace Episcipol Church on October 21, 1863. She was buried in the Clifton Cemetary. *8th U.S. Census*, Houghton County, 1860.

13. The "Marshall" to whom Hobart refers was Colonel William B. Wright, a U .S. Army veteran. Born in New Jersey in 1814, he served in the U .S. Army during the Black Hawk War and the Indian War in Florida. Later he was appointed Ordinance sergeant at Fort Wilkins where he served until 1855. He reenlisted in 1862 and led a recruiting campaign in Northern Michigan. After the Civil War, he operated the Phoenix House in Eagle River, and served as Superintendent of the Poor for Keweenaw County, School Director and Sherff. *History of the Upper Peninsula*, p. 341

14. According to the *Lake Superior Miner*, October 3, 1863, D.C. Wright was appointed minister of the Methodist Episcopal Church at Clifton.

15. Maria Hyde, age 17 in 1860, was the daughter of George W., age 49, and Eva, age 35 , Hyde of Grand Isle, Vermont. Her brother Randolph, age 20 in 1860, was a classmate of Hobart's at Williston Academy in 1859. *Williston Academy Catalogue*, 1859 and *8th U.S. Census*, Grand Isle, 1860.

and was oriented on Lake Erie, Mansfield, History of Great Lakes, p. 600.

Detroit Free Press, April 16, 1864; Canal of Nails, Lake Superior News and

*"There is a comfortable look around a Lake Superior man's dress," wrote Hobart.
But the "rough-looking bluff" of the Cliff Mine on the following page gave him
painful contrast with the hills and valleys of his native Vermont.*

November—December 1863

November 2, 1863

The wind is blowing a gale this afternoon and I can hear the roar of the waves as they dash against the rocky shore three miles away. It must be bad for any Boats out on the Lake. Rain is falling most of the time; it is muddy under foot and it is truly a disagreeable day.

My school was not very large—six night scholars in [all]. Arrangements are being made to secure Miss Nutt to assist me.[1] She has had some experience and will doubtless do very well.

I heard our new minister last evening. He had a very good sermon and showed much energy in speaking. His style is quite different from Mr. Baughman's and I must say that I prefer listening to the sound reasoning of Mr. Baughman, yet I suppose I am not fully prepared to judge as one trial will not show his beauties fully. It was cold as the stoves have not been put up yet. I find that I have a severe cold and my lungs are very sore. Miss Amelia Hutchinson has come from below to work for Mrs. Rawlings. She is a tall red-head without education and very soft I should judge by the kisses she lavishes on the boys. I suppose she thinks herself excusable because she was acquainted with them formerly. But I could hardly justify such conduct by any acquaintance except it be between two lovers. How it might work that then those who have experienced such change could affirm much better than I could. I doubt not, however, it is very pleasant apparition to pass through. It is not our beliefs & convictions that frighten us half as much as our fancies.

November 4, 1863

A beautiful morning. The sky is clear; the sun shines pleasantly and there is a brisk breeze from the South which is not uncomfortable notwithstanding it is cool. How fresh everything in the sky and air looks

Yesterday was a very disagreeable day. My school was small. Several night scholars were in. Had a quiet time in the evening although I was very tired after the exertions of the day. I feel some evenings as if I could drop down I am so tired. Sam James, who was school inspector, is attending my evening school. He is studying arithmetic. I must now go to the schoolhouse. *"Il est temps pour commecer mon ecole pour au jourd hui. Ecrit per Henri."*

Mrs. Carter has gone away on a spree. She has taken her oath against drink and is off tight again. I think it is a strange principle that will influence anyone to sustain or even harbor a woman of so mean a character. She should be despised and shuned by all decent people. There should be some limit to sympathy. It should not be extended too far. It is right to sympathize with one in trouble but if a lady takes drink & is a person of ill fame how could I sympathize with her now if she takes her oath against drink and endeavors by strong efforts to shun the evil she is deserving of some credit—but if she seeks some opportuinty to violate that oath when she is not surrounded by temptation I say she should be shunned by every decent person. If she persisted in such a course I would not sympathize with her enough to protect her from the cold or give her anything to eat. How could a reform be effected if she is fed & sheltered while her earning go for drink. I say hunt her out of the place. Shun her always.

November 12, 1863

I find that I have neglected writing in my journal for want of time. If it were not for my evening school I could fill out one or two pages here each day on some subject to my lasting benefit.

226

But from nine in the morning my toils continue until nine in the evening & am generally very busily employed every morning.

We have had coolish weather for some time. There has been no remarkable change. The Lake has been quite rough. The Boats are on their last trip.

Saturday the teacher at the Central Mine visited me. He is to all appearances a fine young man. We shall have some sparing in spelling this winter, I think. Horatio Halls was one of my first spellers and he has gone to the North Western mine to live and intends giving my pupils a try this winter. I shall endeavor to make all needed preparations to meet him in a warm manner. If I can discharge a few heavy guns I am in hopes of breaking through his coat of mail and sending him back crippled if not whipped. My pupils are fully awake to the business. Frank Ten Broeck is very sick with the inflammation of the lungs. He is inclined to consumption & will doubtless have a severe time. Most everyone has a severe cold. I have had one too.

I have paid one dollars and twenty-five cents to have two flannels made for the winter. I am in hopes of keeping warm during the cold weather that will come soon. I bought the cloth for a pair of apnts for which I paid six dollars and fifty cents. I must have them made soon.

November 14, 1863

I am now attending to distribution of the Books of the Public Library. I have not taught school today. I took a list of the books in the Sabbath School Library at the Methodist church and marked the new books preparatory to giving them out tomrrow. It took me until noon. I shall go down to Captain Paull's this evening for recreation. I wish I could do as I used to when Saturday came—go and visit home and friends. Such an opportunity would be a great pleasure.

I look out from my schoolhouse where my time is mostly spent on the wilderness and rough-looking bluff. I look at the white log huts of the miners and contrast the scene with the valleys & hills around my good home. A feeling gives me longing desires to take conveyance for Yankee land, and once more enjoy home scenes I look back three or four years and say to myself it is strange that I am here writing in this school house. The darkness is coming on and as I write I wonder what fond parents are doing, and Getrie and Florence. Are they all at home enjoying the comforts of a warm fire etc. I cannot tell. I hope for the best. How I would like to call in and give them a surprise. There is beauty in the song "Do They Miss Me at Home." But home is far away and cannot be reached without great expense and exertion. Spring will open the cold barriers that are now closing up the passage of boats and then I think of directing my steps of Home. O may I meet all in health. How uncertain it is; many have died since I left home. May I meet all in health and happiness

Miss Nutt is to be my assistant in school commencing Monday. She is a young lady of good education and has taught some below.

November 18, 1863

We are now enjoying splendid weather. The nights are clear and the sun shines beauitfully every day. It was very warm today. The thermometer indicates a change of over thirty degrees between the temperature of each day and night. This is quite large. It is remark-able that there is no snow on the ground at this time of the year and I for one long to see it a foot deep for this reason. My school-house is very unclean. One hundred and fifty scholars will make much dirt in weather like this—but when the snow falls it will then be clean. The school is in fine condition at present.

Miss Nutt is laboring earnestly to promote the interests of every pupil under her care. I think a better report will soon be given of the primary department. This is right. It is hard to affirm that a teacher cannot make any impression of a scholar towards improve-ment in a year's time. It is a poor recommendation for a teacher. I think this was true with Miss Cundy. My evening school is in very good condition now.

I received a fine letter from my sister, Florence, the other day and a letter from Cousin G. A. Eastman. I wrote a reply to George's letter & will soon to Florence.

Mr. Wright—the new minister

I do not deign here to give a criticism of this gent, merely to make a few remarks. He is a fine-looking man and doubtless has a good education. His forte as a minister is to have a revival and all his labors aim at that one thing. He gives a short sermon on Sunday evening and then tries to create some excitement by having a prayer meeting. We miss the sound logical sermons of Mr. Baughman's Sunday evenings. There was much information in them & they were pleasant to hear.

November 19, 1863

I neglected to write at the time of this date and it is now Saturday and I am attending to the distribution of books. I have had a very pleasant time. The school was not large and had a good time. In the afternoon we spelt down once. Stephen and Annie Paull stood up the longest & both got down on the same word.[2] After spelling down, we had an exercise in speaking. My pupils have made a fine beginning in speaking and writing compositions. I do not know that I ever had a school that made a beginning so willingly, I received fifteen compositions after the first call. This is a fine beginning. They are all working very well and are making fine progress. I am told that Edward Penberthy is to teach the school at the River. I will speak sometime of this work and its author. My evening school is in very good condition. Mr. Rawlings is quite unwell. He has a cold.

Lessons from evening school

The fact that a person will grow up without an education and look back with regret upon his youthful days spent in neglect is truly exemplified in the evening school. I have one [a school] composed of working men from fifteen to fifty. Some come in unable to tell a letter—others can cipher a little or read some. How sadly they regret their misspent time while young or that they had no chance to attend school. They would give most anything to be a good scholar. Some men are coming to me who cannot cipher any who send three or four scholars to day school. The School Inspector sends four children and comes himself to evening school. Parents, give your children good education and they will bless you when old.

November 22, 1863

How pleasantly and quietly I have passed the day without any accident or meeting with anything to disturb my mind. I went to Sunday School. I gave out a very large number of books, and spoke to the School. Mr. Wright, our new minister, was there. He took no part in the school. He is a man of no great mind and aims at one of these exciting revivals which I do not believe in.

I was glad to hear Captain Souden express his mind to him [Wright] very freely. Last Sunday evening he [Wright] made a call on the members to come forward and have a prayer meeting. They do not believe in such a course & did not do so. He spoke quite insultingly about it and the captain took him in hand today. He [the captain] told him [Wright] that he was not a gentleman.

Mr. Souden is a sound man of good information & there are many others. Mr. Baughman's preaching was of the right kind—sound, logical and full of instruction. His sermons were beautiful and very impressive. They were full of reasoning of the best kind. I never listened to a man who could give so beautiful a course of sermons as did Mr. Baughman during the year that he was here. I regret that he is gone. How pleasant to go and listen to an instructive sermon. I would be influenced by good sound reasoning. Excitement would not influence me. The ignorant are very zealous during the excitement. When that cools down they are as cool and indifferent as ever. Some make a good use of it and improve after conversation. I am not a believer in any excitement of this kind, Give me sound preaching.

November 23, 1863

I have just returned from the wash house and it is now ten o'clock. James is working tonight as boss in the wash. He has only a few men to look too and gets along nicely. He is Mr. Davey's assistant in the day time. The night boss was sick to day.

I gave out the tickets in school this morning to all the scholars who had not whispered without leave. This is a system that I have hit upon myself after trying the usual means to overcome the wholesale whispering that is the main feature of too many schools. By this course there is not half as much trouble and my mind is relieved from much of the care, and anxiety attending any other course. I have become a disbeliever in punishment in the school room. I believe in mild means for I have found it the best. I have not been governed by anyone's theory—it is a result of my own experience and I can show as fine a school as anyone. I have no rulers or whips. I have scholars who love me and who are willing to act as I desire. How pleasant.

There is something peculiar in the weather that should be noticed. It is cold but there is very little snow on the ground only two inches in all. For a country as cold as this it is a remarkable thing. It is almost December yet we have no severe storms and cold days. As I write I wonder what kind of weather Vermonters at home are enjoying. I should like to hear from home and also the war news. I suppose it will be sometime before I have a letter as we must now wait for an overland mail. It will be about six weeks before any can reach us.

I am informed by Captain Josiah Halls that their teacher at the Central Mine has gone below as he received a letter informing him of the death of his father. He was a very good teacher I think and we should have had some fine times this winter in the spelling ex-cerise. If Edward Penberthy teaches the school at the River I will show him how a Yankee can train scholars. He is bragging but will sing a milder tune after trying his hand for a while. It is not all success and honor. A person must have judgment & common sense also prudence etc. which I think he lacks.

November 24, 1863

The clouds are thick and heavy; the air seems to be filled with smoke. There is no wind and it is quite a pleasant morning that is it is not very cold. A person having time would find it a nice time to take a walk. How I long to be free, to enjoy a tramp and above all peace of mind. I should enjoy a rest finely, a respite from the labor of the school room. How tiresome the labor—ten months without vacation and an evening school half of the time. It takes the very life out of a healthy person. I feel as soft and weak as a milkweed. There is none of that healthy lively feeling. A sleepy tired sensation is all the time. I must commence school now. Evening.

Mrs. Rawlings as a Mother

This good English lady with whom I stay prides herself as a person who can train a family rightly. This evening there was quite a row with the two boys, Jimmy & William . . . . To boss seems to be the main feature in this family. If one of the older boys is called upon to do anything, he says one of the younger ones must do it.

They are well pleased if they have some one to boss but will never do anything themselves. Ignorant, self conceited things. They seem to know everything and know nothing. It is all right if I split all the wood. And I am busy all the time in evening school or writing. How can I teach all the time and split all their wood. I will not do it. Mrs. Rawlings likes Edward & thinks he is the height of perfection. This is right enough but if she would learn them common sense & decency it would be much better. I never saw a more disobedient set of boys or more disagreeable in their ways. They lack all the qualities of gentlemen. Edward has just gone to teach the River School with the idea that he has an easy task and that everyone will honor him.

November 26, 1863

It is cool still morning the thermometer standing at about twenty-four degees. I took a walk up to the mine with Mr. Rawlings this morning. Last evening I received the returns from the Boston Brokers in relation to my stock. I have seven shares in the North Cliff Mine for which I gave fifty dollars. I do not expect to make anything now. I could have sold out for sixty if I had received returns before. This is Thanksgiving Day, I think, appointed by the President. It is not observed among miners but I think they have a day for it at some other time. I taught school and often thought how it was spent in Vermont. The turkeys had to take it, I think.

Arithmetic

There are very few who know how to give young minds thorough instruction in this important Branch of Study. A self-conceited young man says he thinks he can do all the examples in the Common School Arithmetic and therefore concludes that he is fitted to impart instruction to others. He applies for a School and perhaps on the committee is a relative which of course gives him the place. Now such a teacher is worthless. He know nothing about the correct method of explaining an example or how to convey correct impressions in simple and proper language. To work an example is one thing to explain it so that the young mind will comprehend it is another. A teacher must be experienced and make his profession a study. Give such explanations as convey in full his idea and in the simplest possible form. A scholar should be required to give the explanations himself until he can comprehend every step fully. It is not the mere working of examples that gives a knowledge of figures. It is more. The reasons etc. must be understood and why every step is taken. It is a subject that every teacher should understand thoroughly.

November 27, 1863

This is a stormy day. The snow is falling quite fast which makes it very uncomfortable as it is quite cold. I received a new pair of pants today which cost me about eight dollars. They are made of the very heaviest cloth. I know it is best to buy cloth that is durable and lasting. A cheap pair will not last long. I must now have my scholar spell down and will close school about three, I think.

Prospect of a fight in Schoolhouse /Yankee Spunk dispels the trouble

The "itch" in a school is very bad. It has made its appearance in this District and two of my pupils I sent home who had it. I was told by good authority of whom they took it & was told to send home suspicious ones. I sent home a boy whose sisters were said to have it telling him to remain until it was decided. The uncle came in & proceeded to take me in hand in the Cornish style. I answered him firmly telling him I was not to listen to an insult. He said he would split my Dam[n] head open. I told him I was Yankee enough to have him try it on as soon as he pleased. I shut the door in his face & he went home. In the afternoon the Father came in & told me that I done perfectly right that the Doctor should examine & see.

Captains Harry and Souden visited the School. I think the thing will not spread for I shall look out & prevent it if possible. I am aware that it is not any business to take an insult from anyone when in the school room. I said nothing about it however but Captain Souden told the fellow he would give him a steady home if he done it again.

November 29, 1863

Snow has been falling since yesterday morning and there is about a half feet on the ground now. The thermometer is down to ten degrees and the windows are covered with frost giving that it is cold winter. How dismal it looks shut off from the world below and compelled to stay in this dreary region. To be contented anywhere will wear off some of the rough features of any country. Things will not have an appearance so desolate, and uncomfortable a look. It will be quite pleasant.

I listened to Mr. Wright in the evening. He had a good sermon showing man's accountability to God etc., but it was not a piece or sermon of such interest that is there were very few new ideas in it. It was after the common sort. There is not that power & life that beauty & freshness full of new & beautiful ideas & reasoning that is one of the finest features of Mr. Baughman's sermons. He always had some thing new & interesting. I heard Mr. Johnson (Episcopal) in the afternoon. He had a fine sermon full of interest and new thoughts.

> *In eating you are quick*
> *In going you are slow*
> *Eat with your feet Friend Dick*
> *And use your jaws to go*

December 2, 1863

The sun shines brightly and although it is very cold it is pleasant. It was quite warm yesterday and fine snow balling and I had a battle with the scholars. Last night it froze very hard making it very slippery. It is fine sleighing and the wood teams pass now & then.

Frank Ten Broeck is very sick. He has consumption. The Doctor says one lung has gone entirely. He is around the store some days and then he is very bad again. This is generally the case I think in consumption. Sometimes the person is very sick and at other times he is quite well or at least feels so. I should try and leave this country as soon as possible if I was inclined that way for the air is too bracing and it is too cold here. It is generally believed that this is not a good place for consumption. I am inclined to believe it to be true for almost every person coming here with it lays his bones on this cold point if he remains. Persons have come here for health supposing that the climate would be of benefit but it is too strong, too bracing & unhealthy. There is a curious sickness here now— some call it the "Influenza." I suppose that is nothing more than a cold. Most everyone is or has been sick with it. Some of the boys & girls are unable to speak or make any noise scarcely they are so hoarse. Very many are going around with Flannels on their necks, and are unable to work. I am free from anything of the kind &

hope I may continue to be. I have been quite unwell about the di-gestive organs, & find I must look out about eating as I am so con-fined that I am not very healthy or feeling well.

December 3, 1863

The wind is making music around my old school house giving the place a lonely feeling or appearance. It has been a mild day. Good snowballing for those who like the sport. It is fine sleighing and everyone is alive to have a sleigh ride. Dogs are harnessed to sleighs or small sleds men or women in the sled urge them along by a brisk application of the lash—very pleasant. To see one or two men on a sled drawn by one dog looks rather cruel but for boys it is not as bad for the load is not as heavy. It is quite amusing and fine sport.

Jimmy the Simpleton

In witnessing the actions & saying of this boy of seventeen years I cannot apply any better name to him than the above. There is al-most as much man about him as there is about a milkweed that has grown up in the shade. A self-conceited proud, cross specimen of a windy young or great boy. In the first place, he never reads any-thing & secondly, knows nothing. Thirdly, he assumes to know ev-erything and is as saucy and abusive as he can be. Fourthly, he insults his mother in the most shameful manner & never does any-thing when called upon. His little brothers must do everything and he must boss them and make them do as he says.

I am well aware that he is very good when he has is own way & someone flatters him. But there is very little of that firm principle about him which should be the main or principle groundwork of every young man's action on which to build a good character. How mean it looks in a young man to see him get in a passion & cry about nothing or when called upon to do something by his mother. How would look for a young man of eighteen.

December 7, 1863

It has been a mild day and in the afternoon commenced raining and finally snowed some. It is a wet time, not very pleasant for walking. It is fine sleighing and the stages run through to the Portage quite regular.

Captain Josiah and Mary Halls were here on Sunday. Emily Edwards went home with them to stop a few days. Ed[ward Penberthy] was up boasting about his success as a Teacher. How he could give them the rod. I hope he will learn something while engaged as a teacher. I have had many very good lessons. If could engage in anything that would deprive him of his self conceit it would be a good job.

A Sad Affair

I hear that a drunken husband drove his wife outdoors at midnight with a little boy at the Phoenix mine. The mother and child were without clothing and were found the next morning frozen in the cold snow a few rods from the house without any clothing. It is stated that they were both drunk which I am inclined to believe as they often drink and he has turned her out before. It was not so cold but what she might have found shelter in houses near by if she had been sober. If she was drunk she would not think of he thing. It is a sad affair. How that little boy must have felt taken from a warm bed out into the cold to be frozen to death on the body of his mother. This is one of the results of drinking. It should be put down. A man going to church next morning saw them by the road side. He went to the house & called the husband asking who it was— he replied he did not know — but imagine his feelings on seeing them dead. He is free by a jury.

December 9, 1863

It is a cold morning and the air is filled with "frost." The wind blows quite strong mak[ing] it quite unpleasant for traveling. Snow is falling some and sleighing is very good.

Yesterday it was very mild and fine snow balling. I had a few new scholars yesterday which makes a large school for me to manage. I have hard work and from this constant confinement I feel lazy or as if my life were worn out. I long for some smart exercise, for a change. Confinement with such care as I have is very severe. It can hardly be endured. I think I will take a run down to the Captain's after school.

A Romance

The following is the way of writing a modern romance.: "Albert rode with the speed of an arrow to the garden, sprang like the wind from his steed, climbed like a squirrel over the hedge, writhed like a snake through the palings, flew like a hawk to the arbor, crept to her all unseen, threw himself passionately at her feet, swore frantically that he would shoot himself unless she would hear him; was however immediately heard, seated himself in blessed delight at her side, sank on her bosom, swam in a sea of bliss"—all this was the work of a second.

I have just received a letter from Miss Cundy, formerly my assistant. She is now going to school at Ypsilanti. She affirms that she is doing finely. I hope it may be true. She ought to have a good education which will take her some time to get. Miss Nutt, my assistant now, is getting along finely. She makes the small ones toe the mark. They need it very much. Success to her labors.

December 14, 1863

We are now in the fullness of a Lake Superior winter. The wind is blowing very strong from the north & coming off from the Lake. There is a coldness & freshness that is not felt by land breezes. The air is filled with snow and it is drifting very high. Everything is white. A person traveling a few minutes will be as white as a polar bear. The thermometer is at about ten degrees, not very cold if it were not for the wind and frost & snow that is blowing through the air. It is very blinding and is quite different from any such weather in Vermont. The frost seems to come from the Lake. Three of my little boys came in this morning with their hands frozen. My school was small.

There is a comfortable look about a Lake Superior man's dress. He wears a Mackinac coat with a hood that covers the head. Shoepacks or moccasins on his feet and then places him on a small sled with a dog for a horse & it is a pleasant sight. But very many of the children are very poorly clad. I am glad that I have spent some time here at least one winter. Still there is a dread about remaining through the cold winter. If I should receive bad news from home I could not leave here for there is no way until near spring. Still I hope for the best. May no such news reach me while in this new country.

Ed Penberthy came up yesterday with Mrs. & Miss Vivian. He was in ecstasy & fairly made an ass of himself going on with nonsense & foolishness. Miss Vivian appears like a very fine young lady. She has poor health which is very bad for one of so lively a disposition. Ed is spending his money.

December 15, 1863

It is a cold still morning and the snow is piled up in large drifts and banks. Small pupils are at home these days mostly as they cannot reach the house. I went out and broke roads with my boys. School quite small. Everything passes pleasantly except we cannot receive any mail. No news reaches us. I dislike to live here on this account. Everything is stale and old when it reaches us. Provisions as well as mails are generally unfit for anyone to use. If we could receive mail every evening with the latest telegraphic dispatches fresh from the seat of war, it would be a very great comfort. It is tiresome to wait so long. Perhaps a mail comes in & everyone anxiously looking for news but when the thing is opened it proves to be an old one that met with some delay somewhere on the road. How discouraging.

December 16, 1863

No mail tonight. The stage has come and I hear by rumor that General Burnside has beaten the Rebel Longstreet capturing five thousand prisoners. There is no reason for believing it to be true. I hope it is. I cannot tell why it is that we sometimes receive a letter mail from below and no papers. I should think if a mail could be brought through it would be a full one.

The postmaster

This self-conceited, overbearing, insulting, disagreeable, haughty personage, is the clerk of the mine, Percival Updegraff. He always tries to ride roughshod over the feelings of everyone. A working man is an object of hatred with him and anyone in his employ is treated like a brute. No feelings at all. His brother is in charge of the post office as his deputy. Both of the same pattern. If I had a late paper either would take it home to read & do what they wished with it.

A scene not far from my boarding place

Feeling quite lazy one pleasant morning, I left my room and directed my steps up to the mine for exercise & pleasant or in other words to "tapir off a bit." I stopped at the Fitting Shop & Smith's Shop enjoying a short conversation with A. Stoddard & receiving a few of Mr. Rawlings' sly jokes by way of spice—making the visit very pleasant etc. After running around for some time, I once more started for home for the hour for calling school was near at hand.

I passed on quietly until I came to a French house where there was quite a stir among a number of Frenchmen who were feeling well under the soothing influence of a drop of bitters. They were looking at a fine pig who was nearby, unconscious of anything wrong. Soon they caught Master pig and by dint of some swearing and tumbling succeeded in bringing his huge body low upon the ground. By getting onto him they were able to hold him until the little short dirty woman of the house came in time of need with an exceedingly long butcher knife and stuck it "not into the Bum" but into the neck which soon caused Master pig to die. Things looking rather odd I remained where I could see them preparing piggy for the final scene. Nothing in sight to scold him. He was soon placed up on his feet on sticks when lo, the little dirty woman brought out a bedtick full of straw that was very fine for it had seen hard times doubtless from use. The straw was emptied on piggy & set on fire. Piggy's bristles were soon gone & he as black as a darky. Having fully satisfied my curiosity I passed on leaving them scraping piggy with sticks.

Ye little piggies I caution you to beware
Of old women who would burn your curly hair
From your backs as by this you may see
Leaving you black as black can be.

December 17, 1863

Talk about snowstorms in Vermont. Vermont can boast of some snowy days; it is not to be compared with a Lake Superior snowstorm. It has snowed finely this week but today caps all others in the snow line. It is blowing almost a gale from the north but not very cold. Snow fell about a foot last night and is falling fast today. The air & everything is full of snow. Drifts piling up very high in every corner or behind every building where the wind will not touch it.

It is quite pleasant sitting at my desk with a few scholars very busily engaged in study while I pen these lines previous to hearing lessons. Everything looks snowy out: air, earth, building, forest, everything. It seems as if we should be buried up. How it would seem if a person was out on the Lake. A day like this is a lonely one for me, for my work is not driving which gives me time to think of home. I shall close my evening school tonight until after new years. It has dragged the life almost out of me. I am as weak and tired as anyone can be and get along. I must have liberty soon. How glad I am tonight to think that I close my evening school for two weeks but how can I enjoy myself. There is no way unless I visit the Cornish houses and listen to their curious talk but this comfort is worthless for one is pressed so hard to imbibe of the intoxicating cup.

Can spend some evenings finely with Mr. Rawlings, a man that I respect & love. He has noble principles & is one of the best men I ever became acquainted with. Pleasant and yet possessing remarkable talent and information. His superior cannot be found in this county and as an Engineer he is of the first order.

December 18, 1863

The severe snowstorm that I spoke about in my last sketch still continues with unabated fury. It is colder and the wind is as strong as ever and the snow falls very fast at times. It is piled up like waves of the ocean or small hills. On one side of my school house it is about seven feet deep and under this is the woodpile. "A sweet place I don't think."

I have twenty-five pupils seated near the stove busily engaged in study. Very quiet times inside but very rough outside. It is now afternoon and the snow has subsided somewhat. At least there is very little snow falling although the wind continues to blow lively. A little boy going home from here last evening got into a snow drift where he was found by a man passing by. If he had not been he would have perished as he was in up to his head. I pulled out one or two this morning on their way here. One of my boys told me that he saw an old Irishman in a large bank of snow cursing in fine style. That is smartly, for there is nothing fine about cursing.

I shall go down to Captain Paull's tonight and buy a pair of shoe packs for my feet for I have no boots. My pocket handkerchiefs are all worn out so I bought a silk one this morning. Went to the Captain's in the evening but did not find any shoe packs that would fit me.

Went up to the Episcopal Church to make wreaths in the evening. There were only a few present. It is a small concern and everything has to be done by a few. I am glad that I am not connected with the thing.

December 19, 1863

The storm has subsided and everything has the appearance of the regions of the north. The sun shines brightly this afternoon at times. I am now engaged at the Library. If nothing occurs, I shall go up and help decorate the church in the evening. There are many things against our having a mail tonight; still I hope that we may for it is awful to wait so long without any news. I will now speak of the following subject:

Giblets

Butching day with us has passed and I have learned what the Cornish mean by giblets. Mrs. Rawlings had six geese to kill which she done herself holding them while she cut their necks with the knife. A hog and cow were killed by a neighbor & I cut them up, her boys being too proud & lazy. Giblets for dinner of the feet of the geese. One head of the same etc. in a thick kind of gravy. O, Horrors, how was I to eat the feet and head of a goose. I could not & at once professed a fondness for the gizzard making an exchange with my Cornish mother who could eat a goose's head even to the bill. But the taste of the gravy reminded me of a goose or as Uncle Eli would say it was as strong as [crossed out]. Ladies— please omit or hold your noses when you read it.[3] Feet, heads & all waste pieces are cooked up making the dish called giblets. The good old lady was talking about the guts of the cow for to be used to stuff with sausage — calling them "pudding skins." Sweet pudding, I should think. I was glad when I learned that the butcher threw them away although the old lady sorrowed.

It reminds me of an incident or circumstance that occurred to me on the way to this land of Cornish manners. It was while passing through the State of New York in the night on board of the cars. I was sleepy and tired —feeling somewhat hungry. I jumped off at a station hearing the news that the cars would start in one minute. I rushed into an eating house in a hurry, got though the crowd and sung out for doughnuts, throwing out a quarter to pay for the same. I received a half dozen of what I took for smooth ones & putting them in my pocket got into the cars in times, to get my seat anticipating a glorious eat on the way. The car was filled with Ladies & Gents in a semi-conscious state.

I [started] out with one of my dougnuts and made a grab with my mouth on the sly, but, lo and behold, my teeth made no impression. On examination, I found they were of the real pudding skins stuffed with blood & meat in a hard state & both ends tight. I cut one open with my knife but thought that if I had been a starved dog I should have rejected it. The first favorable opportunity I threw them out the window. I have never wanted any pudding skins since and do not want any more Cornish giblets. The good old lady claims that they make fine Gravy etc. She looks upon them as the finest dish of the season. I doubt whether any portion of the English except the low Cornish consider it so. If they do they have a delicate taste, I don't think.

The wash will not work next week as the engine that stamps the rock or crushes it is going to be repaired. The Wash boys will be into school I think next week. Expect a large school. *Je Fini.*

December 23, 1863

It has been very mild weather for this week and bids fair to continue. Snow falls some every day but it is not cold. My school is small and few preparatory for Christmas. There are many things pleasant about the way the people spend Christmas here, and many things that are wrong. Many families trim a tree in their houses and make it a gala day for the children. But it is generally made a day for carousing and drinking.

It is pleasant to go around and sing Christmas carols but it destroys everything good about it to sing for ale etc. Before night they are all drunk. As a general thing, this is entirely wrong. It is not right to make the day one for drunkenness and carousal. Everyone's mind should be free from all such impure thoughts & contemplate the event that is to be commemorated by fit ceremonies.

A Greenhorn Yankee schoolmaster from the good old State of Massachusetts went over into the State of New York and took a school. He was informed that there was a family of boys by the name of "Litchfield" who would pitch him out of doors. Accordingly he determined to make an impression at once. The first three days passed well—none of the family made their appearance. On the fourth day after school had commenced, a new scholar made his appearance. The master asked his name. The boy replied "Litchfield"; [then] the master caught him and gave him a severe thrashing winding up by saying that if the Litchfields wanted to throw him out they could try it. He was then informed that this little boy was of another family of the same name—a quite innocent little fellow. Yankee schoolmaster skedaddled at once.

A pleasure excursion

I dismissed my school Wednesday night before Christmas—the vacation to continue during the next week. This would of course include Christmas and New Year's. These holidays are observed in this country and no work is done at this time. When miners have a spree, it always takes two or three days to "tapir off" so there is not much doing between these days, except drinking. This is done to excess. I hear that two barrels of beer & gin to one flour are consumed in some places. This is true to all appearance.

Everything passed off pleasantly at the church Christmas Eve. The tree was trimmed finely and all were well pleased. The miners went around singing for beer as usual. Five of my boys went around singing as a temperance party. I gave them seventy-five cents. I visited at different houses and spent the day pleasantly.

Saturday morning Joe Retallick, Ed, John, William Penberthy & myself started for Portage Lake in Anderson's stage. I doubt whether a party ever set out in better spirits from severe confinement. The snow was about four feet deep; still the road was very good. The distance is about thirty-five miles through a dense forest of all kinds of timber. There is one small hut called the Half Way House after passing the Albion Mine two miles distant.[4] Every tree and bush was loaded down with snow, and it was well that the wind did not blow. I never was on a road through a large forest before. The ground is not rough —very level with the exception of a few small hills.

While getting ready here we saw a drunken man in the snow not far from the house. It was bitter cold so we went & pulled him out; he was very drunk. He got mad at last because one of us told him he ought to have a dry shirt on. So we left him, his clothes were all wet and could hardly stand. He was just finishing up his Christmas spree.

We set out from the store singing *John Brown*. I believe we were singing songs all the way through the bush. There was a drunken German in the sleigh behind us who was hollering all of the time. We had a jolly time on our way up. Took some refreshment at the Half Way House. As we were passing the Boston Mine near the Portage we met Mr. Baughman, the best preacher I ever heard.

Stopped at William Trewarther ['s for] a few minutes. We reached the Portage at five and as it was late went to the "Douglass House" for the night.[5] It is a fine hotel situated on the Houghton side of the Lake and will compare with many in Detroit. Here we met with Mr. Merryweather, the Cliff surveyor, who just came in from the bush from an exploring trip.[6] We spent the evening very pleasantly. I believe I was the only cold water man there then. William is one & he stopped at a friend's. I went out & saw Mr. McDonald's people in the evening [and] also Mr. McKenzie, the editor of the *Mining Gazette*. He appears like a fine young man. We went to the Episcopal church next day & to hear Mr. Baughman in the evening. On Monday William & I went to see the stamping mills for crushing the copper rock and washing it, also the engines etc. Balls stamps are working finely. It is a great piece of machinery. I got acquainted with many fine people. We went to Mr. Williams of the smelting works. They are Scotch or Welsh and are fine people. He made me a present of a fine specimen of copper that had been melted. So far as I am acquainted with Welch, they are fine people.

I stayed on night with Fred Hynes at the Pewabic store & one night with Mr. McDonald.[7] Little Mary was taken with the measles, while I was there. She is sorry she cannot come to my school and cried bitterly when I came away.

We had our likenesses taken in a group. The boys all came home Tuesday except Ed & I. We came home Thursday. Had quite a rough time on the way back. There were twelve in the sleigh & four of them were drinking all the way. One was dead drunk. He fell out into the snow twice. We got through all safe. This ride has been quite pleasant to me and I feel much better after this recreation.

I was disgusted with Ed as was all the party. He makes an ass of himself always in public. A double team broke through the ice &

was lost while on its way to the *Dubuque*, a steamer that came up late & was stuck in the ice four miles from the village where she will remain this winter.[8] I shall be unable to write any more under this trip for want of time.

A storm

I never saw anything to equal the storm that followed our return from the Portage. It is true that it has snowed most of the time for two weeks but it commenced blowing a gale and snowing. Thermometer at twenty degrees below zero & continued for four days. Great damage has been done about the mine by freezing, pumps etc.

I have no school as I cannot get any wood there the snow is so deep. Some of the teamsters were nearly frozen to death. It has been an awful time. I hear that one man was lost in the snow & has not been found. Mr. Rawlings' provisions froze in the cellar. I have shoveled snow some since to get to the school house. I hope that we will not have another storm like this one. It snows some almost every day. There is enough for everlasting sleighing I should think. If anyone wishes to see a snow storm come up here and stop one winter.

Notes for November-December 1863

1. The *8th U. S. Census*, Houghton County, 1860, lists a Henry Nutt, age 25, a tinner, and Henry Meeds, age 35, a tailor, and Catherine Meeds, age 29. They lived next door to each other. Miss Nutt and Catherine Meeds were half sisters.

2. Hobart is describing Mary Annie Paull, daughter of Joseph and Mary A. Paull. She had two younger sisters, Sarah, age 10, and Isabella, age 6. *8th U. S. Census*, Houghton County, 1860.

3. Eli Hobart, Amos' brother, was born October 1, 1821, and died July 3, 1887. Percy Hobart Titus, *The Hobart Family in America* (Boston: n.p.,1943).

4. The Halfway House was located half way between Hancock and the Cliff Mine. Arthur Thurner, *Calumet Copper and People* (Calumet: A. Thurner, 1974) p. 2.

5. The Douglass House, named for C. C. Douglass, an early mine engineer and speculator, was built in 1861 by John Atwood at a cost of $15,000. It was considered the finest hotel in the Upper Peninsula and "catered to those who didn't want to leave civilization behind." It was a

three-story hotel with an ample veranda along the front of each story. The Hotel Register, now preserved in the Bentley Historical Library, University of Michigan, Ann Arbor, Michigan, has the signatures of the following on December 26, 1863: Edward R. Penberthy and Joseph Retalleck of Eagle River and John Penberthy and Henry Hobart of the Cliff Mine. *Daily Mining Gazette*, January 10, 1983; *Michigan Gazetteer for 1863-64* (Detroit: Charles Clark, 1863),p. 347.

6. Henry Merryweather is cited in the *Houghton Mining Gazette*, February 21, 1863. He was often a visitor at the Douglass House.See Douglass House Register, Bentley Library, University of Michigan, Ann Arbor, Michigan.

7. Hobart is referring to Samuel and Ellen McDonald, the parents of Mary, one of Hobart's favorite young scholars.

8. The propeller steamer *Dubuque* weighing 384 tons was built in Buffalo in 1857. John Brant Mansfield, editor and compiler, *History of Great Lakes* (Chicago: J. H. Beers, 1899), p. 817.

January—February 1864

Mail in the winter came overland often by dog sleigh. Hobart described a dog sleigh as "Lake Superior style in place of a horse team."

The Methodist Episcopal church built in 1847 remained intact in Clifton until 1914, when the roof collapsed.

January 7, 1864

The old year has gone and the new one is fully on its course. Time passes away rapidly. Many great changes have taken place since I left my pleasant home. Death has taken away many friends. Thousands have fallen on the field of battle. The country has been shaken by the terrible contest for liberty. Mighty changes have affected the nation. The army of Freedom is still battling with strong hopes of victory. Everything moves towards the great final result.

While a year's changes have transpired, I have not seen the light of home. I know not how things look around the place of my birth which many years have stamped firmly upon my mind as home. I long to visit those places once more. To associate with former friends. I will labor faithfully until my duty is discharged; then I will start for Vermont if health permits.

I commenced my school this afternoon. I have not had any for the past few days as the late storm blocked up the road so I could not have any wood brought. The snow is four feet deep. Men and teams have been at work breaking roads for many families have no wood to burn. I never saw such a time in my life. I think every cellar in the place has frozen. There were one hundred and fifty barrels of apples at the warehouse worth four dollars and fifty cents per barrel and they are frozen solid. Potatoes are frozen. My school was very small, of course. A great number of children are sick with the Scarlet Fever, Dropsey, Influenza etc. I am in good condition and hope that I may not be sick. I shall commence evening school Monday.

I saw a man today with the Delirium Tremens. He tried to dig a stump up this forenoon & froze his hands, tore the skin off etc. I think he will lose his hands by the looks. I never witnessed such a sight before. Very many will follow in his tracks until they are in a similar state.

January 8, 1864

It is a mild calm morning but very cloudy. People begin to stir out once more and soon the roads will be good. I expect a large school today. The stove pipe in my room is broken so I have school in one room. Miss Nutt will not return until Monday as there is no room for her.

I am informed that Mr. Wright is going to have his children instructed at home by a young lady living there. I am agreeable to such a change as his boy James is a very unpleasant scholar. He has no courage but gives up at every little difficulty. I am sure I do not want to carry him through on my back and pity the one who takes this womanish boy of fifteen. I commenced teaching at that age and this lady's boy is like a little child. I like to see a young man meet a difficulty with true courage and a determination to overcome it.

I went over this evening to Mrs. Meeds at the request of my assistant, Miss Nutt. Mrs. Meeds is her half sister. They board one of the doctors and the store clerks. They keep a fine house which often reminds me of Vermont. Frank Ten Broeck was there and we spent the evening very pleasantly.

I heard that there was a mail and went over to the [post] office and found a letter from Mother, Gertie & Florence. How glad I was to hear from home for it has been a long time since I received any news. It is very cheering to read Mother's kind letter full of good advice which I shall ever remember & try to heed. Florence wrote a good one. She is at school which I am glad to hear.[1] Gertie's little letter caused me to laugh very much. How I would like to see them all. There is nothing like home which I long to see. *Je Fini Pour Cet. Temps.*

January 9, 1864

The wind is blowing almost a gale this morning from the South. The snow is flying through the air which makes it very unpleasant for anyone facing it. It is almost impossible to make any headway against it. The truth is we are having severe weather. I saw no such storms last winter in this place. To give some idea of its extent, I have eight scholars when there should be one hundred. They are all boys except Mr. James' two little girls who have braved the storm and reached here safe.[2] It is now snowing quite fast.

My assistant

I am fortunate in having the services of a good assistant who takes the care of the primary department off from me. I have not felt any anxiety about that part of school for they are all making excellent progress I find on examination. She is a lady of determination and aims to have everything conducted with a regard to order & discipline. It requires such a person to manage these small scholars who are not aware of what it is to mind. They want drilling and I am sure that they are getting that very thing.

Success to every one who aims to do well and makes strong and repeated efforts to accomplish such an object. It is not due to the laggard or the person who despises labor or an account of self conceit or pride. I detest such an individual. I hate those who are above work or think there is a disgrace in it.

I have often been out here and engaged in work. Some thought I was a farmer as I tried making hay while I had nothing else to do; others thought I was a carpenter; others thought I was a painter. They all say I can teach. And I have no doubt that I am some Yankee. *Je Il fin*

January 12, 1864

It is very mild for the clouds are thick and heavy, shutting out the pleasant rays of the sun. It is always pleasant when the sun shines brightly in a still winter's day. There is something very refreshing to feel the mild influence of its genial rays. But a Lake Superior winter passes away and seldom does the sun cheer the faces of those living here. A cloudy sky is the rule and sunny days are only exceptions.

I put my pupils fairly on the right path today and shall endeavor to raise the steam until it is at a strong pressure when action will be in view. I shall not be troubled with any more vacations but shall attend to school. Yesterday I had no school in the forenoon as the pipe was not ready. Had school in with Miss Nutt in the afternoon.

Sunday evening I heard Mr. Wright preach a good sermon. Showing that the soul lives after the death of the body forever. If it can be shown that they live at all after death there is nothing to show that they will not live forever. The spirits of two persons talked with Christ on Earth many years after their death. So the soul lives. I look around me and see every thing material passing away or changing. The flowers die, the tree decay, everything seems to pass away. But the mind is not subject to this change as it is immaterial. It has not the properties of matter. Inertia is a property of matter. Nothing material can move or stop itself unless acted upon by some agency. You cannot limit the mind. It acts itself thinks etc. Therefore it is not subject to material changes. It is immortal & will live.

January 13, 1894

The only news I have tonight is this. There is a small mail in, no papers, no late letters, just enough to make a person mad. It is a direct violation of the contract for bringing the mail here and I wonder if the persons having change of this matter have no regard for the mail interest of this community.

Had a very pleasant school, most of the scholars are here. There is good interest manifested in study. All seem to labor for some purpose. This is very cheering for the teacher.

Mr. Rawlings went to the Humboldt mine with Captain Sam Bennetts. Mr. Vivian, who was here, is agent of the mine. I cannot tell how he contents himself here as he was very homesick while visiting at Mr. Rawlings. Ed Penberthy goes there on Saturdays to do the clerking. If nothing unusual occurs, I shall visit the old Gent & see how he feels.

Miss Annie Paull

This little girl living about one mile from here is a daughter of the Captain and for a girl of thirteen years living in a country like this is very much like a true lady. I never saw any of that romping and silly actions about her that are the main characteristics of girls of her age. She is a fine scholar & works very hard. She has a younger sister who is one of the remarkable little girls. She has a very large head projecting in front. Learns quick yet is quite unhealthy. I shall always remember these little girls as two of my best scholars here. Always trying to be right in every thing. I trust they may receive good educations for they are very anxious to learn. Their parents are equally anxious to have them.

January 14, 1864

We now enjoy weather of a cold nature without any violent changes either way. There seems to be no prospect of storms or violent changes. The thermometer varies from fifteen to twenty above zero. It is very cloudy and now and then a snowflake falls through the still air. How strange things look. The houses half buried in the snow.

Evergreen bushes look like cones they are filled with so much snow. There is a fine look about these cones of pure whiteness. It could hardly be possible for anyone to pass through the bush the snow is so deep, loading the trees and bushes.

My fine old Cornish lady of boarding, Mrs. Rawlings, now complains of her girl. It seems as if it were a duty that she was obliged to perform or she would not be mistress of the shanty. When she was in Ireland, the servants lived on sour milk and potatoes. This she likes very well. She possesses the true feelings of the English woman. The servant is a slave and must be treated as such. I feel vexed when I listen to such talk and long to her it no more. She is kind to me and has many very good principles. I do not overlook these. I am willing to give credit for every good quality.

I am here at evening school having taken a walk to the mine & wash by way of wholesome exercise. Mr. Rawlings' jigs are working finely. The wash under Tomi Davey's hands is doing well. A. Stoddard, the leading blacksmith, is hammering away; also Stephen Kunkle.[3] Billy P., who has worked in the fitting shop, is driving the pumping engine.

January 15, 1864

Half of the first month of the new year will soon be passed and notwithstanding, the old one went out with very severe weather & the new one came in while the storm raged furiously as if commotion and strife would mark its progress, yet since the storm it has been very pleasant weather.

The year will doubtless be a stormy one to this country in relation to the great strife that is going on and the great events that must transpire before 1865 commences its course. I shall expect that Mr. Lincoln will be chosen president for another four years and the rebels used up as an army.

But I will dismiss this subject and say that I intend holding a fine spelling school next week Saturday evening. I intend to have some pieces spoken and shall give each scholar a ticket who can spell the last six pages in the book. It is amusing to see what an interest is created by offering them some little inducement. I see them carry their books home at night and at noon they are studying the speller. A mild course, showing the pupil what he working for and its importance, is the correct way to deal with pupils.

A person who is qualified for the task of imparting instruction must be able to awaken a thorough interest in study among those whom he proposes to teach. To force scholars to learn is a very poor foundation to look for success. The mind is much easier led than drove into a certain course. It will be of no practical benefit to compel one to learn. They cannot get that knowledge of the subject that they would by studying it for the interest and love of learning and improvement.

January 16, 1864

The thermometer indicates a temperature of twenty degrees. The air is still and bracing. I find that the frost works at my ears after remaining out a half an hour or more. It is in truth quite pleasant but very uncomfortable for anyone who has nothing to do for he would soon find himself chilled through and his feelings would resemble those of a bootjacket more than a man. It would not do to apply to him under such sweet circumstances as there would be very little warmth in his feelings for anything "for money for any good cause." It would be a cool reception for anyone. I will now write a few lines about the important subject of Temperance.

Temperance

Mr. Wright in speaking on the subject quoted a passage which applied to the rum seller but I failed to learn the place in the Bible where it is to be found. The sense of the passage was this: If an ox were to push or gore to death a man woman or child, the ox shall die. If the owner know that this is the custom of the ox, then the ox & owner shall surely die. If a man [were to] sell whiskey not knowing its effects, then he is not to blame—but no rumseller can have this excuse. Its effects are known everywhere. Then the Seller, knowing its effects, shall die if he sells it.

Who can tell the destiny of the man who sells alcoholic poison knowing its tendency and effects. I will not dare to say. Few persons know the strength of appetite and especially that for strong drink. A man may eat nice ripe apples but his appetite cannot be strong enough to compel him to eat them because he likes them until he die. I have a strong liking for good apples—stronger than most persons but I can easily satisfy this by eating a few good ones but an appetite formed for strong drink is beyond the control of the powers of man.

I might mention numerous instances to show how powerful is its tendency but will speak of only one or two. Men of powerful minds fall victims to this debasing habit. Daniel Webster was a man of tremendous power yet he could not resist the desire for strong drink. He was to deliver a lecture to the people of Boston and a conference of the finest ministers in the land one evening at Faneuil Hall. Thousands came and at eight Mr. Webster had not come. In a short time he was led on the stage in a drunken state and placing his hand on a pillar to steady himself proceeded to deliver his lecture in a state of reeling drunkenness. This shows that this powerful man could not control himself.

Stephen Douglas, a man of remarkable powers of mind, while delivering a lecture before thousands at Cleveland, Ohio, kept dipping an orange peel in Brandy and putting it in his mouth & when he went to the hotel lay on his bed with a glass of Brandy nearby to sip. Men of tremendous ower have been led captive by the appetite for whiskey.

Mr. Wright was a sailor in his younger days and a drinking man. He would take an oath to stop & call on God to aid him in his resolution, but the first time he saw it he could not resist the temptation to drink.

A young French lawyer, who was a remarkable one in criminal cases, had a severe case in Baltimore; the highest in the profession were there. He rose and made his plea and gained the case. On his way home his friends told him he must come and drink with them; he must be tired etc. Oh no, said he. I must go home and see my wife & child. No, but you must go & take a little. He did go & stayed until drunk. He went to the former pleasant home—kept on drinking, had the Delirium and wandered forth in the world.

When he came to himself he was in the forecastle of a whaler four days out from New Bedford on a cruise of five years. The pen cannot describe his agony. He might have led his profession. He was glad there was nothing on board to make him drunk & thought his wife & boy might be content to live with him even in the forecastle of a whaler if he would keep sober. But his young wife & bright-eyed little boy never received tidings from him after he left in the Delirium. The whaleman touched at the Azores or Western Islands and "Charley", as he was called, in spite of prayers & oaths got hold of the whiskey. He insulted all on board [and] got knocked down & whipped; when he came to, he begged pardon of the captain, mate & second mate, a tall Yankee. Swore he would take no more. The vessel touched at the Cape Verde Islands & "Charley" drank again, had the Delirium, snakes on him, fiends, spiders, etc. O kill me, what a scene; he broke from his keeper ran on deck out on the yard. Screamed "fiends" twice in his agony so that it would stir everyone through & through & then leaped into the foaming waves, rose to the surface & screamed in such a way that it would ring in a man's ears forever & sunk—a victim to strong drink.

Can anyone describe the awful feeling of Delirium who has not felt it. I have heard from the lips of those who have experienced it a description & have seen persons having it. It is terrible. It might amuse one not knowing its feelings but after it is once felt it is enough. Take a little & it will not hurt you. This is false for it is a poison & will do harm according to the quantity. Some say I can drink & leave off when I chose. The first part is true but I must see good proof before I believe the second part.

With relation to pure liquors there is perhaps very little imported. There are companies in New York who will give a receipt for making all kinds without any of the pure article. It is composed of poison & other impure things. Bedbugs are put into brandy and other vermin during the process of fermentation—a sweet beverage indeed. Porter from London is another sweet drink made out of the water of the Thames. All the filth & everything nasty falls into the sewers under the city. This passes out into the Thames where it is taken up with the water to make Porter. Thick, black, muddy, nasty, filthy slobbering stuff. Beer of this is a nice drink. I have seen men drink it until they were drunk. Perfect swill tubs. It will not make a man drunk like gin but slobbering or muddy drunk. It is totally unfit for anything.

But I will not speak about only one more instance of pure Brandy. The officers of a church in Ohio wanted a pure article for sacramental purposes. They went to an Apothecary's shop or, as the Yankee says, a "Shothercary Pop" and the man in charge said he had a friend in New York who imported the pure article for that very purpose. In a few days they went in & inquired if the Brandy or wine had come. O, yes & taking out the demijohn poured some into a glass. "Here, Brother A— try it." "Yes, it is fine." "Try it, Elder B & also the minister." They all pronounced it a fine article and took it. In the meantime, the wife came in saying they had company & hoped her husband would come in early. She wanted some tumblers & took the one that was used for the wine. A few drops fell on her dress and ate a hole through in six minutes. I think that would be tough for sacramental purposes. I would not insure a man's life who would take it in his stomach. The wines & Brandies are disgusting poisons to an alarming extent.

I will close by speaking about scenes in this country. Things that occur here often. Intoxicating drinks are used to an awful extent here. Drunkenness is a common thing. Sunday is a day for drink & gambling for many. The grog shops are well filled on that day. Two deaths have occurred lately here by drink.

I have given some account of one at the Phoenix. A woman & child froze to death. They had whiskey & the woman sung while all hands danced in the evening. Yet before morning she lay with her child cold & dead by the road side naked. It is strange that she took the child. The man who sold the poison is responsible for that murder.

Another instance. Everyone says why did the man die; what is the use of a doctor if he cannot cure a simple case. The truth was the man's stomach had been destroyed by alcoholic poison & medicine would not take any effect on the system.

I see families broken up. Women drunk, men drunk, fighting, swearing etc. Body & mind ruined and all this is the effect of strong drink. Therefore taste not. Never give way to a desire to touch it. Let it alone. Young men to you comes the solemn warning—beware of the evil. Associate with persons of good & true principle shun the grog shop. Cultivate habits of sobriety and temperance. I have witnessed some of its awful effects. May I ever be able to resist the strong temptation that often comes before me as I labor in the discharge of my duty in this place. Stand firm & true.

January 17, 1864

Snow fell about four inches last night; it is mild today. Messrs Joseph & Nicholas Vivian were here this afternoon. Edward was up last night. I feel lonely in my room today. How I long to see home & friends. May I have health & strength for my work which I often fear.

January 22, 1864

For three days the weather has been very uniform not varying from thirty-two degrees. The wind blows quite strong which gives some indications of a thaw but I think it will freeze soon. I received four letters from Vermont the other day which is the best mail I have received yet. One from Florence, one from Jesse, one from cousin G. A., and one from Miss Maria Hyde of Grand Isle applying for a situation as teacher.[4] I do not know as I can secure one for her. She says she is making preparations to come anyway.

I am quite unwell which I suppose is the result of being vaccinated. I find myself hardly able to breathe or move in consequence of a cramp under the shoulder blade in the region of the heart. I know not the cause but did not sleep last night in consequence of the pain. I find that I am injuring my health by teaching. The Doctor pronounces it the lumbago. I had no school this evening.

A curious scene

Several Irishmen were in one of the drinking saloons a short distance below here and after taking the eye water freely got into a general fight. After bruising for awhile a part of them went away & hid in the bushes on the road where one of the others must pass on his way home. They caught him as he came along [and] buried him in the snow after beating him severely. They then piled cord wood onto him & snow. A teamster passing by next morning saw his boot & dug him out. Strange to say he was alive although out of his mind. He will probably recover. Drink is the cause of this outrage. It will not be noticed.

January 24, 1864

I am some better today and think I shall not be unwell long. It is very mild, very much like a thaw. I believe the mercury is at forty-eight degrees. I answered several letters to day & went to Sabbath School also. I was intending to have a spelling school Saturday evening but was too sick. I will try and have one about Tuesday evening. I cannot tell what is the matter with me but think that it is the Rheumatism in consequence of standing on a hard floor without exercise. At least I am suffering much from pain. I shall take proper exercise and see if I cannot wear it off in a few days. I fancy that I will soon overcome it. I shall give up my school for the evenings soon and devote the time to my own improvement and health.

Dog sleighs

This is a Lake Superior style in place of a horse team. A person not acquainted with this way of riding would suppose that they would make a slim team. But this is not the case. A span of good dogs make a smart team. If well trained it is pleasant riding after them. I wish I had a handsome pair to take below with me. Mr. Bergan has a large dog that will pull a heavy load. To keep a horse team would be very expensive whereas a team of dogs costs very little and answers every purpose of a horse. Every Cornishman is sure to have a number of dogs anyway and if he can make them answer the purpose of a horse it is all the better. Bully for the dog teams of Clifton.

January 30, 1894

It is quite mild yet there is a strong wind from the north. There is a very good crust and the roads are fine. The weather for the week has been quite uniform. Had a small thaw the fore part of the week. The mails come very regular now. There was one in last night with Milwaukee papers down to the 18th. No important news has come. Mr. Watson is going below on business soon.

Yesterday I went with the school to the funeral of one of my scholars, Isabella Everett.[5] She was a bright-eyed little girl of ten with bright red hair which hung in beautiful curls. She was a fine little scholar and went to school last winter & spring. Her father moved to the Phoenix this summer. She had the Typhoid fever and was sick four weeks. Although a great sufferer in her last moments, she died happy kissing her little sisters & saying she was going to Jesus. Such an example is somewhat strange in a child of her age. She was a member of the Sunday School and loved by all. How sad to see the young die when giving promise of future excellence etc. Three of my scholars have died since I came here. No one can tell who may be called next.

I hear that there has been two or three arrests of persons suspected of trying to kill Mr. More by beating him & burying him by the side of the road for dead. He is still living although in a terrible condition. His back & head were beaten with round sticks of cordwood in a shocking manner. I hope the perpetrators of the crime will receive a just punishment. Acts of violence are of frequent occurrence in a country where strong drink is so generally used. Prevent the sale of the "eye water" and there will not be as many black eyes.

February 1, 1864

It has been quite a mild day with very little air stirring. I have had a pleasant school today with most of the scholars present. I received compositions from some of the scholars. I have taken measures to organize a debating society to give all an opportunity to see some fun.

Destruction of the world

The Bible informs us in unmistaken terms that this event will take place by the agency of fire not its annihilation but a dissolution of the elements composing it. Every nation on earth has something of this kind in its history handed down from one generation to another by tradition. It is strange that this should be so unless there were really some truth in the matter. The event is possible. Water is composed of oxygen & hydrogen—both strong elements that are very inflammable. Electricity separates these two elements. The earth is full of electricity. Let it loose & the water is a sea of fire at once. The air can be set on fire when its elements are separated. It is a fact that the center of the earth is a mass of fire; if experiment be true as you descend into the earth, heat increases one degree every fifteen feet. At the distance of seventy miles everything would be a sea of fire. The existence of volcanoes proves this to be true. In the Pacific Ocean there was an Island & a rumbling was heard in the mountain for days. At last a river of fire was thrown up ran down the mountain side & over a precipice of one hundred feet into the sea for days. What could supply this but an ocean of fire in the center of the earth. The event is possible.

February 2, 1864

No change or new occurrence worthy of note in our vicinity. Mr. Trewarther is visiting my school for two days to obtain the *modus operandi* of my System of teaching. He is going to teach at the Central Mine and hearing of my good quiet way of teaching he is here taking notes being well pleased. He is not aware of the many trials he must pass through and the trouble it takes to make a good teacher. Says he, "I can never learn to explain as you do. I had no idea that you took such a course in teaching grammar. Where did you learn to analyze. The books say nothing about it."

I am inclined to believe that he will have good success for he does not claim to know everything. Edward would not ask anything about teaching. He knew everything. I wish I had one month to visit schools for benefit to myself. I shall try and call Edward sometime. I want to see him perform. I doubt whether he knows everything or can teach properly.

I now claim to know from the best of schools, viz experience, how to manage Scholars. When a young man learns what it is to take charge of two hundred and twenty-five pupils of all grades, give correct & proper explanations, guide every exercise so as to contribute to the mental improvement of all, he will know what a school experience is. May I be able to perfect my management of young children until I can give them the best possible advantages and have a true course of instruction for use.

February 3, 1864

Mr. Trewarther left me today at half past three and had not been gone many minutes before Mr. Wright, the minister, came in to see how things move. He spoke to the scholars very kindly commending the conduct of Annie Paull in her classes as noble and worthy of the notice of the school. I consider this black-eyed little girl one of the noblest I ever saw, in her conduct & as a scholar. I shall close evening school tomorrow night.

I received a letter from Albert [Eastman] late in the evening.[6] He is at Poughkeepsie commercial school. There are twelve hundred students in all. It is the largest school in America. The students will form a procession nearly two miles long when out on a sleigh ride. I would like to take such a course. It is well for a young man to understand how to do all kinds of business for he may obtain a good situation in a new country.

There is a fortune to be made if a man is lucky enough to procure a place of work. Many have made a fortune here investing their money in stock. This is an easy way but it also an easy way to lose a fortune. But it is said that a man must run some risk if he wishes to make anything. This is very true in a speculating line of business if not in all kinds.

Spelling schools

As a means of improvement, a spelling school is one of the best. It is also the cause of much pleasure among the young. If properly conducted they give great chance for anyone to become a good speller. My pupils are all learning quite fast. They are doing well. Success to their efforts.

February 6, 1864

I wrote a letter to cousin A[lbert] F. Eastman and one home. I have had no school but am making preparations for a spelling school this evening. We shall have one dialogue by four boys and two girls. I wish I could procure some good ones. For the day I must close and fill out this page tomorrow morning. The spelling last evening passed off very pleasantly. The scholars showed that they had been trained well in everything pertaining to good spelling. There were only a few outsiders present so the dialogues were postponed until next Wednesday evening when we will spell again. Everyone labored hard to become good spellers. I am glad to see them have an interest in the work .

February 9, 1864

Death of Scholars

Last Sunday while at Sunday school Mr. Souden's little boy was taken vomiting.[7] He went home, did not complain much, only crying for water through the night. The next day he died at twelve o'clock. This is very sudden and no one can tell the cause. I hear that little Mary McDonald is dead. I am not willing to credit this yet. I hope it is not so.

She was one of my best scholars. When I was at the Portage she was taken with the measles. She was not very sick when I left and perhaps they have lost their only child— an active, beautiful little Scotch girl. A fine scholar. I thought a great deal of this little girl. How she cried when she saw me last. She always loved to go to my school. Four of my pupils have died this winter. How soon others may be called, or perhaps teachers. There is a solemnity about the vocation of the teacher that renders the business serious. How shall a teacher conduct himself a right. May death invade no more my pleasant school. (March 6, 1864—Mary is well again.)

February 13, 1864

How mild yet not pleasant for a wet snow is falling slowly very much like rain at least in its effects on a person. It is a time when one longs to go out but a position by a warm fire is perhaps much better for health. I have this place in the schoolroom distributing the books of the public library. I have been in school all day. I have severe pain in the legs every afternoon the effects of Rheumatism. I know not why it is that I am obliged to suffer these pains for I can not see any cause. I am told that many have attacks while in this region. I wish I were free from it as it is very unpleasant. I cannot enjoy anything while suffering the pain.

Mr. Souden's little boy died last night after an illness of a few hours. He has lost two this week. Scarlet fever is said to be the cause. The last one was always a sickly child looking like one in the last stages of consumption and although six or eight years old he was a mere baby in consequence of much illness. Johnny is the only child left. They have buried four or five small children. It seems impossible for some to raise a child. Mrs. Johns lost a twin boy last night. He was a week old. I am feeling very lonesome. I am wishing for a mail, for some news from home. It is hardly endurable; still it must be put up with. A good mail with letters from home would cheer me amazingly.

Mr. Wright was in school to see me yesterday. He gave the scholars some good advice. There must be a desire to learn, an effort and when learning is acquired put it in practice. An ignorant man is no better than an ox or a horse. The only difference is an ox can be used as food & the horse can be led and driven. An ignorant man performs his daily labor but contributes nothing to science.

When the Iowa legislature was opened the chaplain made the following sound prayer:

Bless Thou the young and growing State of Iowa, her senators and representatives, the Governor and state officers. Give us sound currency, pure water, and undefiled religion.

Money versus a fool

A young man just commencing life with nothing but the clothes on his back ought to have a true idea of money; for very may prove themselves fools if I may use the word. Most young "sprigs" when they arrive at that age in which they are called upon to account for themselves lose their sense and think that the world is gold and to them will fall the treasure. They fail to have a true idea of its value and therefore convert it to such a use as to make perfect "fools" of themselves in the full sense of the term. When a young man boasts that he does not care anything about money, proves the shameful fact, by putting it in fine linen, Beer, cigars, rings and nonsense, I consider him on the road to ruin or in other words he is a hypocritical fool. There are many reasons for this course in a young man and some of them I notice in the character of the "Eager River Schoolmaster."

I am well aware that a store clerk is very apt to have such an idea and if he has it shows his want of common sense, stability, and manhood. A person full of self-conceit and pride who thinks that everyone is trying to put on style over him, and gets in a row with them in consequence, may be classed as a fool. Such is the character of this Pedagogue. There is one consolation: he is Cornish. All honor to him who is careful with money & knows its true worth.

February 16, 1864

It is the coldest morning we have had since last winter and there is a very strong wind from the north filling the air with frost and snow as about one foot of very light snow fell yesterday. I was up early and the girl had fires built but found it almost impossible to warm the house. Mrs. Rawlings came down in a violent passion, making an awful tirade on the girl. Such senseless jawings I never heard. There was no end to it. So I took two pieces of frozen bread for breakfast and left for the schoolhouse to get out of hearing of her senseless complaints. I have built a rousing fire and the scholars begin to come in, some crying, some half froze etc. The school will be small. There was no mail last night and it is very lonesome without any news. I am not very well and not having much to do I find it unpleasant.

Henry Benneys death [on] February 18, 1864

This boy of thirteen was killed in the mine this morning by falling from a ladder under a projection of the pump rod being crushed to death.[8] The shaft is full of ice & it was very slippery. His feet slipped & he fell striking his father's shoulder in the fall. He was killed almost instantly. His poor father feels very bad & his mother & sisters have met with a severe loss. How they grieve the sad death of they boy who was full of promise and hopes. I am inclined to believe that the managers of the Mine should be held responsible for the safety of the ladder way. They should see that it be free from ice & all danger avoided. Carelessness is the cause of many accidents.

February 20, 1864

It is quite mild and I think the severe storm is past. It snows a very little this afternoon, making it quite damp. I went to the river this morning [and] saw Ed [Penberthy] in school. He performs with a vast amount of show and self conceit.

I recieved a fine letter from home last night. They urge me to return in the spring if possible. The time is passing away fast and I shall soon be a free man again. One half of my last contract has expired and five months more will soon pass away. It is a very long term to teach without vacation; in fact, too long. The confinement is severe.

Mr. Watson & Updegraff start for below next week. Mr. Watson is going to Chattanooga as he has brothers & sisters there. Watson, the agent, went below some time since. Updegraff is gone for goods to come up in the spring. Mr. Green is to remain in the warehouse during Mr. Watson's absence.

February 24, 1864

It is very mild & cloudy—very much like a thaw. It rained quite hard night before last. The snow is very soft & damp. Scholars were snow balling yesterday & many of them have swollen eyes. I like to see them have a good round at snow balling. It is good exercise for them & will do them good.

Annie Paull is quite sick. She is some better this morning. I hope she will get well. I shall have a very large school to day & a spelling school tonight. I had a hard day's work yesterday & expect that it will be so through the spring months. Success to the earnest laborer in any place, if his work is founded on right principles or is of a right kind.

February 24, 1864

It is a beautiful morning. The sky is mostly clear. The sun shines very brightly and we have promise of a pleasant day. The thermometer stands two degrees below the freezing point; but it will soon be very far above. I had a good spelling school last night everything passing off pleasantly. I will have one next week which will be the last I think.

February 27, 1864

I am thinking whether there will be any mail in tonight and if I shall be fortunate enough to receive good news. I look for mail all the time. I dreamt last night that I had closed my works & was taking leave of my scholars before going home. It was pleasant to think of going home but sad to part with my pupils.

Time seems to pass slowly away. I had a letter from John Fay last night. He is attending the commercial school at Poughkeepsie and says it is a gigantic humbug. He is evidently a home boy. I confess I am quite a home boy but I long to see more of the world before squatting down a sober life. I have not satisfied my desire for travel yet. The days are very warm & fine now. The wind was quite strong yesterday & today.

Fire: A old woman's account

When the fire was in oure housen father was scared so that the cough tuck him & couldn't do nothing & we lost a brave many things. I was skared too but I don't know how many things was in the fire. I hered the cry 'fire' & sed 'Faher put on your jacket & run,' but the cough took Father & he was don up.

Notes for January-February 1864

1. In 1859, Florence Hobart, age 12, was a student in Underhill Academy, Underhill, Vermont. In 1866, she was a student in the Ladies Seminary of Williston Academy, majoring in Classics and French. Underhill Academy, *Catalogue* (Burlington, Vermont: 1859); Williston Academy, *Catalogue* (Burlington, Vermont: 1866).

2. Samuel James, age 37, born in Ireland was married to Maria, age 35, and had five children according to the *8th U. S. Census*, Houghton County, 1860.

3. Stephen Kunkle, age 39, and Susannah, age 38, are listed in the *8th U.S. Census*, Houghton County, 1860.

4. Maria Hyde, age 17 in 1860, was the daughter of George W., age 49, and Eva, age 35, Hyde of Grand Isle, Vermont. Her brother Randolph, age 20 in 1860, was a classmate of Hobart's at Williston Academy in 1859. *Catalogue of the Trustees, Officers, Teachers and Students of Williston Academy* (Burlington, Vermont.: Free Press Print:1859); *8th U.S. Census*, Grand Isle, Vermont, 1860.

5. Isabella, the daughter of Harlow and Jane Everett, was 9 years and 8 months when she died. Her siblings were Marritta, Albert, Anna and Emma. After her death, the Everetts had three other children—William, Isabella and Manetta. The wooden gravestone for Jane still stands in the cemetery at the Cliff. See *8th U. S. Census*, Houghton County, 1860, and *9th U. S Census*, KeweenawCounty, 1870

6. Albert, the son of Amos and Saphronia Eastman, of Westford, Vermont, was Henry's cousin. *8th U.S. Census*, Chittenden County, Vermont, 1860.

7. The *8th U. S. Census*, Houghton County, 1860, listed the Soudens with two children, John, age 3, and William, age 1.

8. It is possible that Hobart is referring to a son of John Benney. See note 5 in January-February 1863.

"Snow is quite soft in most places," wrote Hobart on April 4. During his tenure at the Cliff Mine Hobart described the death of several of his students, some of whom were buried in the Cliff Mine Cemetery shown on the following page.

March 3, 1864

Weary & tired from school tonight with my mind completely tired out with the very perplexing cares of eighty scholars. I feel almost crazy & take a walk to the "wash" & machine shop to divert my thoughts. It has been a warm day [with] the mercury going as high as fifty degrees—school very pleasant. Some of the boys have swollen eyes from snow balling etc.

The past two nights we have received very large back mails. The only important news is the escape of a number of the federal officers from the Rebel prison at Richmond. Their escape caps all the Rebel escapes that have yet taken place. I intend to take my school out next week for a ride, & the girls & boys are very much excited about the matter. It is a fine thing. It will cheer them up and give them a fine treat.

Mrs. Souden was in last night & said she did not know what would be done if I did not come back next summer. The children all love their teacher. Little Sarah Paull was quite unwell yesterday with a sore throat. She was not at school today.

Mrs. Carnsew, wife of Captain Will, was here last night.[1] She lives at the Portage. Mr. William Trewarther has come down to work at the Phoenix Mine [and] also John Carnsew.[2] Mr. William Benney of this place has moved to the "Eureka" or Captain Paull's Mine. Jimmy & Mr. Rawlings will go to the Portage tomorrow if nothing happens. The agent, Mr. Watson, has come home. He is blind at present in consequence of riding so long through the bush surrounded with snow & as it was pleasant the light was very trying to the eyes. It must be an unpleasant journey of two weeks etc.

March 5, 1864

Yesterday was my birth day known only to me in this place. I did not inform one person and did not take the English custom of having a general feast. I have had a good walk this morning and feel like enjoying a good ride. Mr. Rawlings and Jimmy are at the Portage.

There is to be a temperance lecture tonight by Mr. Wright at the "Good Templars" Hall. We will organize our Society very soon. Death to all intoxicating drinks.

We often hear very much said in just vindication of secret societies such as "Masons", "Odd Fellow" etc. It is claimed that their object is noble and one of the most worthy that can activate the motives of anyone. I am ready to admit that their work extends to some deeds of charity but that is about their only aim. There is not a noble object rising far above this to which the society bends its noblest efforts to accomplish. No great reform to stimulate them. I cannot compare them to the I. O. of Good Templars who have aside from "charity" and brotherly affection toward each other an object rising far above any petty object, Viz to relieve the distressed from the influence of everything that intoxicates and make the mind pure and free from all rust or any thing that can tarnish the moral character. Their aim and object is the noblest that can activate the breast of man.

Temperance meeting at the Good Templars Hall

The meeting was organized by electing Mr. A. Johns President and myself Secretary.[3] Prayer was offered by the Rev. Mr. Wright who was then introduced by the President as the speaker of the evening. He gave a pleasing account of the rise and progress of the temperance cause. Of the first efforts of Mr. Beecher who appealed to the young men who were on the road to a drunkard's grave—

but they could not stop so long as the temptation was before them. He appealed to the rum seller who was guilty of their ruin. A pledge was taken not to use whiskey, gin & brandy but allowing the use of wine, beer etc. It would be a curious pledge for these days but the change was gradually taken. From this the total abstinence Pledge was taken. Societies organized etc.

In Baltimore the excitement was commenced. An old "Bloat" swore he would take the pledge, went home drunk and told his wife he would drink no more. His wife gave him a kiss and he kept the pledge. Soon the people were wondering why they always saw him sober & it was explained by saying he had taken the pledge. A meeting was advertised to be held & what was once an old Bloat, a pest to Society, came forward a prosperous man told what effected the change etc. Thus the excitement commenced & the whole country has been agitated. It has been made a subject of law & politics has interfered with it.

After Maine unfurled the banner it was said that there was as much liquor sold as ever. General Cary of Cincinnati said he would find out & went to Portland put up at a hotel & calling the bar keeper told him privately he was sick & wanted a glass of gin. None to be had & he went through all the streets into all the groceries & could find none. At last, meeting a sailor he told him he would give him one dollar to tell where he could get a glass of gin. The sailor told him to go to such a dock & have a man row him down the Bay four miles & if the schooner was there he would find a pint bottle in the Captain's chest where he saw it the day before. If there is anyone who knows where it can be had, it is a sailor. General Cary went to the jail & went all through & found every cell unlocked but one & in this was a large demijohn with the snout knocked off. Here was all the gin held prisoner. People all free, no crime & gin locked up.

Every case of assault of murder etc. that has occurred here under my observation was caused by whiskey. It is said that it is not right to legislate on the subject, that the law is too sharp & takes away a man's rights.

There was a man who kept a long-jawed cross dog that would assail everyone that passed. Flight was the only safety. A stout blacksmith who was often assailed took a short club & fixing a good dirk in it, went along whistling. When the dog came out & he run him through killing him. The owner came out saying why did

271

you kill him etc. Why did you strike him with the sharp end of the stick; why didn't you use the butt end. The smith replied why didn't your dog come out the *other end first*. If gin has such evil effects, strike [it] with a severe law. Meet it on the same terms.

A man with nothing to do here says: "O, what a dull place, nothing going on. I will go to the saloon," & he goes. The room is blue with smoke from the filthy black stumpy pipes of the smokers. A friend calls out "hallo there, come & have a glass of beer." Takes one or two & treats, gets tight, goes home in about as straight a course as a Virginia fence takes. Cannot eat anything next day, has the headache etc. One step toward ruin. Do not use Porter Beer which will make one muddy drunk, foolish thick headed etc.. Anything but the bloating filthy stuff or any other poison.

March 6, 1864

How fine and beautiful it is today—the sun shines out warm and pleasantly. It thaws some during the middle of the day. Sabbath School was well attended. I went to a funeral of a German child at the Episcopal Church in the afternoon. There was very little parental affection shown.

Listened to Mr. Wright in the evening on the following subject: "How long will ye halt between two opinions." After the sermon there was a spirited prayer meeting. This is Mr. Wright's practice every Sunday night and many of the able men of the church are dissatisfied with the course. Mr. Baughman's style suited everyone.

March 7, 1864

It is a cloudy, dull, cool, morning and looks quite smoky. It looks like many a Vermont day previous to the sugar season. Yet it would be a long time before sap would run here. Men begin to talk about spring & the arrival of the boats. But they will look a long time. The old Lake is covered with snow & ice. Keweenaw Point protects it from the wind. It is quite strange that there is no good skating in this country but I suppose it is owing to the constant fall of snow.

Public Opinion

An old sailor told me that when he was on St. Paul's Island near Amsterdam the following incident occurred. Old Jack found a large crab & was dancing around it in great glee —finally he took it up & master crab put one of his claws through his finger. Jack went to pull him off & he put one through the other hand & held on. His mates seeing his sad position came to the rescue & four of them were caught & held fast. Oh, worse than the toothache. Well, public opinion in bringing about reform sweeps everyone in. There is nothing that will do so much.

There was a farmer who owned a large, cross, long-jawed specimen of a dog—one of those that are politely called "Bull Dogs." His wife was a great snuff taker. He also had a little boy— black-eyed, curly hair, a lively little fellow. A neighbor lived nearby [was] called big "Bob." He was over six feet high & the dog was always at war with him. He would always bite when "Bob" came around & when hold would not let go. Bob was passing one day & out came the dog & took hold of "Bob" by the calf of the leg. "Get out you rascal," but dog was not to let go any way. The farmer & son came out & kicked him. "Get out," but the more they kicked him the more he pulled on "Bob's" leg. A crowd soon gathered but could not relieve "Bob." Soon the little boy came & said: "why don't you take him off?" "That's the very thing we want to do but cannot. I can't get him off." Says "Charlie" running into the house, "Mother, Mother, where is your snuff box?" He gets the snuff box & empties it into the dog's eyes & on his nose & the dog soon let go.

Look at Intemperance laying hold of its victims. Now get up a strong public opinion & it will act like the snuff on the dog's nose. There is nothing that will effect a reform so soon. When the people are wide awake on the subject, then wise & good efforts will be made to overthrow the evil.

A little boy lay sick with a fever. "O Mother I want to drink some cold water out of a tumbler." Father took the last quarter at the request of the mother & went to buy a glass tumbler but the grog shop was between him & the store & he stopped there & got drunk. The little boy was dying. Says he, "Mother, do they drink rum in heaven?" "No, my son." "Well, I want to go there & drink the sparkling water. Oh, I see an angel coming with a beautiful tumbler overflowing with sparkling water," & he died. The father came home & the wife asked him if he bought the tumbler. "No," says he, "the little brat wants everything," & then struck his son but it was his dead body. Oh, for the pure sparkling water in a beautiful glass tumbler.

Tell the truth

A bright-eyed little boy whose parents were dead had a cruel stepfather & [step]mother. The mother committed a severe crime known only to herself & the boy. The little fellow told of it & the stepfather heard of it & going to the wife wanted to know who had told such a false story about his wife. Says she, "the boy reported the story."

They both vowed vengeance on the little orphan. He was pulled up by his thumbs with a rope until his toes only touched the floor. He was stripped naked & beaten to make him confess he lied, but the little hero said he told the truth. Says he, "I am cold," & the stepfather took him down when he rested his head on his shoulder & said "I told the truth," & then he died. This was the confession of the man who was confined in the penitentiary for life. "Boys tell the truth."

March 15, 1864

Yesterday was a cold stormy day & school was not very large. James Thomas, one of my scholars, was buried; also Mrs. Sampson who died of consumption.[4] Two funerals in church the same time. Death has taken away very many. Little James was not sick only a few days & died suddenly. He was a fat healthy little fellow & quite active to learn. It is sad to see so many little ones dying in a village like this. Be ye also ready.

March 16, 1864

It is a cold morning. The sun shines very brightly but a breeze from the north prevents it from becoming warm. The severe weather is past. There is a spring look about the days as they pass giving assurance that the icy barriers of Lake Superior will soon break away. Mr. Green of the store has gone below on Company business.[5]

Ed, the schoolmaster, & his brother, Jimmy

Monday evening Ed, the self-conceited schoolmaster, was home full of his nonsense and deviltry. Before getting up from supper, William got his guitar & we had a sing. Jimmy the Simpleton had a song book in his pocket & Ed wanted it one minute. He did not hold it to suit Jimmy who got mad & they commenced twitting each other of one thing & another & got into a right down quarrel. Finally Jimmy was going to shoot Ed & Ed got Jim by the throat & was going to smash his "mug" for him. They went for about one half of an hour & finally parted, Jimmy crying in his wrath & Ed boasting what he could do with him.

I sat by the table & witnessed this quarrel between two brothers who were large enough to be men. Simple foolish boys devoid of all sense and every good quality. A fight is a common occurrence with these brothers. A more foolish or half trained lot of boys I never saw & never wish to see again. Jimmy is a great green baby while Ed is a senseless bag of nonsense full of self conceit & foolishness. William is the best one of the three. He learns some & is quite ingenious. But Ed is disliked everywhere he goes. Jimmy is known as a senseless baby. But I will not speak of such senseless fools who should act as brothers.

March 17, 1864

As it is a mild pleasant day and there is nothing of importance transpiring I will give an account of a pleasure trip I took last week Saturday with eighty of my scholars to Eagle Harbor. To provide for this trip three teams would be necessary in order to take the whole school. I went to Mr. Anderson & engaged the teams for five dollars apiece. The day was set twice & the first time he failed to be ready. The scholars were sadly disappointed. The next time he told me that I could not have them for he could make a little more & I suppose that he thought that he could put me off until he had nothing to do. But I was not to have everything ready & then another disappointment. I was told this Friday evening at five o'clock & I started on foot without supper for the River four miles distant, hired two teams for thirteen dollars & Captain Paull lent me his so everything was in readiness for a fine time. I arose early Saturday morning & went around to different places encouraging the scholars.

At nine the teams were ready & with three flags flying we left the Cliff singing "Rally round the flag boys." We went through the villages of Eagle River, Garden City, Humboldt, Copper Falls etc.[and] arrived at the Harbor at half past twelve. Had the large hall warmed & there we all took a fine lunch that we brought with us. We returned our sincere thanks to the proprietor & his wife sung them a song gave them three cheers & came home in fine spirits.

At the store I gave them seven dollars worth of candy & nuts. Had three cheers for the Cliff & went home. The day was beautiful & my scholars had a fine treat. This is a great encouragement to them. They will always remember the ride Mr. Hobart gave them.

March 18, 1864

We are now experiencing a sudden change of the weather in all of its fury. The wind commenced blowing last night a gale from the north & the air was filled with sleet & snow. It is now blowing very severely and the thermometer shows two degrees below zero. Although this is not so cold as it might be yet with the searching wind that is now blowing, it is quite unpleasant. I think that this March will compile our worst weather for the year. We may have some storms but they will not be very cold doubtless. O, for the warming spring rays to cheer the cold region of Lake Superior.

Sunday and its scenes

I went to Sunday School in the morning & it was so very cold that the school was very short. On coming home I sat down with Mr. Rawlings in his office & in the afternoon the fire bell rang rousing all.

The fire

It was in a house some forty rods from our place & on the outskirts of the village. It caught from the chimney & the roof was all ablaze before it was noticed. The wind was very strong and cold but from such a direction that no other houses in danger. If it had been blowing opposite, no power could have saved much of our village. I was there shortly after the warning but the wind was so strong that it burnt down in a few minutes although a large house. I climbed up on the front stoop, smashed in a window & tried to save a watch but a dense column of smoke drove me away. It was an exciting scene to witness. Most things were saved.

March 26, 1864

The miners had a holiday yesterday and I closed school Thursday evening at three for the week. I & William went to the River, bought a can of fresh oysters for $1.00, & in the evening went to John's [Penberthy] & ate them all except half a pint which we left for John & wife when they should come home from church. If we had taken them home we should have not got any.

It was a very warm day. Although not very cold this morning, the wind from the north & some snow falling has caused the mercury to fall a number of degrees.

Mr. Philbrick came through from below yesterday bringing his two daughters with him. They are school teachers. He is head carpenter of the mine & a fine old gentleman. Mrs. Rawlings has been giving her girl fits every few days about some trivial cause and yesterday the girl told her that she would go away. It is misery to hear the old lady let off her wrath—there is no end to it. "If you were my girl, I would break you back," etc. I never heard such a tirade of abuse. I often feel like expressing my opinion of these scenes but always keep silence although it is torture & misery to hear them. The old lady & Jimmy are just alike, always mad about nothing & it is impossible to please them. How unreasonable an ignorant person can be. I have seen so much of this lately that I am disgusted beyond endurance.

Ed has had a fall out with Miss Mollie Vivian who was an angel with them all a short time since there was not enough that they could do for her then. His having a quarrel with this young girl shows the spirit of his mother & brother Jimmy. Ignorance. Large bumps of self conceit & pride in a young man make a most disgusting disagreeable customer. A person that will always be hated wherever he goes.

March 28, 1864

What a morning! The wind is blowing a hurricane, snow flying through the air, but there was only one or two inches on top of the hard crust and this is in the air all of the time except behind some hill or house where is falls in a storm & piles up in huge drifts. I ran down to the schoolhouse to build a fire and encountered one of these pleasant places on the steps & door of the front room. The snow was falling in very sweet showers to encounter. The mercury is at twenty-nine degrees so it is very mild. The wind blows from the Lake & with the broad level expanse of Superior to sweep over, it comes in terrible power against the bluff piled like hills along the shore now. It is getting very mild as this storm continues and rains some this evening but not enough to make any great impression on the snow banks.

I received a paper from home and it seems that they are making sugar. I have now missed two sugar seasons here at the Cliff Mine. Negro sugar & molasses is all the go here and talk about having a dislike for the pure Maple free from all impurities, as it is where made by the true Yankee. The Mrs. of the house is cooking off as the days roll by with a storm on a small scale. That is a little correction etc. She & "Millie," the servant, went in big guns last night but it passed off in wind & gas.

Sunday was "Easter," a day for eating eggs in the mining country. But very few were to be had & these at sixty cents per dozen which is quite too much. Georgie Kunkle, one of my pupils, brought me a yellow one which was double yolked.[6] It was a treat. I assure you. Live on Lake Superior & see.

April 4, 1864

The people here enjoyed two fine sermons by Mr. Baughman and one by Mr. Betts last Sunday. Mr. Betts' remarks were very interesting and practical. He spoke on the following text—Job 22:2. Viz "Can a man be profitable unto God as he that is wise may be profitable unto himself." He had two objects in view to correct a common, fatal, error that is prevalent in the minds of most persons, and point all to the true source or merit viz Christ. The error that is so very common and exerts its terrible and fatal effects on the mind is as follows. Most persons believe that they make God obliged to save them on account of some good work they do. How common this error and yet it is a fatal one. Most persons, nay, all desire happiness. It is a prominent feature of the mind.

Most persons are apt to press their opinions as the only ones worthy of merit and often exhibit some willfulness in sustaining their views. It would appear as if they were worthy of merit or should be rewarded for their opinions. This is contrary to the true spirit of love & justice. With men, one is obliged to help another. Obligations bind the human family together as brothers. We see this in all the business of life.

But while we are under obligation to assist each other, no work we can perform can oblige our Father or place him under obligation to save us on account of the merit of any good work. He created us, supplies our wants, but above all gave his Son for us, therefore we poor finite creatures cannot discharge our debt of gratitude to him. Time is too short to fulfill our obligations to him. The true source of merit is Christ, and if we are saved at all, it will not be on account of our virtues but through the blood of Christ. By all means, do good works & promote truth.

Riches

There is a beautiful definition to this word which should make a true impression on the mind of every thinking person. Especially the sordid and avaricious worshiper of the almighty dollar. It means adaptation in one sense. Therefore, a man cannot be said to be rich unless he is adapted to or money is adapted to his wants. Load a person with gold & unless he can make a proper use of it, he is not rich. Money is of no practical or right use if a person is not fitted to use it. If a person is sick, his stomach all out of order, the best of food is no use to him. He turns away in disgust from it. Doctor him, cure him & then it will be of use to him. So riches or money is of use to one when he becomes adapted to make use of it. There is a fable that runs thus:

A certain person who became deeply anxious to obtain Gold prayed to "Jupiter" that what he touched might turn into Gold. Accordingly when he touched his chair, it turned into Gold; also his clothes & everything he laid hands on. Soon he became hungry but when he touched his food, it turned into Gold and he died in the midst of his Gold for bread to eat. He was not rich although covered with Gold.

An honest old Quaker once met while on a ride a fast young man in a sleigh in a very bad place to turn out. The young Gent quietly folded his hands took out a paper & commenced reading. After a while the good Quaker said, "When thee Last finished that paper I will thank thee for the loan of it." It is needless to say that the young man turned out and let the old gentleman pass by. Be accommodating at all times & in all places. Do good at all times & in all places.

The most important event of the week past was the organization of a Good Templars Lodge in this place on Friday evening. It is a secret Society sworn to use no kind of intoxicating drink as a beverage & to oppose its use in all lawful ways. It is secret & no one can enter but a Good Templar. I am worthy Secretary of the Lodge and have entered into the work with strong efforts & a determination to do all in my power to promote the cause. We are engaged in a noble work & have taken solemn oaths in the three different degrees of the Lodge. I trust I may live & lead a temperate life. I am decidedly opposed to tea, coffee or any beverage of the kind. Give me the water in a glass sparkling bright.

It is foggy, wet or damp kind of weather now. Snow is quite soft in most places. School moves lively. Everything looks fine, and prosperous. Miners now pay fifteen dollars for board, Provisions, and especially clothing is very high. It is impossible for one man with a family to save anything. I think that things will raise or be much higher when new goods come. I shall buy as little as possible and save all I can.

Mr. Struckmire's little boy is to be buried tomorrow. He died with the scarlet fever. I think, it has been & is quite unpleasant weather, the thermometer indicating about forty degrees above zero, very cloudy, and the snow under foot is getting very soft. It is truly unpleasant weather. I wish we might have a heavy thaw and remove the great body of snow that lies on the ground now. It is warm enough to make sugar and I can imagine how things look at home. Someone must take my place in the work. I do not know as I feel like engaging in the business of making sugar now for my saga as teacher has made me quite soft physically saying nothing about the mental powers. I am not strong & hardy but quite womanish or soft. A summer's work would do me some good I think.

April 6, 1864

Yesterday the mercury indicated a temperature of sixty degrees in the afternoon but it was not high any great length of time, ranging between that and forty. Snow is getting very soft and wet feet will soon be the general complaint unless care be taken to prevent it. I fancy that this will soften the ice on the Lake so that it will not take much to break it up. If so, the Boats will be up about their usual time. I receive no mail of late but look anxiously for some news from home.

I received a letter from Miss Hyde of Grand Isle in relation to a situation last week, but such a place is not open as Mr. Philbrick has two daughter here who are teachers of some experience. There is much talk about having me remain and scholars beg me to come back. I would like to please them but I cannot say at present.

Nothing of importance has occurred today. Mail this afternoon but nothing from home. Roads very bad & sleighs will soon stop running.

A story is told of a professor in college who became quite fascinated with a young girl in the school. A young student also took great interest in young Ellen also, and would manage generally to have a seat by her side at prayer time, the two desks being near each other. Professor was to have prayer in his usual turn. He had a habit of opening his eyes every few words & this morning in question he had commenced his prayer & was proceeding finely, keeping his eyes open most of the time. Young student sat next too Ellen & was giving her a kiss when Prof opened his eyes & was saying "O Lord." "See him kiss her" came next. It is quite likely that services were unusually short and student was more careful in future. Profs should keep their eyes closed during prayer.

April 8, 1864

It is quite cold and snowing some this morning. The wind is in the north and it seems quite wintry. Good Templars meet this evening to confer degrees. I shall not have a very large school today I think.

Our meeting passed off without any trouble. We put Brothers Wiley & Johns through the three different degrees. Our regular Lodge meeting comes every Saturday night. Degree meeting are generally held once a month. Mr. William Summers received a bad cut on the hand in the mine.

A story

It is told of a young man whose home was in Ohio that he became a preacher went away & while away, hanged his coat taking up with some ism or other. After many years he returned to his former home & was called upon to preach in the old church. The old friends all came in to hear him. After preaching a while he undertook to enforce his new ism & called for those who would be in favor of his cherished views to come forward to the altar. A man in the back part of the house had a large black dog which he had trained to go & shake hands with anyone. When converts were called for & silence was prevailing, the master told his dog to go & shake hands with the preacher. The dog went down the aisle & placing his paws on the alter handed one of his paws to the minister. He did not receive any more converts in that place.

Tresider's speech

I have failed to have an opportunity of reading this grand "sally" of a young Cornishman but it is a tale thing I learn. Full of Gas and things about which he has read. Success to him for he is determined to be a big thing.

April 23, 1864

It is a long time since I wrote in this book during this time some changes have taken place but no very important event. It has been very warm fine weather—the sun has shone most of the time and the snow has gone away gradually until much of the ground is bare. The old Bluff has shaken the immense snow banks from its rocky sides. The road is free from snow. It has gone so very gradually that there has been no heavy flood of water & rain. The little hillock just below the schoolhouse is bare and the boys are enjoying a game of ball.

Captain Souden has gone to the North Cliff Mine to take charge of it. His family are here yet. Thomas George has been promoted to fill the Captain's place in this mine. There is much talk about when we shall have the first boat. Some bet quite heavy in the oyster line.

John Penberthy is going to the Portage to clerk for Leopold receiving $900 per year. I think that the ice is nearly gone on the Lake. I have not received any letters of late which makes the time see quite long. We are now enjoying a Lake Superior spring. Very invigorating weather it is true but there is a great scarcity in the eating line—no meat, stale butter, old molasses & white bread which I like if there was some corn bread once in a while. But I get tired of it without milk, no pies or anything inviting. One of my little girls brings me an apple once in a while which is a fine treat. I have had one or two eggs just enough to inform me that they go fine but that I cannot have them. The warehouse pork would do for one to eat who had lost the sense of smell. In any other circumstances it is no go.

Notes for March-April 1864

1. Will Carnsew, born in England in 1820, lived in Portage, Michigan in 1860. He and his wife, June, had two children. *8th U. S. Census*, Michigan, Houghton County 1860. He was a mining captain for the Cliff Mine in the 1850s. Pittsburgh & Boston Mining Company. Annual Report, November 1856 and November 1857, located in the State Library, Lansing, Michigan. He was active in the Grace Episcopal Church in Clifton. See Brockway Scrapbook, Bentley Library, University of Michigan, Ann Arbor, Michigan.

2. According to the *9th U.S. Census*, Keweenaw County, 1870, John Carnsew was born in England in 1832.

3. Johns may have been James Johns, a hotel keeper in Eagle River in 1860. *8th U. S. Census*. Houghton County, 1860.

4. James, age 4, was the son of William S. and Elizabeth Thomas, according to the *8th U. S. Census*. Houghton County, 1860. Mrs. Jane Sampson, age 35, was the wife of Richard Sampson, a miner, age 38; their children were John, age 8, and Richard, age 5, according to the *8th U. S. Census*, Houghton County, 1860.

5. E. M. Green was the shipping clerk at the Cliff Mine in the 1860s. See the Pittsburgh & Boston Mining Company Annual Report, 1863-1864, located in the State Library, Lansing, Michigan.

6. George Kunkle was the son of Stephen, age 38, and Susannah, age 38, according to the *8th U. S. Census*, Houghton County, 1860.

Spring on Lake Superior, said Hobart, came like "freedom to the caged prisoner."
The painting on the following page by Robert S. Duncanson, The Cliff Mine,
Lake Superior, 1848, shows the bluff as one looks northwest.

May—June 1864

May 7, 1864

On account of pressing business day and evening, I have been wholly unable to write as I should. The weather has been mild. Quite a rain yesterday. There are very few snow banks in sight at this time yet there is plenty of snow in the bush. There is some floating ice in the Lake [and] a heavy bank along the shore. We had a boat last year the first of May but there is no prospect of one now. There is no special news.

A very sad accident took place the other day at noon. The rocks came down the Bluff and a rock of about seven tons dashed in the side of a house standing at the foot of the Bluff and killed a little girl asleep in the bed. One woman was in the house at the time but escaped. The house was knocked to pieces and everything in it. The rocks often fall down the sides of the Bluff in the spring, after being loosened by the frost. A house was knocked to pieces in the same way some time since in the night and a family of eight in bed thrown out into the road and not injured.

Cornish Wrestling

I witnessed a few tumbles in this way for a prize of thirty dollars. There was a crowd of men and women, ladies etc. present also

285

several barrels of ale on the ground. The wrestlers took off their shirts and put on a very loose jacket made of bagging tied with cord up & down in front. It was then a rough and tumble game, twisting each other in all shapes. Most of them were full of "Beer," swearing, fighting etc. I never witnessed such a tight, rough set of men in my life. I cannot tell all the Cornish talk and will not try. Some were very good on a hitch.

May 12, 1864

It has been a very fine day, warm, pleasant and plenty of cheering sunshine. It was quite windy yesterday. The *Iron City* was in at the Dock today. She passed up the day before yesterday but could not come in on account of a severe wind. Very little was brought up for this place, just a few oranges selling for twelve cents a piece. A few men came up for the Mine. Also a clerk "John" has gone to the Portage to clerk for H. F. Leopold & Co. for nine hundred dollars per year.[1] A few cattle were brought up and are selling at twenty cents per pound killed & retailed out. Things must be very high. Board at the Hotel is thirty-five dollars per month and will be twenty here. I must lose some money by engaging for ten months which would have been fine for me if things were as low now as they were then.

I am very busy, so much so that my Journal is almost a failure. I am Secretary and Librarian of the Sunday School, Librarian of the Township Library, Secretary of the Good Templars Society, President of the Band of Hope, a juvenile temperance society of seventy members. All this business is outside of the School. My time is well taken up. Our Good Templars Society is a fine thing and is doing much for the Temperance cause. May it prosper. I trust that I shall never dishonor it or do anything to violate its sacred principles and truths. The principles of a good templar.

May 13, 1864

How cheering and pleasant the sun breaks out this morning. It will be a very warm day. I close school this afternoon for the week. I think that I shall have some execise or a ramble tomorrow. I hope the mails will come regular soon. I must now attend to "Lodge" minutes. Had a spelling school in the afternoon and a very fine time of it. William Benney drew the ticket for spelling the school down. Many of the scholars were not there as it is a very busy time. Two or three of the best boys have gone to work. Miss Nutt talks about going away.

May 18, 1864

The weather is fine and pleasant. There is very little wind and it is very warm every day. The ground is becoming dry and warm. The leaves are beginning to spring from the trees, the grass is looking green and bright and with the invigorating air of our Lake Superior clime, it is cheering to the person caged up here through the long winters. It is like freedom to the prisoner. I shall not try to find time to go and see a boat for it is not worth the trouble.

Things are high and I have spent thirty-six dollars for clothing. This I am obliged to do as I have nothing to wear. I am sorry that I am under a contract for I shall lose much by it. I cannot prevent it now but will work out my time. I am now President of the Band of Hope which is prospering finely. It is a noble thing and will do much Good. All the little boys & girls are much pleased with it. I will make it prosper under my care, and trust it will after I finish my work. I enjoy the meetings of the Good Templars Lodge very much. It is a noble Society and has a fine object. May it continue to prosper as it has so far.

May 21, 1864

The weather is very hot ranging about eighty degrees for a number of days. It is somewhat cloudy and often a brisk little breeze springs up a few drops of rain falls, but the "good shower" that all would like to see does not fall. It was very unpleasant in bed last night and when I got up this morning I found a large bed bug—perhaps come to warn me of a fate similar to last spring, when I was sorely bitten by them. The bed was full of them and the curtains also. I shall try and avoid a like fate this spring, but I will drop the subject thinking and hoping that some scourge may come to destroy the whole race of bugs.

The bushes on the side of the Bluff look quite green and fresh which is one of the best evidences of the coming spring. It is refreshing to see this change in the aspect of nature. Flowers are now beginning to blossom and fill the air with their sweet perfume giving please [pleasure] to anyone who walks out to enjoy the spring air.

The mine is prospering finely; about thirty new men are at work here now. The surveyor gets about fifteen dollars per day which is very good wages. Captain Souden will move to the North Cliff Mine very soon. He is agent and Mr. Osborne is mining Captain. Men are now getting the North American Mine ready to work by pumping out the water.

Our Lodge in the evening passed off pleasantly and without trouble. Things were done decently and in order. Thus the noble "Order" will continue to perform the great work for which it was intended. We number about fifty strong members ready to work for the overthrow of the evil of "Intemperance." And our efforts are not all in vain. We have taken some from a bad end and hope to take more. Success to the Good Templars.

May 23, 1864

It is a cool cloudy damp morning. Rain fell some last night but not in a very large quantity. It makes the fields look very green and beautiful, the buds on the trees to start with new life and vigor. How cheering to see the first evidences of summer, the summer in which I hope to see home once more. I notice some things about our Lake Superior weather that are quite different from the warm showers of Old Vermont. We seldom if ever have any of those storms that pour down in torrents that we do in Vermont. We have had no rain of any amount here this spring. The woods are not covered with verdure yet only a few bushes among the rocks where it is warm. It will be a long time before the leaves will be out in full beauty. I shall not engage in planting this spring but will avoid anything of the kind.

I have not written a letter for some weeks and in fact I have no time. I have the minutes of the Lodge of Good Templars to write; also, Band of Hope; and some time about the Sabbath School is required each week. In our Sabbath School we are to have a paper once every month made by the officers and teachers. I think this will be a fine thing and will draw the attention of the people to the school as the exercise is to be public. If properly conducted it will, no doubt, have many beneficial results which can not be derived from our present faulty system. There are very many isms in our Sabbath School which I dislike. I hope they will be put down sooner or later. Clifton Lodge of the I. O. of G. T. and the Band of Hope are having fine prosperity. May they continue to increase in strength.

June 8, 1864

During the past few days since I wrote, I have been very busy in school and while out of school working to prepare the "Band of Hope" with their new Regalias and writing on Lodge matters. I have not felt any appetite to write or compose. I have wrote only two letters for many long weeks. One home and the other to Uncle John Shipman.[2] I have not heard from home or any friend and I am quite lonely. I hope I shall receive some news very soon.

At my home everything moves after the old style. Mrs. Rawlings has no cow and I get no milk which makes me feel quite sour. Mrs. Rawlings is going to Portage Lake very soon to stop one month. We shall not hear her ceaseless murmurs, then I suppose. Mrs. Rawlings is busy with his work. Quite a number of new men have come up this spring. The most of them are "Old Sods" from Cornwall.

There is one thing worthy of notice with these young Cornishmen. They are nearly all "local preachers."[3] Nothing that I can discover goes to show that they have any education. They can exhort and groan and make a noise but there is nothing refining about them. I listened to one last Saturday evening who went into the pulpit with his hat on and in witnessing his contortions, I was reminded of some pictures in the "college maul", a paper from Burlington College.[4] Violent Gestures. Great noise, Cornish Eloquence. Bustin sermon etc. But I do not speak about this in derision only as a comparison with intelligent preaching such as would come from the lips of Rev. Mr. Baughman of Portage Lake.

June 9, 1864

It was truly a warm day yesterday. I found it very unpleasant in the school room. I think the thermometer rose as high as ninety degrees in the sun. In the afternoon we had a small thunder shower and some hail fell during the storm. In the evening William and I went to Captain Paull's. Captain is doing all he can to have me remain here. He is well pleased with the school and wishes me to come back anyway.

It is quite cool this morning and there is a breeze from the Lake. The sky is clear and there is a promise of a fine day after the cooling shower. The leaves are coming out on the trees and everything looks green. It is indeed spring but from my confinement I hardly realize it. I have two girls in school now who are studying French. I am getting along finely and have a full school.

There have been one or two very narrow escapes from death in the mine. A rock of one ton came out from one side of a drift and caught Mr. Samuel James against the other side right across the kidneys & hips.[5] He was fairly crushed and is in a very dangerous condition. It is a wonder that he was not killed at once. A large rock rolled over Mr. Pommy but did not injure him seriously as others prevented him from being hurt by laying up so as to form a hollow. How many dangers are in store for the miner. I think that I will go down into the mine next Friday night with Captain Sam Bennetts & William Penberthy.

Went up to Brother Charles James in the evening with Ellen and Melissa Philbrick and Brother William and had some eggs and milk or "Eggy hot," as it is called. Miners just from the mine often when going into the dinner room say, "Dance youee—Pasty for dinner," or some expression very much similar. Can you "clunk" a pasty [is an expression] which means to swallow one. "Bravish old pasty youee, eh old man," etc.

June 17, 1864

Hot, suffocating weather, causing a person to feel very lazy and indolent and unfit for any work. The thermometer ranges as high as a hundred degrees yesterday in the sun. What weather for teaching. Few scholars and very lazy ones at that. The leaves on the trees are of a dark color and the bluff looks very beautiful clothed in the rich foliage of the bushes and trees. A good ramble looks as if it would be pleasant to one confined for months in the school room with its impure air. But I cannot enjoy that pleasure at present.

I have received one letter from home during the past few days. The Vermont soldiers were cut to pieces in the late battles with Grant & Lee. Father and Mother urge me very strongly to return home soon. My school will close in twenty-four days.

I shall be to the Good Templars Lodge as Secretary tonight. It is a degree meeting. The regular meeting will be tomorrow night. I enjoy these meetings although they cost me much labor. I have all the writing and business to attend too and find my time very well occupied.

June 20, 1864

It is very hot unpleasant weather. I find day after day the same disagreeable feeling. It was ninety degrees this morning and as strange as it may seem, we have not had one good shower this spring and the mercury has been as high as one hundred and ten degrees. This is awful weather for one to enjoy in a school room. I must say that it is a little irksome although I have become very much attached to the business and regret that I may have to give it up for the drugery of the farm. I must not yet.

The amiable "John Spir"[Spears][6]

It is not my aim to show any disrespect or say any thing against my Cornish brother for such I call every good strong working Good Templer. We hold the pleasant relation of brothers and sisters, that is, all members of our Noble Order and are bound to assist each other whenever assistance is demanded. But I must speak of Brother John. He is a full or pure blooded Cornishman, short in stature and quite a "Cousin Jack" in appearance. Speaks pure Cornish and is quite simple and ignorant. He was a hard drinker until he joined our Order, and I have often seen him drunk & in a shameful condition, even dancing with his clothes off.

He is now firm. He was married night before last. He was always telling about bringing his spark from the old country and everyone knew the fact. Says John: "Cusent ee see old man. I get a nice little spark at home & I spect she here soon." Well, John's spark came & in one half of an hour they were united. John had got tired & wanted to go to bed but some of the Boys must have a spree so John did not get to bed until very near morning. "Twoudent do youee cusent ee see she is tired."

John has her at home and very many have gone to see her. But Brother Spir [Spears] says, "Twoudent do for so many come to seen she. Cusent ee see she's just come from the old county." Well, John, I wish you success with your cosy little wife. Be firm in the principles of Good Templarship & you will prosper. "Ay old man, she will make you happy although she came a brave way."

June 21, 1864

How very similar to the past few days only it is quite cloudy this morning, but it soon cleared away and now the same suffocating, warm, unpleasant, sultry kind of days. I can hardly keep my eyes open which I attribute partly to the severe heat and partly to the fact that I set up until three with a "Good Templar," a young lady, of course, and an old hand at teaching. She is from Wisconsin and is a lady of fine principles and accomplishments and good health.

It is the first time since I left Vermont that I have met with what I might call a fine young lady. It is true there are young girls and Cornish girls but I cannot appreciate their excellent pasty qualities. I know a lady and especially one of some mind. When I hear a young lady of about one hundred and eighty pounds saying now "heree he ain't good for noffing for such a brave miss as she." "Thee art a nice man" & etc. and this is an uncommon display of the mental powers of some. I am sick. An order of the brute creation and very little above that kind of stock. What a shame cannot read nor write. They can make a pasty that a strong "Cousin Jack" can clunk without knowing any difference between it and a good rousing pie. A hog had very little choice so it is here.

There is something cheering, something noble, something attractive in the manner & conversation of a young lady of pure mind, well cultivated and possessing the true American stamp to a person who has listened to the Cornish twaddle and nonsense for nearly two long years. I am reminded of good company of good society etc. What a difference.

June 22, 1864

It is as warm as ever. I am sick and expect to have school before noon. I have felt miserable and took a strong dose of medicine last night. It has only weakened me without any operation therefore I shall feel quite miserable until it operates. I dislike very much to take any such medicine when in school but must as I am quite out of tune.

Captain Souden has been discharged from the North Cliff Mine. He was accused of writing a certain letter to the *Miner's Gazette* not approving of Watson's course of conduct. Captain Souden is free and an independent man. He has more sense and good information than the whole nest of Watson's "clique." I am sorry that he is going away for it is a pity to lose a good man from any place. I trust that he will better his situation or have a better one. Success to an energetic worker of sound priciples.

The mercury is at one hundred and ten at twelve noon. This is very warm. It is too much heat for school. I have nineteen days more before my time is out. It will pass off without my thinking of it. There is to be a show or sleight of hand performance at the Good Templars Hall this evening.[7] I judge that is a small thing. Josiah is now at work about the algebra and nothing else. The school is quite small now, owing to various causes.

Sam James is recovering from his bruise in the mine. He will not be able to do anything or even walk for many weeks and perhaps months.

The Band of Hope will meet here tonight. I shall have all the business to perform as the first Superintendent is on night shift. This is the case generally so it does not trouble me much. I will make things move. Success to the Band of Hope.

June 23, 1864

Hot, hot as ever. Mercury at one hundred degrees this morning. I went to the store and bought a shirt & suspenders for seven dollars and twenty-five cents. I could not do without them.

The Band of Hope met last night. Had a very fine meeting and a pleasant time. After the meeting I went to the Hall and saw a scientific performance including some magic and sleight of hand. It was a very good thing. I am quite weary of my labors as teacher. It is so very warm and [I] look for a change. I must have a fishing tour in the bush soon. But I suppose that the flies are very savage. If we could only have some rain it would do much good. I think I will go on the Bluff this evening. Perhaps there will be some one there who has a specimen of copper for me.

Good Templar

The aim of a Templar is not only to do all within his power or means to injure and prevent the use of any liquors, to prevent its sale etc. but as a Society their efforts extend to deeds of charity. Every member of the order is bound to assist another in distress to extend the hand of sympathy etc. I have a case in point. Our worthy Brother William Osborne is sick. He is supplied with watchers and all he wants by the Good Templars of this place. The committee visit him and he has whatever he wants. If I were in a strange land and in trouble, I should make myself known as a Templar and any Brother present are bound by the most solemn ties to render me assistance. It is a noble order and has a noble object.

June 24, 1864

How pleasant the wind is in this hot weather and in spite of breezes the mercury is up to one hundred degrees but this cooling breeze from the Lake makes it very pleasant. I am quite certain that it is full as warm as it is below generally. It is indeed worthy of notice that we have not had any rain this spring. Hot sultry unpleasant weather most of the time.

I just learned that there has been a very severe fire at the Central Mine, destroying the Stamp Mill, wash, saw mill, four dwellings & thousands of dollars worth of wood.[8] It will be a damage of over one hundred thousand dollars to the company. This is killing to the profits of the mine. I did not learn the cause of this fire.

A. Trewarther, who left this Mine to teach at the "Central", is coming back to run an engine. He is sick of the drudgery of a teacher's life. The Board at Eagle Harbor raised their teacher's wages to sixty dollars per month on account of the high price of things. This is an honorable act and should give the stingy "Board" of this District an idea of their true duty. Honor to an act of that kind. It shows a just appreciation of the services [that] should be fully appreciated

It is the teacher who works for the best interests of his pupils and who is always ready to assist & promote their interest and that of every good reform. I love such an individual for he is doing more to advance the cause of truth and universal education than the mass of the laboring people. It is a noble cause and should stir the noblest feelings of the heart. If there is no pecuniary reward; to the true man, there is a conscious satisfaction of having led the youthful mind in the true direction and accomplished good that is permanent & lasting.

June 25, 1864

The wind is blowing almost a gale this morning sending clouds of dust into the air and fine sand. The road is so very dry that the sand is flying in all directions. It is very bad for the eyes. I do not think that I shall walk out much today in this storm of sand & dust.

Brother William Osborne is in a very dangerous condition. He has the "Quick Consumption," to all appearance. He used to walk to the North Cliff Mine getting very warm and then to into the mine. It is not well aired and very bad so much so that a light will not burn in some places. He took a severe cold, I think, and as he is now, there is very little prospect of his recovery. He has a wife and one little boy. He has always been very unfortunate in life. Brother Wiley is with him today. Rev. Mr. Wright is getting quite smart again. James Penberthy was taken this morning with something like the "colic." He is quite sick. I was unwell myself this morning. The weather is quite too warm for health. I trust that there will be a speedy change soon.

I saw William Van Orden's sister pass last night.[9] She is up on a visit from New York City to see her brothers who are stopping at Captain Paull's as clerks. They are relatives of Kennedy who stands at the head of the "Police Force" of New York City. William Van Orden is a very smart young man having a thorough knowledge of most kinds of business.

Scene in Detroit

Last week a young man was running through the street in the Delirium Tremens in awful agony thinking a number of men were going to kill him. He was confined & thought snakes were on him. He begged for water but would not drink. It was an awful sight. Shocking.

June 28, 1864

The weather has changed so it is quite mild and pleasant and not so very disagreeable and hot. This change took place Saturday night and was so violent that there was quite a severe frost. We got no rain. Sunday was a very pleasant day.

I set with William to watch Brother William Osborne's corpse. The funeral took place yesterday. The I. O. of G. T. and O. F. formed in procession as he was a member of both Orders. I acted as one of the bearers. He was taken to the O. F.'s burying ground at Eagle River. His wife is a very dangerous state. She fainted at the church and also at the grave. It is a very sad case. He died like a true Christian—happy and firm in his belief. How consoling are the truths of Religion.

June 29, 1864

Quite windy and warm. A few drops of rain fell this morning but only a few. The sky is very clear and there is a prospect of the same warm weather that we have experienced all along. How long this will continue without any change I cannot tell. But I sincerely trust that it will not be very long.

I intend to go into the mine tonight after the meeting of the "Band of Hope." Captain Sam Bennetts will conduct our party down. William Wylie, William Penberthy, Isaac Bergan and perhaps P. V. Carbines will go with us. We will have plenty of oysters after coming up. I trust that we may all come up safe and that no one of us may be hurt.

I have just received a letter from the Grand Secretary of the Good Templars Lodge enclosing the Charter of our Lodge. *Je fini pour ce nuit, je pense. Bon soir mon plume.*

June 30, 1864

I was in Cliff Mine as far as the one hundred and twenty level. We had a very pleasant time and got to the surface about three this morning. I am feeling quite tired. I cut out a chip of copper from a mass at the one hundred. "Jack" Richards held the chisel.[10]

We had some oysters & pineapples on coming to the surface. It is a long road to the one hundred and twenty, and especially coming back. The ladder way is very good most of the way. At the one hundred and twenty level there is a beautiful show of copper. Large masses of copper being cut etc. Some are still in the rock & small drifts are being dug in behind them to throw them out with a sand blast. William Simmens was working in one of these.[11]

Edward Richards showed us down viz Brothers William Penberthy & I constituted the party. We were at Number 4 shaft looking at the skip in one hundred and ten fathom level when Captain Samuel Bennetts came down. We then went all through below. I think I will go down some day and see the work in a day shift. I used three candles while down last night.

Mining is very dangerous work and there is a very great cost in opening a mine. The drifts in Cliff Mine are very long. It is a very large mine and it takes a long time to follow through the long range of levels. It is very tiresome work to a person who is not accustomed to the business of climbing. If I were to work in a mine, I should prefer to work in one not so very deep unless there was a chance to ride down. There will be a man engine at work here this fall. Mr. Rawlings is putting it into operation as fast as possible. It will be a fine piece of work when completed.

Notes for May-June 1864

1. H. F. Leopold was a member of a pioneer family of the Keewenaw. The Leopold brothers opened general stores in Eagle Harbor and Eagle River and in 1858 erected the first store in Hancock. *8th U.S. Census*. Houghton County. 1860 and Clarence Monette, *Hancock, Michigan Remembered* (Monette: Lake Linden, 1982), p. 8.

2. John Shipman was married to Rachel Hobart, sister of Amos Hobart, and aunt to Henry.

3. For an account of the Cornish tradition of lay preachers, revival meetings, and hymn singing, see John Rowe, *Hard Rock Men: Cornish Immigrants* (New York: Barnes and Noble, 1974), p. 15 and Fisher, "Michigan Cornish People," *Michigan History* 29 (1945), p. 383.

4. Burlington College is the University of Vermont, chartered in 1791 and located in Burlington.

5. Samuel James, age 37, was married to Maria, age 35. By 1860 they had five children. *8th U. S. Census*, Michigan, Houghton County, 1860.

6. John Spears was born in England in 1832. He and his wife Jane had two children as of 1860. *8th U.S. Census*, Houghton County, 1860.

7. There is no reference to the name of the performer; however, on September 5, 1863, the *Lake Superior Miner* announced that "Whitney the Necromancer performed to a full house at Good Templar Hall at the Minesota Mine in Rosendale."

8. For an account of the fire, see *Lake Superior Miner*, July 2, 1864.

9. According to the *8th U. S. Census*, Houghton County, 1860, William Van Orden was born in 1839. His occupation was listed as clerk.

10. Jack Richards was listed in the *8th U. S. Census*, Houghton County, 1860, as age 24, and as a native of England. He lived with a brother, William Richards.

11. William Simmens, a miner, was born in England in 1830. He and his wife Elizabeth, age 29, had four children as of 1860. *8th U. S. Census.* Houghton County, Michigan, 1860.

The painting shows the area of Vermont where Hobart was returning; he said he regretted giving up teaching "for the drudgery of the farm." Hobart recorded the death of the child whose grave marker is shown on the following page.

July 1, 1864

It is a very beautiful morning although quite cloudy at times; still there is no prospect of any rain. It is quite smoky and there is strong evidences of large fires back in the woods. It is a very dry time and fires sweep over thousands of acres.

I was busy last night in a degree meeting of the Good Templars Order. Had plenty of business. The regular Lodge meeting will come tonight after which I must watch with Mr. Wilson's little boy who died this morning.[1] He was sick only a few days with some kind of fever. Mrs. Wilson is a woman of very feeble health and this sad event will doubtless have a very bad effect on her. She is a true Christian and will look to the true source for comfort in this sad bereavement. It is solid comfort in time of some affliction to possess a sure faith and strong hope.

July 3, 1864

Saturday I spent at home not doing much anyway. I was here at the Library at the proper hours. Today I have done very little. I went up in the morning and attended the election of teachers in Sunday School. I resigned my office as Secretary & Librarian. The meeting was a pleasant one and some good changes were made in the exercises connected with the school. I sincerely trust that the school will prosper finely and increase in number. The efforts of many in the school are well deserving success and prosperity. I trust that they will meet with the praise their labors demand. I am glad that I am through for I have labored very hard.

July 5, 1864

It is a very cool morning; cloudy, small prospect of a shower. The thick black clouds begin to roll up from the west, distant thunder can be heard. It comes nearer & now we are having as fine a shower as I have seen for many long months. The ground which has been baked and dried by the heat of the spring months is now moistened by a cooling shower. It is not enough but I hope it is the forerunner of many more pleasant, cooling, showers of rain.

The "Fourth" was celebrated in this place in the Cornish way. There must be no change. Whatever was done by preceding generations must be done today. I dislike this principle which ex-cludes everything like change or improvement. The same kind of Cornish cake & lemonade, the same detestable way of giving it out and the same hoggish way of receiving it. It is the most disagree-able sight I ever saw. They are like hogs in every sense of the word.

Of course being the only genuine Yankee in the place, I had to read the "Declaration of Independence." Also helped pass the Lemonade & Cornish Cake. I could not enjoy myself at all. I am disgusted with the want of public spirit in the place. There is not public spirit or anyone who wishes to build up the place and contribute to the public good except Captain Souden. He is now going away.

At the Boarding House there was a fight in which one chap was well beaten. The cause was a dispute in gambling and the parties being well soaked with Beer. At the Hall there was a grand "Ball" by the Germans in the evening. Beer was the principle feature in-cluding much noise and some small fighting. The noblest sight among the crowd of whiskey-soaked, beer bellies of the blear-eyed set of Cornish topers, was now and then three of four "Good Tem-plars" together with eyes clear and bright and minds also, enjoy-ing as a temperate man only can enjoy the scenes of the day. It is a cheering sight for one interested in reform. I am glad that our soci-ety is beginning to make its mark that we will do much good. A stranger to the drunken scenes that I have witnessed on Lake Su-perior would never know how to appreciate the great reforms re-sulting from the earnest efforts of pure, sound "Good Templars." We initiated a young man about twenty-four years of age last Sat-urday night who has been a terrible drinker and engaged in fights in consequence of his drunken habits. He is taken from ruin and we are taking very many from an awful ruin.

I received a very pleasant letter from cousin George Eastman this morning who is now in Titusville, Pennsylvania, making one hundred dollars per month. It is in the oil region. I trust that he may prosper finely and receive extra pay. I think I may perhaps visit him.

A new agent for this mine arrived here today. Watson is to re-main as general Superintendent of several mines and have sub agents under his control. I should not enjoy such a birth I assure you. Compelled to obey the dictates of such a man would approach very near to slavery. I have nothing to say about him however. I am aware of the fact that the officers of this Mine are linked together like a band of rogues and their highest aim is money and nothing else. Men are abused in a shameful way as a result of this action. No regard is paid to Sunday, or decent respect to others. The clerk is a rascal to the bone.

July 6, 1864

It is a damp, cloudy, cool morning, just such as very frequently follow a shower of rain. A person feels like getting near the stove or taking some cozy corner enjoy a quiet snooze. Perhaps this is fancy of mine, feeling tired and a little lazy. Well, it is not very strange that I feel tired and sleepy as I was up until twelve last night having a cozy talk with a fine school man of the "Hoosier" style. This, of course, would cause me to feel quite lazy and another very good reason is my school is small, so there is very little inducement to drive business. I might remark by the way that I feel quite sleepy about two days in each week. Perhaps there is some good reason, but I will not explain the matter or as Brother John Spir said when asked the password of our Lodge by an outsider, "Cusent ee see old man I shant split."

Well, I will speak of other events. The formidable I. R. Tresider is up once more but not to make any speeches. He has had one or two fits and is not in very good health. He intends entering the Michigan University in one year.[2] Sam James, who was so very seriously hurt in the mine, is able to walk around some. He is recovering very fast. I hope he will be able to work as his family are in a very pitiable condition.

Mr. Dunn, who lived just opposite of us, has gone to the Bay State Mine as Captain Abraham Trewarther will occupy his house and drive No. 5 engine on the Bluff for raising masses of copper. There is a teacher wanted at the Central Mine—pay sixty dollars per month. Captain Josiah Halls has gone to New York to take charge of a mine. I think it is nearly opposite to our place.

July 7, 1864

A cold, cloudy, rainy, damp morning in which the "flannel" feels quite pleasant —much more so than the "cotton" and by the way I wear flannel as my cotton shirts are scat up and they are so very costly, I will not buy any more. My "flannel" cost six dollars, not a very mild price. Goods of all kinds [and] also provisions are being raised in price daily. Butter is over five cents per pound. Boots ten dollars per pair. Coats from sixteen apiece. Hats from two dollars, to six dollars, a piece. Vests five dollars. Pants twelve dollars. And these are the common stock, nothing extra. It is by the closest economy that I save any thing. My expenses were about per month for two months this spring when I was compelled to purchase new clothes.

Mrs. Rawlings will come from the Portage this week. There is to be a very great change in this place. About fifty men have gone already have gone and more are going. Miners do much better at all other mines. Messrs. Thomas & Isaac Bergan, members of our Lodge, are going. It will injure our Society some as it takes away some of the most active members. I shall go and the main business of the Lodge rests on my shoulders. The "Band of Hope" will lose its leader and founder. It numbers seventy members. I sincerely trust that it will be fully sustained and so good a cause be maintained.

How few there are that take any interest in the great reforms of the day or in sustaining the best interest of Society, truth and justice. I ever wish to see my name connected with all great practical reforms on the roll of those who sustain morality, virtue, truth and Christianity. I hope, above, all never to see it where hundreds are seen in the country viz. O, the Books of the whiskey dealer in debt for Paddy's eye water or a "Bill of Ale." Sustain the right, oppose the wrong.

James Watson

It is my honest intention to express my mind freely on this page in relation to the honorable gentleman whose name stands at the top of this page. I shall do it without prejudice or any desire to find fault yet I wish to speak of his faults in plain terms. It is one thing to act the gentleman and another to claim all the rights and privileges of one and fail to perform the duties of one. It is one thing to meet a man face to face & inform him if he is trespassing, it is quite another to slander him behind his back. It is one thing to be a man when in a position of influence and quite another to fancy one's self so mighty exalted and elevated as to consider every intruding and visitors a nuisance.

The position of J. Watson is merely agent of Cliff Mine and it should be his aim to extend a hearty welcome to visitors unacquainted with mining to grant them the privilege of visiting the mine for there is nothing about the business that should be kept secret.

I heard last night that Mr. Watson made this remark about me one year ago, viz: "If I catch him about the mine I will send him from the place." The cause of this remark was the fact that I went around to see what & how the work was done, being a stranger. I never in any shape whatever interfered with the workmen or work and I look upon this remark as a shameful thing. After being in the place one year gaining the friendship of all I see no cause for this remark. He is very fearful that something will occur and makes a rascal of himself in consequence. I care not for any agent & will visit the mine as often as I please. He was in poor temper at the time I judge or he never would said it. I detest the man when actuated by such silly, soft, jealous, sneaking principles.

July 11, 1864

It is a cloudy, still morning, very cool and some prospect of rain. It rained very hard Saturday night commencing just before we closed our Lodge meeting. Brothers Simon Crane, John Benney and John Trewarther stopped at our place in consequence of the rain.

Mrs. Rawlings came home last night in very good spirits. All well at the Portage. The steamer *Illinois* is on the reef at the River filled with water. All attempts to get her off have failed. If there should be a storm she would be a total loss. An attempt was made to pump her out with a twelve inch lift but it could not be done so they have sent below for a steam pump.

There is an artist here taking pictures. I had a sharp discussion today noon with an Englishman who advocates the secesh doctrine quite strongly. He is a man of sound information but I cannot swallow his views so we had it sharply although strangers. This is the first time that I have had an opportunity to oppose the wrong. I shall have my eye on the chap again and give him a few broad sides every favorable time.

There was a breakage at No. 4 engine of one of the cog wheels and Mr. Rawlings and the shop boys have had to work two days and nights. William Trewarther has come from below & is clerking for Captain Paull. He took a commercial course at College and is going to make a book keeper.

A meeting was held at the Bay State Mine Saturday evening to take measures to support a school. I expect a strong effort will be made to secure me as teacher. Everyone wishes me to come. I have a number of chances and shall doubtless accept one of them if I can do well.

Je fini pour au jourd hui.

July 12, 1864

I am feeling in moderate spirits this fine day but quite different from happy my money matters are in such a reckless state. I shall have very little money when I get it in funds that will pass. I cannot prevent it as my expenses are very high. I have spent a very large sum in clothes board etc. I shall not be deceived again I trust.

I was over to Mr. Philbrick's last night eating "little neck clams and pine apples," had quite a treat and pleasant talk on spiritualism and war matters. Mr. Philbrick is a genuine Yankee from New Hampshire, a member of Methodist Episcopal Church and a man of good principles and motives. I must commence my work.

Thomas Howe, Agent [3]

There is some rejoicing to know that Cliff Mine is to have a new agent and there would be much more if there was to be a new clerk. Mr. Howe is a Brother of the clerk or secretary of the Company. I shall not pass my opinion of him yet. I hear he is a very pleasant man but I notice one fault. He is a drinker to all appearance. I trust that he is a clever man and amiable.

Watson says he is to remain as head agent but I do not believe one word of it. I believe that he is nearly through with this career of harshness & cruelty. Watson has been over strict in his management. He is disliked everywhere he goes. The agents and leading men in the mining business shun him whenever they meet. There is a strong feeling against the business men of the Cliff mine. I know not the cause but judge it to be on account of the unfair dealing and roguery that is the main feature of their action. The cross disposition & uncivil way they act to all they have business with.

July 13, 1864

It is a beautiful morning, some breeze stirring and some few clouds in the sky. There is no very good prospect of rain. The *Illinois*, the boat

I came up on, is still on the reef at Eagle River. Her freight has been removed but not her machinery. She will doubtless be a total loss if not taken off soon. She is breaking into two parts through the center in consequence of resting on the rock & filling with water.

I went to Captain Paull's last night and spent the evening having a dish of bread & milk according to promise. William Van Orden's sister is there on a visit. I received a paper last night from home bringing the news of nomination of "Father" as State Senator. I am glad to hear the news. I trust he will be elected and do justice in his office. I am in hopes to receive one or two letters before leaving this place.

P. V. Carbines

The above person has just come from London where he has been a machinist. I know nothing of his former reputation as a gentleman but if I am to judge by his talk I should set him down as an associate of the lowest characters of London. He appears like a city flop and deserves a worse reputation. He has made one or two remarks about two ladies in this place in connection with me that has given me a very low opinion of him. They are school teachers just from Wisconsin & belonging to our Lodge & being genuine American girls of fine talents, I have often visited them. I have not justified any saucy remark. I have only to answer the rascal in the proper place which I will do as soon as convenient.

July 14, 1864

It is very hot, the sun shines bright. There is a suffocating feeling about the atmosphere that makes a person feel lazy and gives him a disposition to spend his time lounging about without anything to disturb the quiet repose & ease of his sleepy faculties. I feel as if a close of my school would be new life to me. I am weary and weak from the tiresome work. Still I cannot say as I want to go home and go to work at once in the hay field. I do not feel able for anything of that kind.

I met the Band of Hope last night and had a very fine meeting. We are to meet once more on Saturday next at four PM. to have the last meeting while I remain as president. I shall send an account of the organization and progress of the Band of Hope to the *Peninsular Herald*, the only paper devoted to the cause of Good Templars in the state. Success to the Band. I am informed this morning that there are good reasons for believing that the *Illinois* is off from the reef there was only three-and-a-half feet of water in her yesterday evening. In the morning there was eleven feet.

A Business Man

At the present time almost every man is what may be called a business man. But I wish to refer more particularly to a man who comes in contact with or transacts business with the laboring class of community. The position of clerk in Cliff Mine will illustrate what I wish to express. It is his duty once per month to give men money for their work. He looks upon them as dogs, insults and abuses them so that very few are willing to go into the office. A business man should be kind, obliging, willing, pleasant and a gentleman.

July 15, 1864

I commence school in a very sleepy condition from the fact that I watched with Mr. Wright who is quite sick with fever. I was up all night wetting clothes to put on his head & attending to his wants in various ways. I shall have a school only one-half of the day. Weather very warm and pleasant, rather hot, somewhat cloudy. It is quite a mild day, some considerable of a day. I will "tapir off" & write when I can keep my eyes open.

July 16, 1864

I cannot keep my eyes open today very well as I watched again last night. Had rain during the night and it is cloudy and smoky to day. It is quite warm also. I will simply give a short account of closing my school.

Closing school

I have neglected to fill this out in season and will only say that I closed school without any exhibition giving each pupil his reward. Every pupil is anxious to have me return again and the final close caused them sadness. I dismissed the Band of Hope receiving a present of three dollars from them as a token of respect with which I purchased a fine "Gold pen." My last business with the Lodge I went through with & they will send me a 3rd degree Regalia worth ten dollars as a token of respect.

I received my pay and bidding all my friends good-bye took my way for Eagle River in company with Brothers William & Josiah. We spent the evening in quiet conversation & I took leave of William at ten PM. The *Meteor* came in at two in the night & Josiah & myself went on board.[4] I took some notes & will be guided by them in my writing on this book.

Notes Taken on My Way Home

July 27, 1864

On board steamer *Meteor* in the engine room. I left the Cliff yesterday at noon in company with Brothers William & Josiah, having bid all my friends farewell during the past two days. As there was no boat in when we arrived at Eagle River we spent the evening there with Edward. Brother William went home at 10 PM ; Josiah remained to go as far as the Harbor with me.

The beautiful propeller Meteor

"Captain Ryder" came down during the night having a pleasure party on board.[5] At eight the next morning we left the River for "Isle Royale" directly opposite. My ticket for Portage Lake cost six dollars. It is very foggy and quite cool, there is no breeze to disturb the Lake which is smooth. The whistle is blown every few minutes to avoid a collision. After a few hours drive we are near the shores of this beautiful Island. The Captain goes on shore in a small boat to look for a convenient harbor. We work our way up in the fog judging the distance by the echo of the whistle; very soon we are within six rods of the Rocky shore & the mate in a careless way ran the boat on the rocks doing no damage however. The ladies were frightened a little.

We enjoyed a fine dinner and sail along shore for Rock Harbor which we make about two miles distant. We enter this Harbor, the fog disappears & we sail in about four miles with the most beautiful scenery on all sides. It is a fine island covered with a thick forest. We landed in a small boat & pick a few greenstones. Just as we were about leaving the island a party came on board who were exploring there for mines.

We went for Eagle Harbor just at dusk & Josiah & I went to bed & slept soundly until morning when we arrived at Eagle Harbor which is nine miles from the River. The propeller *Dubuque* was there, unloading.[6] We were here all day taking in copper. The beautiful propeller *Lac*

La Belle came in kiting in the afternoon & I got the first paper I have seen for nearly two months.[7] We left Eagle Harbor at a half past 4 PM for Copper Harbor. Josiah went back on the *Lac La Belle*.

There is no fog, clear fine weather, the Lake is very smooth and there is a ringing to the clear spray as it is thrown out by the boat. I believe that there is no water so beautiful as the pure sparkling water of Lake Superior. Copper Harbor is a very safe port being guarded by a reef of rocks. There are a few bushes on this reef. We sail in at the lower point & go up the Harbor about three-quarters of a mile to the dock. There is only one good house in this small place. Very little business is done I judge by the looks of the dock & storage house. A portion of this side of the bluff has been over-run by fire lately. I think there are no good mines here, and they are back some distance.

Left for Portage Lake arriving there in the morning. I went up to "John Penberthy's." In the afternoon I crossed the Lake in the ferry for Mr. McDonald's where I met Miss Cundy, my former assistant, looking in very good health. Little Mary [McDonald] threw her arms around my neck and almost cried with joy she was so glad to see me. Miss Cundy is looking well and having good success in school. She intends returning very soon. I spent all day Saturday looking about the place and as it was pay day the "Eye water" was plenty and there was quite a number of fights. I saw one fellow cut up in a shocking manner.

Sunday I went to the Episcopal Church with Mr. Williams & John [Penberthy] & family. John's little boy was christened. Coming home got very wet from a shower. Went & visited Miss Cundy in the afternoon. Met with Brother John Trewarther. The *Pewabic* came in Monday morning & John & I took passage for Marquette, where John was to stop a while.[8] I went up & bid little Mary good-bye just before starting.

Portage is a place of great business. There is much excitement now in relation to the silver lead region. Speculators are very plenty. There is a very fine Hotel on one side & they intend building a very fine school house to cost twenty thousand dollars. It is to be a stone building.

August 1, 1864

Trip to Detroit on board the beautiful propeller *Pewabic* of a thousand tons burden.

Pewabic

I cannot give much of an account of this fine boat but what is said of her may be said of the *Meteor* & *Lac La Belle* as they are all after the same pattern. This is the first season that they have run. The *Pewabic* is a large boat driven by two screws which are driven by two beautiful engines. She will accommodate four-hundred passengers and is well provided with life boats, life preservers and fire engines & hose. She is beautifully ornamented inside and painted black outside. There is a deer's head, neck & horns on the top of the pilot house that is a fine piece of workmanship. She is commanded by Captain McKay, a fine sailor and gentleman.[9] He has red hair and long red whiskers. The officers are all very pleasant and I heard no rough language while on board. The living is very fine. I should prefer to go on the *Pewabic* to any other boat on the Lake. Well, John & I took a glass of lemonade, bought a story of the barber and took a read upon the hurricane deck where we could see everything along the shore.

The weather is very fine and we make our way through the entry into the Lake without any trouble. A short distance out we passed the *Northern Light* bound up.[10] In a short time we passed the *Michigan*.[11] They saluted us with the whistle and we replied with the same. It was a pleasant trip, the Lake being very smooth and beautiful weather. We arrived at Marquette at about six PM.

John and I bought a blueberry pie, ice cream, lemonade and enjoyed a farewell treat. We went around and saw all the fine sights. There is quite an extensive business done here. There were about twelve schooners here taking in iron. We were here all night and took on board four-hundred tons of coal. The mines are about twelve miles back and there is an incline track to the wharves, the ore coming down in cars which are drawn back by steam engines. A passenger train runs back also for the accommodation of visitors. John left me here. I secured a good berth and went to bed but slept very little as there was a dance on board.

August 2, 1864

We started early in the morning notwithstanding there was a thick fog which caused the whistle to be blown every few minutes to avoid accident. At twelve noon the fog disappeared and we are making fine headway. Have had a good dinner and am feeling bully. Land is in full view on our right which has not been the case before today.

We arrived at the Sault about seven PM and remained here all night taking in coal. Had a dance in the evening. I went through the place to see the curiosities. Bought a little Indian's basket made of bark for "Gertie."

There is a kind of yellow fly that comes into the cabin in such swarms as to stop the dance. They would cover a person & are very troublesome yet they do not bite, "a mercy." It is amusing to see the darkies fight them, and an old grayhaired copperhead was nearly smothered with them. It was a pity that they could not bite him, as long as he had such principles until he could see what was the true cause of our war.

August 3, 1864

Left the beautiful village and more beautiful falls of St Mary's down the River passing a tug pulling up a number of schooners in tow. Indians along the shore, wild ducks also. Weather fine, a small breeze, sun shines very brightly. Partook of a good Breakfast, I went in quite strong for tripe and some of the luxuries.

Lake Huron is very calm and we make fine time. I slept most of the afternoon and through the night. In the morning of Thursday I find it quite foggy and we are near the mouth of St. Clair River feeling our way, blowing the whistle. There is a dense smoke occasioned by fires back in the bush. A boat passes to our right blowing her whistle constantly. We are trying to enter the mouth. It is almost suffocating at times. The sun shines brightly in the east.

We now commence sounding & find six fathoms and now it is only two-and-a-half & land just in sight on our right. We run along near the shore & soon come to the St. Clair River which we enter stopping at Port Huron to land a few passengers. What a pleasant change to one who has been confined to the rocky bluffs of Lake Superior. I have not witnessed for two long years such a pleasant sight as I now behold on either hand. I see beautiful villages, orchards, fields of grain etc. It is a pleasant view to me and reminds of the fact that there is a much better place to live than the country of Lake Superior especially for a young man. How grand these orchards look with fruit in abundance. There are many small steamers, tugs, schooners, ferry boats etc. We just now pass a small tug having five schooners & a scow loaded with wood in tow, and here comes another with six schooners in tow. Now the light sidewheel steamer *Rein Deer* of East Saginaw passes us with a load of passengers.[12] She stops at the different ports along the River. She is built for a river boat drawing five or six feet of water. She is made after the pattern of the Mississippi boats.

We pass one small island in the River, one house on it & part of it cleared. The wheat crop is fine, corn poor, grass & oats quite fair. Steam saw mills are in full operation all along the shore. Here comes another tug with four schooners in tow, bound up. We enter Lake St. Clair. For the last eight miles we have been passing through a marsh swarming with wild ducks. There are two lighthouses at the mouth of the river built of stone in the water.

We pass a number of propellers & steamers bound up crowded with passengers. The *Rein Deer* which has been after us now comes just opposite only six rods away and is trying to pass us. Now for a race although our noble boat is very heavily loaded drawing twelve feet of water she keeps the lead. It is exciting, three thousand passengers all on our deck, one hundred on the other. If one gains a little then comes a cheer and so it goes.

Captain McKay sits near the pilot house puffing a cigar & says not a word. We are running fifteen or twenty miles an hour and the spray rolls away from our noble propeller in fine style as she cuts the water with her heavy load. It is a splendid time for our crew. We keep just a few feet in the lead through Lake St. Clair and enter the Detroit River. Crowds along the wharves give rousing cheers as we pass. The *Rein Deer* gains a little as we approach the city but we fasten to the dock first and give three rousing cheers for the *Pewabic* & three groans for the *Rein Deer* as she passes. We made up a purse of a few dollars for the fireman who was nearly roasted keeping up steam. Crowds came on the wharves at the city as we came in and the daily papers speaks of the race between the boats that came in kiting.

I put up at the Michigan Exchange; had a room in the fourth story.[13] I bought a ticket for Burlington [Ontario] for twelve dollars & stopped here two days to see all the fine sights. Can ride all the city for five cents on the city railway. I went to Young Men's Hall to a very fine theatre in the evening.[14] I was well pleased with my visit and took the Grand Trunk railway for home Saturday morning.

At Port Sarnia my baggage was opened & examined. Had a rough ride all day. It is warm, sand & smoke flying, the road is very rough. I dislike the route. It is an English concern, poor accommodations and saucy employers. I arrived at Oshawa station at seven PM. Took my satchel and went down the track one mile to Uncle Shipman's where I was made welcome.[15]

Cousin Hobart is a fine steady young man and is quite a reader. Wilbur is in New York on the Canal. The family are all well. Uncle Shipman has a very pleasant little farm here that is smooth, good house, fair barn, shade trees & things comfortable. He raises grain. I have helped him draw in barley for the past two days. He will finish today.

I am very lonely here as I am anxious to get home having started. I think that I will go to [New] York State next week for pleasure. I expect a letter from home very soon. I hope that I shall receive one by tomorrow as I am tired of waiting.

We have just had a shower [on] August 13, 1864.

August 14, 1864

It is a very warm day and I stop at home reading, resting etc. I went down with Cousin Hobart to the Lake and had a genuine bath. There was a swell of about three feet and it is quite pleasant swimming in the water in such a time or very fine to stand & dive in under a large wave. The Lake water is very pleasant, and never very warm except very near the Shore. Uncle Shipman and family or wife went to church in the afternoon.

I took a snooze after reading the papers and becoming quite disgusted with an account of a McClelland [General George McClellan] Mass Meeting in the city of New York. The main feature of this meeting of rank Copperheads was their very expressive sympathy for the almost immortal Hero "Mac" and their heavy denunciations of the present administration. It was certainly a large meeting. I noticed that one speaker spoke about dammed drums disturbing him and very shortly after he said that they wished to elect a "Christian" for the next President. I should judge that there was some need of such a man. The Copperheads wish to sustain the Government if their words are fine and sympathize with Rebels whose aim is to overthrow it. If there is any class that should be punished it is the copperheads of the North.

August 15, 1864

I went to the Post Office and found a welcome letter from home which I have just answered. Friend John M. Fay called to see me but I have not got there yet. He will soon marry the fair Miss Julia Martin, I think. It is a very warm day and I am in the house writing and reading. I shall start Wednesday morning for Rochester on a visit and to see the country. I will give some account on my return here for home. I shall cross Lake Ontario in the snug little steamer *Empress* from the Port of Oshawa.[16] I hope I shall have very good time and see much of interest.

Il Est temts pour fini.

Trip To Danville, New York

August 22, 1864

I partook of a fine breakfast Wednesday morning & in company with cousin Hobart went to the Oshawa wharf where I took passage on the steamer *Empress* for Rochester. The *Empress* is a very fine little side wheel boat [that] runs quite well. There were a very few passengers, one little rogue of a boy belonging to the Captain.

We kept along in full view of the Canada shore but owing to the smoke I can form only an imperfect idea of the looks of the country; in truth I only wish to as I am fully satisfied with what I know already of this land of "copperheads & traitors." I can distinguish large fields of wheat & barley which proves it to be quite a grain country.

The shores along before Oshawa are perpendicular & in many places about twenty to thirty feet high; they look as if washed away by the waves & show a clayey soil. I notice a very fine farm house just on one of these points surrounded with an orchard of thrifty fruit trees. Just in front of the house stands seven tall "Balm Gileads" covered with beautiful leaves towering up to a great height. Just the other side of the ridge the land is quite level and covered with woods, yet it seems to be quite thickly settled.

We arrive at the little Port of Bowmansville in about a half an hour where we where we take in wood & land some freight.[17] In about thirty minutes we are off with a strong wind ahead. Arrived at Port Hope at a half past ten. It is quite a large place & one person remarked that it was like Jerusalem in one respect viz. It is surrounded by hills but he knew that it was different in every other. I think he was right. It looked quite strange to see the British flag floating over the place. The rail road extends along over a kind of "bay" built on the top of high "abutments." There are some large brick dwellings & stores.

The little steamer *Rochester* came in while we were there.[18] She is just from the American side. In a short time we are off & pass the propeller *Hercules* with a large raft of logs in tow.[19] Very near the point a mile from the Port Hope is a lighthouse built out in the water a great distance from the shore. I should judge that it would be a very lonely place to live in. Do very well for an old "maid or Bach."

We arrived and left Cobourg at a half past eleven for the Port of Charlotte on the American side nine miles from Rochester.[20] Had a very pleasant trip without any sickness, arriving there at five PM. I took the cars & arrived at Rochester and found lodgings at the Exchange Hotel for the night taking the cars next morning for Wayland Station in Livingston County & then the stage to Dansville. I spent the day here in this beautiful little village situated on a stream in a valley. I have never seen a more beautiful place in my life. There is a fine village among shade trees in a valley the hill extending to the height of four hundred or five hundred feet high in a beautiful slope along which are fine farms, houses, orchards groves & in about the center of this hill is the Dansville Hygenic Institution of Dr. James C. Jackson & its beautiful grounds surrounding it.[21] I cannot think of a more pleasant "Home."

I went up to the Institute and was welcomed by Dr. Hurd. I went over the grounds and all through the bath & packing rooms. It is a very large building with large wings & lecture rooms attached. It is painted in fine style & well furnished. The baths are given between ten & twelve AM. & then there is an hour and a half for rest, all retiring. They have two meals a day & in their system of diet, exercise, etc. lies their success.

There are a very large number of patients there, & all wear white, wet, cloth on the head. The ladies all adopt the new style of dress which consist of pants & a short dress. I saw Miss Harriet Austin, M. D. It is certainly a very comfortable dress. Dr. James C. Jackson spoke to me kindly but owing to business I had no long conversation with him. The attendant that showed me the different apartments told me about their success. They lose no patients, but cure [them]. I firmly believe in their system & plans. It is truly one of the greatest cures of the ages & founded on the best principles.

Some of the ladies would amuse themselves with cards & walking, & one thing & another. They are all cheerful & happy & everything is made pleasant. They have lectures every morning & no pains is spared to make it truly a "Home." The table is set in beautiful style with all kinds of fruit & each patient has his diet as prescribed by the doctors. I partook of a meal which was cooked in their style & it was certainly good. They correct all evil habits etc. I was never more favorably impressed with any system than the one practiced here.

Back of the Institute was a grape yard of nearly an acre & many fruit trees. It commands a most beautiful view of the village & whole valley, which seems to be right below. If disease can be cured at all it is here & the past success of this institution & its reputation all through the state is sufficient proof that it is one of the greatest Institutions of the age.

I returned to Rochester in the evening. I passed through a very rich fertile valley fine farms, fruit trees, grain fields, all along the way. It is worth a journey to pass through this very fine valley. There is nothing in Canada that can compare with it in richness and fertility. Rochester is a fine city full of business at all times. If a person wished to form an idea of its population let them stand in the Arcade Post Office and from morning until night there is a perfect rush in at one door & out at the other.

While in this city I heard a lecture on the war one evening that paid me my trip. It was by Brigadier General Hithe of Kentucky. He was a young man about twenty-two and quite small & odd in appearance yet had a keen eye & was a forcible speaker. He was always a temperance man & never tasted liquor or cider & was never sick a day in his life. He was a slaveholder also his father & his mother too. He was educated as a slaveholder & was the very man to give the Copperheads a lecture. There could not be a more fit person. He voted for "Bill" & done all he could to oppose Lincoln's election. He is now one of the noblest patriots that has gone forth in this war in defense of the right.

He entered in the 102nd Illinois as a private. The officers & two-thirds of the privates of that regiment were pure Democrats. He being the strength of the Bill & Everet party. The colonel Bill McMartry was an out & out Democrat. He believed if there had been no such party "old Bill" would never have been born & when it dies "old Bill" will draw his last breath.

He was promoted to Captain, Colonel, then Inspector of General Rosecran's command & then Brigadier General when he was severely wounded in the hip, shoulder, & hand being temporarily disabled, but being unwilling to cease battling in the struggle, he was lecturing until the first of September when he would join his command.

He knew the government needed men or it would not call & could go & went. When the Emancipation Proclamation was made he looked upon it as wise. If the President is sworn to protect the government he shall use all means in his power. He said there was not a particle of abolitionism in it. There was not anything that indicated it. Jeff Davis himself did not object to the government. It was only to the manner it was conducted. This is just what the copperheads are doing so they are Rebels of the meanest kind. He said the slaveholders did not want their sympathy, they hated them. He alluded to them in a most cutting way, using powerful arguments. The whole speech was a masterly thing & filled with amusing incidents. I will not try to give any account of it. There was a large audience & immense cheering. The close was really affecting. It was the best treat I have listened to for a long time.

I took the cars from Rochester Saturday evening & the boat from Charlotte arriving safely home at Uncle Shipman at five on Sunday evening. I was quite sick coming over as it was rough & rained all the way. It is cold & wet today.

I have been at the Post Office & found a letter from home. I shall start tomorrow morning for Vermont. I have had a fine visit at Uncle Shipman's & they have taken great pains to make my stay pleasant. I like the place & find that the little enterprise there is here is carried on by Americans. All the manufacturing business is in the hands of genuine Yankees. They are the men for business & where they are there is business & enterprise.

Notes for July-August 1864

1. The wooden marker for John T. Wilson, age 4, is in the Protestant Cemetery at Clifton. He died July 1, 1864. Buried with him in the same plot was his sister, Carrie Wilson, who died November 27, 1872, age 11 months, 22 days.

2. Michigan University refers to the University of Michigan, Ann Arbor, whose regents had their first meeting in November 1837.

3. Howe was the brother of Thomas M. Howe, the longtime officer of the Pittsburgh and Boston Mining Company.

4. The propeller steam vessel, the *Meteor*, was built by Walbridge and Whiting in Detroit in 1863. *Detroit Free Press*, July 3, 1863. The *Meteor* went to Detroit, Cleveland and Lake Superior mining ports. It collided with the *Pewabic* in 1865 in Thunder Bay, Lake Huron. *Detroit Free Press*, August 13, 1865. The *Pewabic* sank but the *Meteor* continued to ply the waters of the Great Lakes for years after. In 1867 it carried a piece of mass copper weighing 1,111 pounds. Grace Lee Nute, *Lake Superior* (Indianapolis: Bobbs-Merrill, 1944), p. 123.

5. George Ryder served as captain of the steamer *Mineral Rock* in 1861, the steamer *Marquette* in 1862, the *City of Cleveland* in 1862-63, and the *Meteor* in 1864. *Annual Directory, City of Detroit, 1863-64* (Detroit: Charles F. Clark, 1863).

6. The propeller *Dubuque*, 384 tons, was built in Buffalo in 1857. John Brant Mansfield, editor and compiler, *History of the Great Lakes* (Chicago: J. H. Beers, 1899), p. 817.

7. The steamer *Lac La Belle* , 850 tons, was built in Cleveland in 1864. It sunk in Lake St. Clair in 1866 with two lives lost. Mansfield, *History of Great Lakes*, p. 846.

8. The propeller *Pewabic* was built in Cleveland in 1863. It was sunk in a collision with its sister ship,the *Meteor*, in Lake Huron in 1865 with a loss of seventy lives. Among the survivors was Hervey Parke, former clerk of the Cliff Mine and later founder of Parke, Davis pharmaceutical company in Detroit. *Detroit Free Press*, August 13, 1865. Mansfield, *History of Great Lakes*, p. 873. See also, Samuel T. Douglas, "The Pewabic Disaster," *Michigan History* 16 (1932), pp. 431-438.

9. Captain George Perry McKay was born aboard the steamer *Commander Perry* in 1838 and died in 1918. He was in command of the *Pewabic* on the night it collided with the *Meteor* in 1865. Fred Landon, *Lake Huron* (Indianapolis: Bobbs-Merrill, 1944), pp. 272-276.

10. The *Northern Light*, an 857-ton steamer, was built in 1858 by Saffrinier and Stevenson of Cleveland. It operated between Cleveland and Lake Superior. *Detroit Free Press*, May 7, 1858; Mansfield, *History of Great Lakes*, p. 867.

11. The *Michigan* was built in Detroit in 1833 by Oliver Newberry. This 156-foot, 472-ton steamer usually operated between Detroit and Buffalo. Mansfield, *History of Great Lakes*, p. 858.

12. The *Reindeer*, a schooner of 207 tons, was built in East Saginaw in 1863. Mansfield, *History of Great Lakes*, p. 879.

13. One of Detroit's most celebrated hotels was the Michigan Exchange, a large, six-story hotel, that was located on Shelby, Woodbridge and later Jefferson Avenue in Detroit. It was first opened in 1835 and enlarged several times in subsequent years. Silas Farmer, *The History of Detroit and Michigan* (Detroit: Silas Farmer and Company, 1889), p. 482. An illustration and description of the Michigan Exchange is found in Charles Tuttle, *General History of Michigan* (Detroit: Detroit Free Press Company, 1873), p. 737.

14. The Detroit Young Men's Hall was located in the Biddle House Hotel, on Jefferson Avenue. *Annual Directory, City of Detroit, 1863-64* (Detroit: Charles F. Clark, 1863).

15. John Shipman married Rachel Hobart, the sister of Amos Hobart, Henry's father. Hobart and William Shipman were Henry's cousins. Percy Hobart Titus, *The Hobart Family in America* (Boston: n.p., 1943).

16. The steamer *Empress* burned, in Kingston, Ontario in 1868. Mansfield, *History of Great Lakes*, p. 822.

17. Bowmansville, Ontario is located in Durham County, Ontario, forty-two miles southwest of Toronto, and east of Oshawa, and near Port Hope, Ontario.

18. The steamer *Rochester* was built in Oswego, New York in 1843. Mansfield, *History of Great Lakes*, p. 881.

19. The propeller *Hercules*, 373 tons, was built in Buffalo in 1843. Mansfield, *History of Great Lakes*, p. 836.

20. Cobourg, Ontario is located sixty-nine miles northeast of Toronto on the north shore of Lake Ontario, Northumberland County, Ontario, Canada. Charlotte, a port and resort village in Monroe County, New York, is located at the mouth of the Genesee River, seven miles north of Rochester.

21. For an account of the Dansville Health Resort, known in 1858 as the Jackson Water Cure, as well as biographical accounts of James C. Jackson, F. Wilson Hurd and Harriett Austin see A. O. Bunnel, editor, *Dansville, 1789-1902* (Dansville, New York: Instructor Publishers, 1902), pp. 27-31, 99-113, 177-181, 249-250. See also William Conklin, "The Jackson Health Resort: Pioneer in its Field." Typescript, 348 pages, New York State Library, Albany.

Epilogue

Above are picnickers in 1904 at Shaft No. 4 of the by then deserted Cliff Mine. On the following page is a view of the village of Clifton circa 1900 with the belfry of the Methodist Church in the background.

321

Henry Hobart's Life After the Cliff

Henry Hobart's journal gives the reader vivid details of his everyday life and the scope of his interests. It is a far greater challenge to trace the career of Henry Hobart *after* he left Clifton in 1864. Hobart returned to his family in Westford, Vermont and most likely he accepted a teaching position in one of the communities in the Burlington, Vermont area. His journal, however, makes no reference to his future plans for life in Vermont.

Vital records of Vermont reveal that Hobart married Julia Wires, the daughter of Junius and Jane Wires of Cambridge, Vermont, on September 2, 1868.[1] Immediately following their marriage, Hobart and his wife moved to Wisconsin, settling in the small farming community of Menasha, near Oshkosh, in the eastern central part of the state. In the fall of 1869, they moved to Winneconne, Wisconsin, where Hobart was placed in charge of the District No. 3 School. Hobart was appointed Superintendent of Schools for Winnebago County, Wisconsin in 1872. [2]

As superintendent, Hobart continued to develop his philosophy of education In a speech before the Winnebago County Teachers Association on January 13, 1872, Hobart argued that "thorough discipline and order was of great importance, and the methods pursued should be of a kind to prepare the pupil to become a law-abiding citizen." He also urged that "scholars should be held to an account for their conduct during the day and be required to give a truthful report of the same."[3]

The active temperance movement in the area must have pleased Hobart. When the Winnebago Temperance Society met in Winneconne in February 1872, Hobart was elected secretary. He was also a founder and officer of the Independent Order of Good Templars Lodge, founded in the same year.

Hobart served as principal of Neenah Wisconsin High School from 1874 to 1882.[4] He was president of the Winnebago Teachers Association and sought to improve professional standards of teachers. Among his projects with the association was a campaign for improved methods in the teaching of spelling and the prohibition of the use of tobacco by teachers "unless ordered by a physician."[5]

In 1882, Hobart resigned his position as principal of Neenah High School and announced his plans to move to Calumet, Michigan, about

323

twelve miles south of Clifton.[6] By 1882, Calumet was one of the most prosperous mining towns of the Keweenaw Peninsula. Although the reasons for his move are unknown, it is possible, like others, he was attracted by the climate and clean air of the Lake Superior region.

The Hobarts remained in Calumet from 1882 to 1887, when they returned to Oshkosh, Wisconsin "on the advice of Julia's physician."[7] Hobart accepted a position as general manager and later district agent for the Northwestern Mutual Life Insurance Company, one of the largest insurance companies in the Midwest.[8]

Retiring from the insurance business, Hobart took up a position as secretary of the Badger Canning Company of Oshkosh and, in 1905, its president. He retired from Badger in 1908 and became president of the Central Lake Canning Company of Central Lake, Michigan.[9]

Julia Hobart died in Oshkosh in 1903 at the age of sixty-one; Henry lived until July 25, 1920, when he was stricken by a cerebral hemorrhage, at the age of seventy-nine. He was survived by his sister, Mrs. Gertrude A. Reynolds of Hermosa Beach, California.[10]

One gap in background information of Henry Hobart has been the lack of descriptions of the young schoolteacher by his contemporaries. The only clue is a statement in his Journal for October 20, 1863, shortly after he "was taken sick with a billious attack resulting in Yellow Jaundice severely." He observed: "I think I am gaining in flesh for I now weigh 163 lbs. Hope I may gain until I reach 200 when I will be quite a man physically."

Regardless of his height and weight, the Journal testifies to his work habits, his long days of teaching and preparations and his extra jobs of painting the school house and his work on the farm, harvesting the crops and cutting hay. The Yankee work ethic was another life style transplanted on the northern Michigan frontier by Henry Hobart.

There is no information available on the disposition of Hobart's personal property or his residence in Oshkosh. Hobart's journal about his years in Clifton from 1862 to 1864 was acquired by the Burton Historical Collection of the Detroit Public Library from Mrs. George Williams of Oshkosh in August 1952.[11]

Cliff Mine

In 1864 when Henry Hobart left Clifton to return to his home in Vermont, the Cliff Mine was still profitable. Although production was down by 750,000 pounds compared to the previous year, the demand for copper kept profits high. The company declared dividends totalling $320,000, more than any other year in the mine's history.[12]

Curtis Hussey and other officers of the Pittsburgh and Boston Mining Company watched carefully development at Cliff Mine. They had realized huge profits on their investments in the mine, but recognized the decline in world copper prices and increased costs of production below 1400 feet made the future uncertain.[13]

In 1869, the output of the mine dropped to 711,361 pounds, and for the first time the mine did not show a profit. A short time later, on June 24, 1870, the company's board of directors suspended all mining operations effective at the end of the month. This action allowed time to transport all copper to Eagle River for shipment by steamer to lower lake ports. Included in this final shipment was a mass of native copper weighing 4,920 pounds, cut from the lowest level of the shaft.[14]

The company stopped the pumps and slowly the underground shafts and drifts began to fill with water. The editor of the *Portage Lake Mining Gazette*, under the headline, "The Fate of the Old Mine is Sealed," lamented the action: "Too bad after such splendid results, yet there is wisdom to stop work when there is no apparent chance of profit." [15]

Thus ended, in the summer of 1870, the profitable operation of one of the most famous copper mines in North America. In its twenty-five years of operation, the Cliff Mine paid more than $2,627,000 in dividends on investments of $110,905, a profit of nearly two-thousand percent.

The Cliff Mine properties were sold to Marshall Simpson, of New York City, in December 1871 for $100,000. Simpson began exploration at different depths in the mine, up to a thousand feet.[16] The discovery of large copper masses at the nine-hundred and one thousand-foot levels buoyed hopes for the future of the mine. The optimism, as it turned out, was short lived. Even in 1874 and 1875, when Simpson's company produced more than one million pounds of ore, the mine failed to make a profit. Simpson laid off the miners, shut down the stamp mills in 1876 and, in 1879 put the Cliff property up for sale.[17]

The history of the Cliff Mine after the 1860s was one of financial downturn and deterioration of the physical assets such as the stamp mill and warehouse above circa 1900.

In 1892, the Cliff Mine and properties were sold to the Tamarack Mining Company. They were later acquired by the Calumet and Hecla Company. It was not until 1903 that Calumet and Hecla, by that time one of the world's largest mining companies, re-explored the northern section of the Keweenaw Peninsula, including the Cliff Mine. The results were disappointing. Even the new diamond drill technology was unsuccessful in finding the legendary Kearsarge Lode or other major lodes. In 1913, Calumet and Hecla closed all operations at the Cliff and sealed the shaft openings.[18]

A final attempt to operate the Cliff Mine occurred in 1927 when a subsidiary of Calumet and Hecla, under Rudolphe Agassiz, re-opened the Cliff and the Phoenix mines "as a initial step in a huge program of exploration in Keweenaw County."[19] Once again, the Avery Shaft was opened, water pumped out and new drifts excavated for more than 1300 feet. Agassiz found no new veins or masses of copper. On February 3, 1931, he ceased all work, and the Cliff Mine was sealed for good.

The Village of Clifton

The village of Clifton, totally dependent on the Cliff Mine, met a similar fate. Even before the Pittsburgh and Boston company suspended operations in 1870, the populaton of Clifton plummeted. During the Civil War years, a steady stream of miners and their families left Clifton for jobs in other mines in the Keweenaw Peninsula, western states and South America. By 1870, the population of Clifton had dropped to 615. Forty-eight houses were listed as "empty" by the census taker. In 1874, there were 250 miners employed; one year later, there were 225. The village soon became deserted except for a small staff to watch over the mine buildings and machinery and keep away the "buzzard tributors."[20]

The mine buildings—such as the stamp mills, engine houses, blacksmith's shop, warehouses and stores—were boarded up, waiting for some future mining operation. The harsh weather of the Keweenaw and lack of maintenance took their toll. Roofs caved in and fires and vandalism brought premature destruction. Soon, only the stone buildings and foundations were left. By 1903, all the mining company machinery was shipped to Hancock and sold for scrap metal.[21]

*Miners like those above left their homes in Clifton as the operations at the Cliff
Mine wavered and ultimately failed completely. Hobart who left Michigan for
Vermont in 1864 lived in nearby Calumet, Michigan from 1882 to 1887.*

Buildings in the village deteriorated or were demolished. Some of the frame houses were sold, dismantled and moved to other locations. Others collapsed or, like the doctor's residence and office, burned to the ground. There is no record of the fate of the schoolhouse.

A record of the churches was kept. In 1899, the Catholic church was dismantled and moved to Phoenix, Michigan where it was rebuilt for the parishioners there. The Grace Episcopal Church was leased to the Odd Fellows for a meeting hall in 1872. In 1913, sections of the same church were taken and used to build the chapels of St. Andrew in Florida, St. Mary's in Painesdale and St. Peter's in South Range, all communities in the Keweenaw Peninsula. The Methodist Episcopal Church remained intact in Clifton until 1914, when the roof collapsed.[22]

By 1900, Clifton was a ghost town. The few remaining buildings were boarded up, but served as a constant reminder to travelers between Calumet, Eagle River and Copper Harbor of the once famous Cliff Mine. As the buildings disappeared, little was left except the stone chimneys and, at the mine site, piles of waste rock and tailings. The bluff above the village became a popular gathering place for former mine workers and others, who met there to visit, picnic and enjoy the view of the peninsula. Fortunately for the historical record, they also brought their cameras and took pictures of the remaining mine buildings and village before the structures fell into ruin.

Today, all that remains of the Cliff Mine are the huge piles of waste rock, the foundations and chimneys of mine buildings and the shaft openings, now cemented shut. A small stream that once powered mine machinery still flows at the base of the cliff. From the cliff base to the top of the bluff, the markings of wagon trails are still visible. At the foot of the bluff, several hundred yards apart, are the deserted, almost hidden remains of two cemeteries where the Protestant and Catholic families of Clifton laid their dead to rest. Many of the wooden gravestones are still standing and bear silent testimony to the difficult and often dangerous life in a copper mining frontier village.

Although overgrown with aspen trees, the foundations of the houses, boarding houses, schoolhouse and other buildings remain in place. They are easily visible in the fall before heavy snow covers the site and in spring before trees and underbush leaf out. The view from the top of the bluff still provides the same panoramic view of the Keweeenaw and Lake Superior as Hobart described in the 1980s.

Joseph Rawlings's stepson Edward (with beard, seated at extreme right) stayed in the area and is pictured with family.

The log dwellings remained long after the mine was closed and the village abandoned. The Methodist Episcopal Church mentioned often in Hobart's journal is seen in the background.

The Rawlings-Penberthy Family

The Rawlings-Penberthy family with whom Hobart boarded in Clifton, remained in the village until 1869 when they moved to nearby Ripley, Michigan. After leaving Clifton, Joseph Rawlings served as engineer and clerk at various foundries in Ripley until he retired in 1896, at the age of seventy. During retirement he worked part-time "drafting and amusing myself by writing at odd times both in prose and rhyme." His "Recollections of a Long Life" published in 1967 in Roy Drier's *Copper Country Tales* and his "Reminiscences" found in the archives at Michigan Technological University provided informative and objective accounts of life in the copper mines of the Keweenaw and in Rawlings' birthplace, Cornwall, England.

Rawlings also left his mark in the Upper Peninsula as a brilliant mechanical engineer and cartographer. Rawlings' wife, Johanna Penberthy, died in 1893 in Ripley and in 1900 Josiah moved to the Mass Mine in Marqutte, Ontonagon County, with his son, Samuel, who was employed there as an engineer. After the turn of the century Rawlings summed up the years of his life and explained his close association of his children, Samuel and Eliza. But his reflections of the past were not at all pleasant. Perhaps remembering the difficult times in the frontier communities and mines of the Keweenaw, he concluded: "I would not care to live my life over again."[23]

The Penberthy boys, with whom Hobart lived while at Clifton, also had successful careers, mostly connected with the Upper Peninsula of Michigan. Edward, who was the same age as Henry Hobart, and had been his companion and rival, worked at the Cliff Mine in various capacities. For two years, during 1864 and 1865, Edward taught school at Eagle River. He then became purchasing agent for the Foley Mercantile Company and the Lake Superior Copper Company. For many years he managed the Penberthy Brothers General Store in Hubbell, Michigan and he served as postmaster and town clerk of Houghton from 1886 and 1890.

In 1876, Edward married Ellen McKernan and from that bond, six children were born: John Edward, Alice, Emma, Grover Cleveland, Stanley and Philip.[24]

The lives of other members of the Rawlings and Penberthy families and other members of the Cliff Mine community—all brought

331

together by the copper mining boom—could be traced to show the contributions they and their descendants made to the business, educational and public life of their communities.[25]

Notes for Epilogue

1. Vermont Vital Statistics Office, Montpelier, Vermont.

2. *History of Northern Wisconsin* (Chicago: Western Historical Society, 1881), p. 1174; *Winneconne Item*, September 16, 1871, July 20, 1872.

3. *Winneconne Item*, March 2, 1872.

4. *History of Northern Wisconsin*, p. 1174.

5. *Winneconne Item*, March 2, 9, June 1, and October 26, 1872. For an account of the educational policies in Winnebago County see Robert C. Robertson, "The Social History of Winnebago County, Wisconsin." Master of Arts thesis, Department of History, University of Chicago, December 1939.

6. *Oshkosh Northwestern*, July 26, 1920.

7. Ibid.

8. Ibid.

9. Michigan State Gazetteer and Business Directory (Detroit: R.L. Polk), Biannual volumes 1905-1921.

10. *Oshkosh Northwestern*, July 26, 1920.

11. The Hobart journal was purchased on August 5, 1952, for the sum of forty dollars. Accession Files, Burton Historical Collection, Detroit Public Library.

12. Horace J. Stevens, *The Copper Handbook: A Manual for the Copper Industry of the U.S. and Foreign Countries* (Houghton: 1900), pp. 49-50.

13. Ibid., p. 51.

14. *Portage Lake Mining Gazette*, June 30, 1870.

15. Ibid., June 2, 1870.

16. Michigan Commission of Mineral Statistics, Annual Report for 1880, located in the State Archives, Lansing, Michigan; Oliver Farwell, "Copper Country History." Manuscript. in Copper Country Vertical File, Michigan Technological University Archives, Houghton, Michigan; *Portage Lake Mining Gazette*, September 15, 1870, June 20, 1871.

17. Michigan Commission of Mineral Statistics, Annual Report for 1880, located in the State Archives. Donald Chaput, *The Cliff* (Sequoia Press: Kalamazoo, 1971), p.102; *Portage Lake Mining Gazette*, January 11, 1883; *History of the Upper Peninsula* (Chicago: Western Historical Society, 1883),p. 344; *Portage Lake Mining Gazette*, October 29, 1874, April 19, 1877, May 30, 1890, June 13, 1890, July 17, 1890, November 7, 1890; C.E. Wright,

Mineral Statistics for the Year 1881, p. 78; A. P. Swineford, *Mineral Statistics for the Year 1883*, pp. 29-30; *Ontonagon Herald*, April 17, 1886, September 18, 1886.

18. *Mining World*, September 12, 19, October 3, November 21, 1903; - A.L. Carnahan, "Development of Lake Superior Copper Mines during 1904," *Portage Lake Daily Mining Gazette*, August 28, 1903, January 10,1904; February 7, 1904, March 31, 1904, April 13, 1905, May 28, 1905, December 29, 1905, January 31, 1906, January 3, 1907, September 29, 1907, November 27, 1908, July 24, 1909, January 14, 1910, November 19, 1910, August 3, 1912, July 25, 1913.

19. Cliff Mining Company, Report, March 1931, located in the State Archives; *Boston News Bureau*, March 3, 1927, May 26, 1927, November 21, 1928.

20. Michigan Commission of Mineral Statistics, Annual Report for 1880, pp. 19-20.

21. *Mining World*, November 21, 1903.

22. *Pathfinder*, March, 1905; *Hancock Evening Journal*, Deember. 18, 23, 1908; *Houghton Daily Mining Gazette*, December 5, 1953, September 2, 1955, August 6, 1966.

23. Joseph Rawlings, "Recollections of a Long Life," p. 127.

24. Samuel V. Rawlings to Edwin J. Penberthy, December 31, 1922, January 28, 1923, March 14, 1923. Letter in possession of S. Josiah Penberthy, Birmingham, Michigan, *Memorial Record of the Northern Peninsula of Michigan*, pp. 482-483.

25. S. Josiah Penberthy, "A Medical Man Who Operates: Grover Penberthy," in possession of S. Josiah Penberthy; "Surgeon and Soldier, Beloved by the Rank and File," *Detroit Medical News* 25 (May 14, 1934), p. 9.

Illustration Credits

State Archives: pages 17, 97 (inset), 134, 135, 197, 198 (bottom), 224, 268, 284, 300 and 328.

The Michigan Technological University Archives and Copper Country Historical Collections: pages 27, 33, 47, 53, 58, 76, 97, 98, 177, 198 (top), 225, 248, 269, 321, 322, 326 and 330.

Courtesy Mrs. Violet Hobart: pages 16 and 20.

Courtesy Department of Transportation: page 176.

Collection of the Family of F. Ward Paine, Portola Valley, California: page 285.

Collection of Shelburne Museum, Shelburne, Vermont: page 299.

Collection of S. Josiah Penberthy, Farmington Hills, Michigan: page 330 (inset).

The map on page 8 was drawn by Elizabeth Pilon. It is based on a map created by William T. Woodward.

Bostwick, Lucius, death in Civil War, 167, 175n.24

Bowmansville, Ontario, 315, 320n.17

Brewery, in Eagle River, 40

Brockway, Daniel: proprietor of hotel at Eagle River, 44, 78, 85; biographical sketch of, 93n.1

Bruce Mines (Ontario), 60

Brule, E., agent of Mining Emigrant Association, 60

Burlington, Vermont, temperance societies in, 68n.7

Burrows, Mrs., 138

Burt, William, 48

Bushnell, Jesse, 87, 95n.18, 126, 185, 217, 258

Butler, General, speech by, 42, 130

Byron, Lord, 137-38

California, Cornish miners in, 59

Calumet, Michigan, 323-24

Cambridge, Vermont, 323

Canadian, immigrants at Clifton, 60

Carbines, P.V., 296, 307

Carnsew, Capt. Will, 283n.1; Mrs. Will, 269; John, 283n.2

Carter, Mr. and Mrs. Richard, description of and drinking habits of, 25, 144-46, 152, 152-53, 158,173n.6, 220, 226

Cary, General, temperance leader, 271

Cass, Lewis, expedition of 1820, 48

Catholic Church, at Clifton, 39

Catholic Priest, views on public school, 90

Cemeteries: in Clifton and Eagle River, 37

Central Lake (Michigan) Canning Company, 324

Central Mine, 34, 152, 162, 164, 215, 222, 227, 231, 260, 303; and Charles Lewis, 87, 89; fire at, 294, 297n.8

Chadwick, Hattie, death of, 167

Chapman, George R., 91, 96n.24

Charlotte, New York, 316

Chase, Peter, founder of Williston Academy, 19

Chesapeake (steamer), 52

Chittenden County, Vermont, Hobart farm in, 19

Christmas, celebration of, at Clifton, 44, 78, 242-44

Church, Chauncey, death of in Civil War, 167, 174n.24

Cilley, J.S., as principal of Williston Academy, 88, 96n.20

City of Cleveland (steamer), 213, 222n.11, ran aground at Eagle Harbor, 136, 172n.1

Civil War: news and accounts of, 41, 43, 78, 82, 119, 124, 142, 155, 169, 187, 202, 219, 269; draft act of 1863, 21; draft in Keweenaw County, 214; recruitment at Cliff Mine, 42; exhibition, at Clifton, 191; panorama, at Clifton, 46

Clarke, Robert, writer for *Harper's Weekly*, 66

Cleveland, Ohio, 52

Cliff Mine: Avery Shaft at, 327, cemetery at, 269; closing and sale of, 325; production of, 55, 56; re-opened, 327; visit in, 82-83, 161-62, 296-97; visitors to, 66; work force at, 62-63; working conditions at, 37-38, 65-67. *See also* Mine accidents

Clifton: blizzards at, 34; cemetery at, 267n.5, 268, 329; churches at, 38, 327-29; clothing and wearing apparel in, 88; dentist at, 37; description of log cabins in, 86-87; drinking at, 41; fire at, 107-108; as ghost town, 329; isolation of, 34; location of, 17; medical facilities at, 36-37; newspapers received at, 36; population, in 1870, 327-29; public library at, 26, 199, 227, 301; rivalry with Eagle River, 115-116; Sunday activities at, 38-40; recreation at, 38, 43; winter weather at, 31

Clifton Catholic Church, removed to Phoenix, 329

Clifton Cemetery, 37, 223n.12

Clifton Grace Episcopal, church, abandoned at, 329

Clifton Public School, addition to schoolhouse, 80, 117, 143-44, 172, 187, 190; attendance in, 26, 28-29, 78, 80, 81, 82, 86, 88, 104, 109, 110, 127, 137, 153, 162, 163, 177, 179, 203, 240, 250, 269; budget of, 26, 28; use of corporal punishment in, 230-31; discipline in, 233; incident at, 112-13; repair of schoolhouse at, 149, 152, 157-58, 193, 199; singing class at, 123; teachers' salary at, 28. *See also* Evening School; Spelling contests

Clothing, cost of at Clifton, 146, 153-54, 227, 241, 304

Clothing styles, at Clifton, 237

Cobourg, Ontario, 316, 320n.20

Company store, at Clifton, 65

Copper: cutting of, 61-62; transportation of, to Eagle River, 62

Copper Falls, 31, 170, 276

Copper Harbor: 191, 200, 276, 310; Fort Wilkins at, 50; immigrants at, 60; Raymond claim at, 52; U.S. mineral agent at, 49-50

Copper mass, size of, 62

Copper mines, description of, 61

Copper mining, description of, 205-207

Cornish: at Clifton, 207; criticism of, 185; drinking habits of, 180-83; families at Clifton, 57, 59; food and cooking, 23, 24, 177-78, 206, 241-42; hostility with Irish, 40; as lay preachers, 38, 165-67, 297n.3; life and customs, 44, 45; migration of to the Upper Peninsula, 59-60; patriotism of, 43; pole-climbing by, 45; religious activities of, 38; views on Civil War, 188; wrestling, 45, 285-86

Cornish pasty, 206

Cornish phrases, 25, 66, 82, 86, 102, 105-106, 115, 116, 121, 124-25, 135-36, 147, 148-49, 153, 216-17, 266-67, 290-91, 303

Cornwall: decline of copper mines in, 59; immigration from, 57-59

"Cousin Jack", 153, 174n.15

Cows, purchase of, 155

Crane, Simon, 305

Cundy, Miss (sister of Solomon Cundy), 91, 117, 131, 137, 138, 139, 164, 172, 179, 185, 189, 310; student at Ypsilanti Normal School (Eastern Michigan University), 201, 237

Cundy, Solomon, as clerk at Portage, 85, 95n.16

Cunningham, General Walter, 51

Fay, John M., 145, 173n.7, 185, 266, 315
Fire, at Clifton, 276-77
Fish and fishing, near Clifton, 46, 141-42, 201
Fitch, Mr., 163
Foley Mercantile Company, 330
Foodstuff, cost of, 153-54, 304
Food poisoning, 214-15
Fort Michilimackinac, 48
Fort Sumpter, bombardment of, 138-39
Fort Wilkins, 50
Foster, General, 139
Fourth of July, celebrated at Clifton, 43, 70n.39, 163, 172, 178, 180-81, 196n.1, 301-302
Frank Leslie's Illustrated Weekly, cited, 36, 42, 131, 133n.22, 138
Funky, Mr., 157

Garden City, Michigan, student visit to, 31, 276
George, Capt. Harry, 96n.23, 160-61, 204, 233; home of, 91
George, Capt. Henry, 57
George, Capt. Thomas, 57, 282
George, Tommy, 211, 222n.8
Germans, at Clifton, 60, 207
Godey's Lady's Book, 36
Good Templars, Independent Order of,: as temperance organization, 25, 37, 70n.40, 270; aid to sick fellow members, 45, 293-94, 295-96
Good Templars Hall, at Clifton, 270, 293
Good Templars Lodge, founded at Clifton, 41, 280, 281, 286, 287, 288, 289, 290-91, 292, 301, 302, 305, 308, 323
Goldsmith, Oliver, poem by, 111, 132n.11

Goniwan, Henry, accident of, 66
Grace Episcopal Church, 38. *See also* Episcopal Church
Grand Isle, Vermont, 21, 110, 218, 258
Gratiot Lake, 201
Gratiot River, 149, 151, 174n.11
Green, E.M., 57, 162, 265, 274, 283n.5
Green Bay, Wisconsin, mail delivery from, 34-35
Greelee, Dr., dentist at Clifton, 37, 83, 94n.12
Greeley, Horace, 66

Halls, Capt. Josiah, 91-93, 117, 132n.14, 162, 210, 215, 231, 236, 303; at North Western Mine, 144, 169-71, 191, 202, 214; visit with, 82; biographical sketch of, 94n.11; at Central Mine, 152
Hales, Miss, 138
Halfway House, 243, 244, 245n.4
Halls, Horatio, 105, 132n.4, 210, 215, 227; in spelling bee, 107
Hammond, Col., 51
Hankinson, Rev. J.T., 195, 196n.7
Hanley, John, 86
Hanley, Mike, 86, 95n.17
Harper, Miss. 87, 91
Harpers Weekly Magazine, cited, 131, 133n.22
Harpers New Monthly Magazine, 36
Harris, Mr., murder trial of, 41, 87, 95-96n.19, 107
Harvey, C.T., as mail contractor, 35, 81, 94n.8
Hays, John, 52, 54, 55, 71n.51
Heaton, Abraham S., 37, 106, 126, 132n.7
Henry, Alexander, 48
Hercules (propeller), 320n.19
Hithe, Brigadier General, 317-18

Hobart family, 68n.1
Hobart, Amos, letter from, 19, 136
Hobart, Mrs. Amos (Clarissa
　Fullington), 19, 35
Hobart, DeForest, 19
Hobart, Eli, 245n.3
Hobart, Florence, 19, 79, 88,
　94n.4, 203, 228, 250, 258;
　biographical sketch of, 19
Hobart, Gertrude, 19, 35, 228, 250
Hobart, Henry: dental treatment
　of, 88-89; diary of, 18; elected
　president, Winnebago
　Teachers Association, 323;
　general manager of
　Northwestern Mutual Life
　Insurance Company, 324;
　illness, yellow jaundice,
　199-200; lumbago attack, 258;
　marriage of, 323; pay for
　painting school, 203;
　philosophy of teaching, 28,
　212, 230-31, 321; as secretary,
　Badger Canning Company,
　324; student at Williston
　Academy, 21; appointed
　Superintendent of Schools,
　Winnebago County, 323;
　temperance leader in
　Wisconsin, 323; death in 1903,
　324
Hobart, Rachel, 297n.2
Hooker, General, 139
Hotels, 63
Houghton, visit to, 65
Houghton Township, election at,
　115-16
Houghton, Douglass, geologist
　on 1832 expedition, 49
Howe, Thomas, agent of Cliff
　Mine, 54, 306, 319n.3
Humboldt Mine, 31, 252, 276
Hunting, 169-70

Hurd, F. Wilson, 316, 320n.21
Hussey, Curtis, 52, 54, 55, 325
Hutchinson, Amelia, 225-26
Hyde, Maria, of Grand Isle,
　Vermont, 22, 218, 267n.4, 281
Hyde, Randolph, of Grand Isle,
　Vermont, 223n.15, 267n.4
Hynes, Fred, clerk in Portage,
　168, 244

Illinois (steamer): at Copper
　Harbor, 170; report of sinking
　of, 203, 305, 306-307
Indians, mining of copper, 48
Influenza, epidemic of, 29, 37,
　234-35, 249
Irish: hostility with Cornish, 40;
　immigrants at Clifton, 60, 207
Iron, discovery of, 46, 48
Iron City (steamer), arrival of,
　142, 162, 210, 286
Irving, Washington,
　Knickerbocker's History of New
　York, 123, 133n.20
Isle Royale, 127, 309

"Jack," "old Indian named," 120
Jackson, James, 316, 317
James, Samuel, 204, 293, 303;
　injury to, 290, 297n.5; as
　school inspector, 226
Jeffrey, Louisa, 212-13, 223n.9
Jenkins, Henry, accident to, 66
Jennings, Capt. Edward, 55
Jennings, Capt. William, 160-61,
　174n.20
Jericho, Vermont, J.H. Bostwick
　family of, 174n.24
Johns, Mrs., death of son of, 263
Johns, A., 270, 283n.3
Johnson, Rev. William. 141, 154,
　173n.3, 180, 234

Keweenaw Peninsula:
description of, 204-207;
teaching at, 17-18
Knights of Pythias, 36
Kunkle, Stephen, 253, 267n.3
Kunkle, George, 278, 283n.6
Kunkle, M., 145

Lac La Belle (steamer), 310, 319n.7
Lake St. Clair, 313
Lake Superior, harsh winters of, 50
Lake Superior, agates, search for, 151
Lake Superior Copper Company, 331-32
Lake Superior Miner, 36
Lake Superior News and Mining Journal, 36
Lamb, Mr., 193-94
Lawbaugh, A.I., 37, 69n.23
Leopold, Henry F., 120, 132n.17
Leopold, Samuel F., 133, 132n.17
Leopold, Aaron F., at Eagle River,132n.17
Leopold, H.F. Company, of Portage, 282, 286, 297n.1
Lewis, Charles, death of, 89
Liberty pole, climbing of, 124
Libraries, Hobart's views on, 214
Lice, on students, 29, 213, 233
Lloyds Military Magazine, 81
London News, 36

McCoskey, Bishop Samuel A., at Cliff Mine, 39
McDonald, Mary, 244, 262, 310
McDonald, Samuel, family of, 104, 131n.3, 244
Mc'Grah, Mr., student at school, 116
McKay, Capt. George, 311, 313, 319n.9

McKenzie, Henry, editor of *Mining Gazette*, 190, 196n.5, 244
McLean, Judge, governor of Indiana, 138
McMartry, Col. William, 318
Magic show, at Clifton, 293, 297n.7
Magician, at Clifton, 46
Mail service, at Clifton, 34-36, 42, 79, 136, 138, 178, 238, 247, 252, 258, 259, 269, 281
"Man machine", introduction of at Cliff Mine, 66
Marbles, game of, 125
Martin, Julia, 315
Marquette, Michigan, 46, 134, 154
Marxhausen, C., editor of *Michigan Journal*, 60
Masons, 36
Mass Mine, 331
Medical facilities, at Clifton, 37
Meeds, Henry, 245n.1
Meeds, Mrs., 250
Menasha, Wisconsin, 323
Merryweather, Henry, 244, 246n.6
Meteor (steamer), 309, 311, 319n.4
Methodist Episcopal Church:
abandoned, 329; at Clifton, 25, 38; completion of, 156; as leader of temperance movement, 38; photograph of, 33, 321
Methodist Sabbath School, 111, 124, 129, 187, 258, 288
Methodist Sunday School, 44, 99, 111, 117, 180, 193, 229-30
Methodist Sunday School Library, condition of, 191
Metsger, Daniel, 112-13
Michigan (steamer), 311, 320n.11
Michigan Exchange Hotel, in Detroit, 313
Michigan *Journal*, 60

Dr. Philip P. Mason is Distinguished Professor of History and Director of the Archives of Labor and Urban Affairs at Wayne State University, Detroit, Michigan. He received his B. S. degree from Boston University and his M. A. and PhD. degrees from the University of Michigan. In 1985 he received the Distinguished Faculty Award from Wayne State University. He is the author of *Schoolcrafts's Expedition to Lake Itasca; The Discovery of the Source of the Mississippi*, *The Literary Voyager*, *History of American Roads*, *Harper of Detroit* (co-authored with Frank Woodford), and *The Ambassador Bridge*. He has served as President and Secretary-Treasurer of the Historical Society of Michigan and President, Executive Director and Fellow of the Society of American Archivists. He is presently completing a history of Grace Hospital.

Saralee R. Howard-Filler, Managing Editor, Book Program, Bureau of History, edited the manuscript and designed the camera-ready version of the manuscript on the IBM compatible CPT 9000 system loaded with Ventura Desktop Publishing software.

Susan Cooper Finney, Exhibit Designer and Graphic Artist for the Michigan Historical Museum, Bureau of History, served as design consultant for the book's interior and cover.

CPSIA information can be obtained
at www.ICGtesting.com
Printed in the USA
BVHW080328110922
646700BV00005B/210

9 780814 323427